THE EXTENT OF SINGAPORE'S INVESTMENTS ABROAD

"To God Be The Glory"

The Extent of Singapore's Investments Abroad

SAMUEL BASSEY OKPOSIN
Co-ordinator, MBA Centre
Universiti Telekom (Universiti Multimedia)
Malaysia

Ashgate

Aldershot • Brookfield USA • Singapore • Sydney

332.6735957

© Samuel Bassey Okposin 1999 O4|e

Published by
Ashgate Publishing Limited
Gower House
Croft Road
Aldershot
Hampshire GU11 3HR
England

Ashgate Publishing Company
Old Post Road
Brookfield
Vermont 05036
USA

British Library Cataloguing in Publication Data
Okposin, Samuel Bassey
    The extent of Singapore's investments abroad
    1.Investments, Singapore 2.Singapore - Economic conditions
    I.Title
    332.7'35957

Library of Congress Catalog Card Number: 98-074637
JK
ISBN 0 7546 1010 1

Printed and bound by Athenaeum Press, Ltd.,
Gateshead, Tyne & Wear.

Contents

v

List of Tables

Foreword

The 1997-98 Pacific Asian crises have served to refocus attention on the regional patterns of rapid export-oriented manufacturing based growth. In particular, the differential impact of the crises has underlined the differences between the Pacific Asian economies. This is important because much of the vast literature that the region's 'miracle growth' has given rise to has tended to stress the similarities in terms of policies and patterns of growth. This is most clearly the case in such studies as the World Bank's (1993) *The East Asian Miracle.* In many ways Singapore with its almost completely open trade and financial regimes is much closer to the open economy model of the Pacific Asian economies presented by such agencies as the World Bank. However, the international agencies also, until the 1997-8 crises, underplayed the developmental role of the state in Pacific Asia, yet in Singapore the state has perhaps played the most all pervading role in development anywhere in the region outside of the socialist bloc.

For all the Pacific Asian economies, foreign investment and transnational activity have played significant, but far from uniform roles in development. Again Singapore is at the extreme with by far the most internationalised economy in the region and the greatest dependence on foreign investment and enterprise. However, particularly since the early 1980s, Singapore, like the other Newly Industrialised Economies (NIEs), has become a substantial exporter of capital to other parts of Pacific Asia. This has been very largely a consequence of the upgrading of their production facilities and the decanting of labour intensive and low-tech manufacturing activities in the face of rising costs and government policy aimed at moving to higher levels of value-added production.

The export of capital and manufacturing processes has been a major factor in the rapid development of export oriented manufacturing in Indonesia, Malaysia, and Thailand during the late 1980s and in the Peoples' Republic of China (PRC) and Vietnam during the 1990s. These developments have resulted in a marked increase in the level of regional integration, the regional share of Pacific Asian trade increasing from 34 per cent in 1980 to 55 per cent in 1996. Much of this increase in intra-regional trade reflects the emergence of a series of nested regional divisions of labour which principally reflect differential costs and factor availability. Within these structures many individual firms, both regionally and extra-regionally based, have disaggregated their production, spatially separated it and adopted regional modes of operation in order to take advantage of differences in comparative advantage.

In these developments Singapore has come to occupy a unique position. As well as sharing its position in the regional divisions of labour with the other NIEs the city state has established a pivotal role in Association of South East Asian Nations (ASEAN). In terms of most measures of development, it is by far the most developed economy in the region and has been able to develop its strategic and transhipment functions established in the colonial period in the fields of manufacturing and finance. This has been a major component of Singapore's development policy which has emphasised the attraction of foreign investment and transnational activity. Since the early 1980s, for example, incentives have been offered in order to attract the regional headquarters transnational companies. Thus Lee Kuan Yew envisaged Singapore functioning as a conduit through which foreign investment and transnational corporations:

> ...can serve not only their home market, but also the regional and world market. Furthermore, they can tap the region's bigger and cheaper labour pool. Labour-intensive parts of a product can be done in neighbouring countries and exported to Singapore for more capital- or skill intensive operations (speech delivered in Tokyo and reported in the *Far Eastern Economic Review*, 18 August 1989: 77).

The regional role of Singapore has been enhanced by the rapid opening of the former Asian socialist bloc to international capital and the incorporation of Laos, Myanmar and Vietnam into ASEAN during 1996-7. In addition, Singapore has become the focus of a much more localised division of labour involving the adjacent areas of the Malaysian state of Johore and the islands of the Indonesian Riu archipelago. This development initially involved the relocation of manufacturing activities from Singapore in order to take advantage of lower costs some 30 kilometres from the city state. Subsequently, foreign investors have been attracted directly to Indonesia and Malaysia territory despite costs in the latter being the highest in ASEAN outside of Singapore. The costs being offset by the advantage of location adjacent to Singapore's sophisticated technical, service and communications facilities.

The general background to the relocation of manufacturing from Singapore has been well documented, particularly with respect to government policy which from 1979 onwards encouraged and, to a degree, forced technical upgrading. As the Director of the Economic Development Board stated in 1984:

> We decided that making radios was not a job for us, nor did we want workers in the rag trade. We want technical services (cited in Smith *et al* 1985: 87).

A combination of direct promotion of such activities as aerospace, wage increases, training programmes, incentives and restrictions on cheap immigrant labour reinforced the tendency for costs to rise and resulted in significant technical upgrading and the elimination of exporting of labour-intensive low-tech activities. How these changes in the economic and policy environments impacted on the individual Singapore based firms and their decision making processes have been little investigated. In this respect Samuel Okposin's study provides much valuable insight. A particular strength is the manner in which the firm level material is linked to the overall outflow of capital, the macro-level conditions and the established theoretical explanations for the export of capital.

Professor Chris Dixon
London Guildhall University

References

Smith, M., McLoughlin, J., Large, P. and Chapman, R. (1985) *Asia's New Industrial World*, Methuen, London.
World Bank (1993) *The East Asian Miracle*, Washington.

Preface

For nearly four decades, economists and international development agencies have characterised Singapore's economic miracle as a success story of international trade and foreign direct investment (FDI). Recently, the Organisation for Economic Co-operation and Development (OECD) classified Singapore among its list of developed countries. Surprisingly, Singapore remains a popular destination for foreign capital inflow. Whereas Singapore remains a major importer of FDI by transnational corporations (TNCs), it is also a net exporter of capital to the neighbouring countries. The question then is if Singapore is a net recipient of FDI, why is it also a net capital exporter. Thus the objectives of this book are fourfold. Firstly, to examine the causes of inward and outward direct investment in Singapore's economy. Secondly, to investigate the motivation for Singapore firms to invest abroad. Thirdly, to provide a theoretical explanation for overseas direct investment from Singapore. Finally, to examine Singapore's overseas direct investment strategies, strengths and weaknesses; and to consider if the current trend of outward direct investment will continue into the next millennium.

Singapore's investments abroad are particularly interesting because when people think of Singapore they have a picture of inward rather than outward direct investments. Currently, the city-state is the biggest recipient of FDI in ASEAN. It is this unusually high level of foreign activities *vis-á-vis* other East Asian newly industrialised economies (over 3,000 foreign subsidiaries, representing the highest concentration of foreign activities in one location) that makes Singapore an unusual case.

The extreme openness of the Singaporean economy to international trade and FDI is a characteristic, which is not shared by most Asian countries except for Hong Kong. However, unlike Korea, Taiwan and Japan where the power of the state is rooted in the success of the local entrepreneurs, in Singapore, the success of the state is closely tied to foreign capital. Thus, Singapore has the weakest indigenous group of entrepreneurs in the whole of Asia. Foreign investors account for over eighty per cent of manufacturing investment in Singapore. Such a dominant level of direct investment requires fundamental investigations as to what are the causes of foreign FDI inflow and outflow in Singapore. Moreover, Singapore is not endowed with any natural resources except its labour force and locational advantage as an entrepot. In fact, the city-state is the smallest nation in Southeast Asia, and is extremely reliant on its neighbours as well as developed nations for its food imports.

The methodology that is adopted in this book is a modified Kojima theory. It is argued that Singapore's direct investment abroad is determined by two sets of phenomena. Firstly, the objective conditions of profitability for capital as largely determined by factor prices. That is, labour-intensive firms in Singapore which are losing comparative advantage, will relocate to countries which are gaining comparative advantage in the same industry. Secondly, the subjective motivation of Singapore-based firms for FDI as influenced by state policies and firms' desires to invest in places other than Singapore. It is concluded that profitability, a limited domestic market, product diversification and risks, labour shortage, trade barriers, culture and religion and tax incentives are some of the other determinants of overseas direct investment from Singapore.

Acknowledgements

I would like to thank very much Professors M. Cowen, J. McConville and Dr P. Alizadeh for their precious time during the preparation of the earlier draft of the book. I also wish to thank Professor C. Dixon for helping with the final draft of this book and for writing the Foreword.

I thank Professor J. Fox for proof reading this book at its final stage. I must record my appreciation of the invaluable comments which I received from the following professionals, managers, economists, and academics: Associate Professors B. Kapur, M. Asher, Pang Eng Fong, Khoo Cheng Lim, Dr C. Yeoh, Dr C. Grundy-Warr, Dr S. Liow, Dr L. Theng, Dr J. Sen, Dr Y. Lee, B. Darrington, L. Ng, Y. Mace, and S. Kumar.

I am grateful to Professors G. Jasmon, S. Richardson, J. Fox, M. Ismail, A. Gumel, M. Kanbur and all my colleagues in the Faculty of Management, Universiti Telekom (Multimedia University).

My appreciation goes to Drs. A. Ajibewa, G. Tasie, Ms J. Munster, Mr Foh Hee Loong, Ms Goh Bee Liam, Mr Azman. I am indebted to Ms Lim Wei Ling for the statistical input of this book.

Furthermore, I especially thank Manu Bhaskaran, Managing Director, Group Head of Research, SocGen-Crosby, Singapore for allowing me access to their database. I am also grateful to Poline Ang.

Above all, I express my gratitude to my parents and all members of my family most especially, Lim Yian Ling, Daniel, Emma, and Jane for their understanding, love, patience, care, support and prayers.

List of Abbreviations

NIES	Newly Industrialised Economies
PRC	Peoples' Republic of China
ASEAN	Association of South East Asian Nations
FDI	Foreign Direct Investment
OECD	Organisation for Economic Cooperation and Development
TNC	Transnational Corporations
US	United States
H-O	Heckscher - Ohlin
GNP	Gross National Product
CPI	Consumer Price Index
PAP	Peoples' Action Party
STUC	Singapore Trade Unions Council
NWC	National Wage Council
EDB	Economic Development Board
JTC	Jurong Town Corporation
SISIR	Singapore Institute for Standards and Industrial Research
NTUC	National Trade Unions Congress
SIFS	Small Industries Finance Scheme
ESIFS	Extended Small Industries Finance Scheme
CPF	Central Provident Fund
ULC	Unit Labour Cost
UBC	Unit Business Cost
GIC	Government Investment Corporation
LDC	Less Developed Countries
CPI	Consumer Price Index
IS	Import-Substitution

GNS	Gross National Saving
IDI	International Direct Investments
GLC	Government Link Companies
RD	Research and Development
OLS	Ordinary Least Square
NUS	National University of Singapore
NTU	Nanyang Technological University
SMA	Singapore Manufacturers Association
GSP	General System Preference
ASD	Appreciating Singapore Dollar
GS	Government Support
HOC	High Operating Costs
DPR	Diversification of products
HLRC	High Land / Rent Costs
HLC	High Labour Costs
LDM	Limited Domestic Market
GIRS	Government Industrial Restructuring Strategy
LS	Labour Shortage
TAX	Tax Incentives
FIC	Favourable Investment Climate
TB	Trade Barriers
PT	Proximity To Singapore
GI	Good Infrastructure
SLCR	Shared Language, Culture and Religion
ACL	Availability of Cheap Labour
CLR	Cheap Land and Raw Materials
LM	Large Market
PS	Political Stability
EC	European Community
NAFTA	North American Free Trade Area
UN	United Nations
SFI	Singapore Food Technologies
NTD	Novo Technology Development

List of Appendices

The Author

Samuel Bassey Okposin received his Ph.D in Economics from the London Guildhall University, United Kingdom. He is currently the Co-ordinator, MBA Centre at the Faculty of Management, Universiti Telekom (Universiti Multimedia), Malaysia.

Prior to working at Universiti Telekom (Universiti Multimedia), Dr. Okposin has worked as a lecturer in Economics at the Faculty of Economics and Business, University Malaysia Sarawak (UNIMAS). Also, he has worked as visiting lecturer with London Guildhall University and Birkbeck College (University of London).

His research interests include Foreign Direct Investment Analysis, Industrial Economics, Multinational Corporations, International Economics, Microeconomics, Development Economics and Macroeconomics issues and policy.

1 Introduction

ABSTRACT

The main argument of this book is that a firm's FDI is determined by two sets of phenomena. Firstly, the objective conditions of profitability for capital as largely determined by factor prices. That is, labour-intensive firms in a country which is losing comparative advantage, will relocate to a country which is gaining comparative advantage in the same industry. Secondly, the subjective motivation of firms for FDI as influenced by state policies and firms' desire to invest in places other than the existing location or domestic economy. It is concluded that there is a "special correspondence" between a country's comparative advantage and outward direct investment on the one hand, and the international division of labour between the investing and the recipient countries on the other. By special correspondence I mean the interrelationship between a country's factor costs in international division of labour and outward direct investment.

Introduction

The objectives of this book are fourfold. Firstly, to examine the causes of inward and outward direct investment in Singapore's economy. Secondly, to investigate the motivation for Singapore firms to invest abroad. Thirdly, to provide a theoretical explanation for overseas direct investment from Singapore. Finally, to examine Singapore's overseas direct investment strategies, strengths and weaknesses; and to consider if the current trend of outward direct investment will continue into the next millennium.

The Singaporean case is particularly interesting because of the unusually high level of FDI by TNCs[1] and because Singapore is also extremely open to international trade. The openness of the Singaporean economy to international trade and FDI is a characteristic, which is not shared by most Asian countries except for Hong Kong. However, unlike most of the Asian countries, Singapore is not endowed with any natural resources except its labour force and locational advantage as an entrepot. In fact, the city-state is the smallest nation in Southeast Asia, and is extremely reliant on its neighbours as well as developed nations for its food imports. Also, the country relies heavily on foreign investment and international trade for its economic growth.

However, Singapore's experience could be very relevant for other countries considering a liberalisation of policies toward FDI for development in at least three aspects.[2] Firstly, it shows the role of the state in laying the ground for economic growth and actually creating the country's comparative advantage. Secondly, it shows the importance of FDI by TNCs for development purposes. Thirdly, it shows the fact that a country's comparative advantage is never static, but evolves with capital accumulation and technological change where, as labour becomes more expensive in Singapore and capital is cheaper, firms in Singapore use less labour and more capital by substituting capital for labour. Thus methods of production for Singaporean firms becomes more capital-intensive, while labour-intensive firms relocate production to countries that are gaining comparative advantage in labour for similar industry. By so doing, Singapore is able to maintain its comparative as well as competitive

---

[1] The term TNC is loosely used here to mean any firm with two or more operations outside its native country.

[2] Naya, Seiji and Ramstetter, Eric D. (1988), "Policy Interactions and Direct Foreign Investment in East and Southeast Asia", *Journal of World Trade*, 22 (2), pp. 57-71.

2

advantage as both a recipient and donor of FDI in the region.[3]

In the 1960s and 1970s, FDI inflow in Singapore's economy was determined by two major factors. Firstly, the relatively higher rate of profitability for capital, which depends on the relative labour costs and high productivity, output in labour-intensive industries. By contrast, most western countries at the time were characterised by increasing unionisation, expectations of rising living standards, and an increasing burden of employers' statutory obligations, which raised labour costs and reduced firms' profitability. Thus, firms in most of the western countries relocated production to Singapore in search for cheaper labour, access to regional markets and outstanding governing policies that ensure greater profitability. Secondly, Singapore's open investment policy and generous incentives which was one of the best in the whole of Southeast Asia ensured the timely and most needed FDI.

As FDI became more complex and competitive in the late 1980s and the 1990s, the main determinants of inward direct investment included: the relative wage differentials between Singapore and other Asian countries, the increasing importance of higher productivity, quality exports, infrastructure, research and development (R&D), and the outlook for Singapore's strategic plans of becoming the hub of Asia. In the past, because of the intense competition for FDI by other countries, the Singapore government's response has been to introduce more favourable industrial policies and incentives for TNCs.

Over the years, this has led to the steady decline in the role of local participation in industrial production and the relative weakness of the indigenous entrepreneurship. The deficiency between foreign and local firms in Singapore's economy and in particular, the manufacturing sector is evident in the shares of manufacturing investment, employment, number of establishments, labour productivity and exports. Thus among the Southeast Asian countries, Singapore has the weakest local entrepreneurship.

However, the question of whether excessive dependence on TNCs leads to the crowding-out of local entrepreneurs is still a topic of considerable debate

---

[3] In recent years, however, the emphasis has shifted from comparative to competitive advantage. By comparative advantage I imply that a country will gain most by exporting commodities that it produces, using its abundant factors of production most intensely, while importing those goods whose production would require relatively more of the scarcer factors of production. Unlike comparative advantage that deals with locational or static factors, competitive advantage deals with product quality and consumers acceptance. The competitors are the TNCs from countries around the world who are aiming at gaining market share on a global basis and together they form what is known as the "New World Order".

among economists in Singapore.[4] As is pointed out by Lim, the group of study which argues that there is a serious deficiency points to the dominant roles of foreign firms in the manufacturing sector and the paucity of local industrial entrepreneurs. However, those who argued against the crowding-out effect base their perception on a wider spectrum of the highly successful role of ethnic Chinese communities in the development of much of Southeast Asia including Hong Kong and Taiwan.[5] The conflicting perceptions are sometimes due to the different interpretations of the term "entrepreneurship". If entrepreneurship is judged by the ability to engage in trading and small scale business, and the ability to undertake risks in speculative ventures, then there is no such deficiency in Singapore.[6] However, if entrepreneurship is defined in terms of the ability to perceive opportunities in industrial ventures and to innovate, and the willingness to organise resources, scout for technology and develop export markets for long term profits, then it should be admitted that the pool of local export-led industrial entrepreneurs is limited.[7]

Keeping the above-mentioned distinction in mind, this book examines what motivates foreign and local firms based in Singapore to invest abroad. Chapter 2 examines three major theories of FDI and introduces a theoretical framework for examining outward direct investment from Singapore. The first approach is the neoclassical microeconomic theory which posits, that under perfect competition it is the differential rate of return which causes firms to invest overseas. Although the theory has been criticised as unrealistic in a world dominated by TNCs, it is argued that, the approach shows the interrelationship between a country's factor costs and its outward direct investment. The second approach is the intangible-asset theory, which claims that the possession of firm-specific advantage was the *sine qua non* for FDI. This theory is rejected on the grounds that all investing firms are required to possess firm-specific advantages. The third approach examined is the macroeconomic theory of FDI, which claims that there is relationship between a country's comparative advantage and FDI outflow.

The book is based on the modified Kojima's macroeconomic theory, which argues that there is a correspondence between a country's comparative

---

[4] Lim, Chong Yah (1988), *Policy Options for the Singapore Economy*, Singapore: McGraw-Hill, p. 268.

[5] Ibid.

[6] Ibid.

[7] Ibid.

advantage and outward directs investment on the one hand, and the international division of labour between the investing and the recipient countries on the other. In chapter 3, a close investigation of the role of the state as a major determinant of the Singapore's comparative advantage and success is made. Chapter 4 examines the strengths and weaknesses of Singapore investment strategies; the extent and geographical distribution of Singapore's direct investment abroad. It distinguishes between foreign TNCs and local firms, as both groups of investors have some different, yet similar motives, for investing capital overseas. An empirical test for the motivation of a firm's desire to invest in other countries is conducted in chapter 5. Chapter 6 concludes on the outlook for the next millennium.

Foreign Direct and Portfolio Investment

For the purpose of this research, the term FDI is used to refer to the amount invested by a foreign enterprise which is "sufficient to assure not only an ownership interest, but also partial or complete control"[8] of the subsidiary. As pointed out by Ragazzi, the main distinction between FDI and portfolio investment is that the former entails control of an overseas project, while the latter does not.[9] Since portfolio investment decisions are short term in nature, they are often determined mainly by expected rate of return and the risk of the investment (for instance, speculation), while FDI, which are long term, are determined by objective as well as subjective factors.[10]

Until World War I, over ninety per cent of investment was recorded as portfolio.[11] Also foreign investment was considered to be determined by interest rate differentials. Worse still, investment was disaggregated and classified along the following lines: economic enterprise and government bonds; entrepreneurial and government investment; private-listed and government-listed

---

[8] Richardson, J. D. (1971), "On 'Going Abroad': The Firm's Initial Foreign Investment Decision", *Quarterly Review of Economics and Business*, 11(4), pp. 7-22.
[9] Ragazzi, Giorgio (1973), "Theories of the Determinants of Direct Foreign Investment", *International Monetary Fund Staff Papers*, 20(2), pp. 471-98.
[10] Ibid., p. 476.
[11] See Wilkins, Mira (1988), "The Free-Standing Company, 1870-1914: An Important Type of British Foreign Direct Investment", *Economic History*, 41 (2), pp. 259-82; Jones, Geoffrey (1988), "Foreign Multinationals and British Industry before 1945", *Economic History Review*, 41 (3), pp. 429-53; Turrell, Robert Vicat and Van-Helten, Jean Jacques (1987), "The Investment Group: The Missing Link in British Overseas Expansion Before 1914?", *Economic History Review*, 40 (2), pp. 267-274; Bloomfield, Arthur I. (1963), *Short-Term Capital Movements Under the Pre-1914 Gold Standard*, New Jersey: Princeton University Press; Kenwood, A. G. and Lougheed, A. L. (1992), *The Growth of the International Economy 1820-1990*, London: Routledge, p. 27.

investment. Even where terms such as "portfolio" and "direct" were employed, the definitions, which were used at the time, were not the same as those, which are applied today.[12]

In the early 1950s and 1960s, direct investment was defined to include the extension of a business through overseas branches or subsidiaries. The finance of these affiliates would normally come from the parent company (not necessarily from a Stock Exchange floatation) and the investment would involve effective control of the overseas undertaking. Portfolio investment on the other hand, referred to investment through the medium of securities traded on the Stock Exchange. According to Svedberg's analysis of the old definitions, "the *medium* through which shares were distributed plus the *control* by the investor of the undertaking in which the capital became embodied, were the *two* criteria usually used to separate direct from portfolio investment. Nowadays, only the latter criterion is used. Consequently, investments which were floated on the Stock Exchange Market and controlled by the foreign investor have been counted as portfolio when the old definition was applied, but should be regarded as direct by present-day standards".[13]

Thus to reclassify nineteenth century investments according to modern composition of direct-portfolio investment, most standard international economics texts would need to be re-written. The correction has already been evident in Dunning's research in 1983, where he suggested that the 1914 estimate of FDI (10 per cent of FDI and 90 per cent of portfolio investment) was inaccurate, and the new estimate which takes into account the modern definition is 35 per cent of direct investment and 65 per cent for portfolio investment.[14] Similarly, Svedberg in an earlier work argued that if modern definition of FDI were applied to 1914 investment then direct investment would constitute more than 70 per cent[15] of the total flows.

Though the modern definition of foreign investment has enabled the distinction of FDI and portfolio, its major contribution has been to provide insight into the nature and causes of FDI flows. The understanding of this distinction will enable us to understand the historical causes as well as circumstances that have led to Singapore becoming a significant location for FDI in Asia.

---

[12] Svedberg, Peter (1978), "The Portfolio-Direct Composition of Private Foreign Investment in 1914 Revisited", *The Economic Journal*, 88, pp. 763-777.

[13] Ibid.

[14] Dunning, J. H. (1970), *Studies in International Investment*, London: Allen & Unwin p. 2; Dunning, J. H. (1983), "Changes in the Level and Structure of International Production: The Last One Hundred Years", in Casson, M. (ed.), *The Growth of International Business*, London: , pp. 84-139.

[15] Svedberg, Peter (1978), *op. cit.*, p. 765.

The History of FDI in Singapore: A Colonial Legacy

The impressive economic transformation in Singapore and the dominant role of FDI by TNCs can only be understood when discussed in its historical context. In fact, its colonial legacy shows that its development has been linked to and depended on foreign enterprises. According to its founder, Sir Stamford Raffles, in June 1819, Singapore was meant to be "a great commercial emporium"[16] for businesses. In other words, Singapore's development was to be paid for by enterprises while it served the interests of business. It has been a symbiotic relationship which remains true even until this day.[17]

The pre-1819 history of Singapore is not altogether clear due to the sketchy and contradictory records available. The main written sources now available are accounts by Chinese travellers, Portuguese historians, and the "Malay Annals" or "Sejarah Melayu", which is the earliest Malay account of historical events. In the 13th century, the Venetian traveller, Marco Polo referred to the island-city as "Chiamassie" and in the latter part of the 14th century, the Javanese historians made reference to it as "Temasek". By the end of 14th century, the name "Singapura" first began to be used.[18] Although little is known about the inhabitants during 13th and 14th centuries, it is suspected that the Chinese, Indian and Arab traders who visited the island settled with native inhabitants, creating settlements and civilisations wherever land or trade offered a livelihood.[19]

What is clear is that Singapore was founded in 1819 by Raffles, an agent of the British East India Company (a Charter Company), to enable the British to have a trading port in Southeast Asia, in rivalry with the Dutch East India Company which controlled Malacca, and much of the region, including Java,

---

[16] Turnbull, C. M. (1977), *A History of Singapore, 1819-1975*, London: Oxford University Press.
[17] Chow, Kit Boey and Tyabji, Amina (1980), *External Linkages and Economic Development: The Singapore Experience*, Economic Research Centre, Monograph Series 8, p. 2; Chong, Li Choy (1986), "Singapore's Development: Harnessing the MNCs", *Contemporary Southeast Asia: A Quarterly Journal of International and Strategic Affairs*, 8 (3), pp. 56-69; Regnier, Philippe (1987), *Singapore: City-State in Southeast Asia*, London: Hurst & Company, p. 17.
[18] Joo-Jock, Lim A. (1991), "Geographical Setting", in *A History of Singapore* by Ernest Chew, C. T. and Lee, Edwin (eds.), Oxford: Oxford University Press, p. 3.
[19] Hughes, Helen (1969), "From Entrepot Trade to Manufacturing", in *Foreign Investment and Industrialization in Singapore* (eds.), by Hughes, H. and Seng, Y. P., Canberra: Australian National University Press, p. 1.

Moluccas and the Riau islands. In 1867, it gained the British Crown Colony status and membership of the Straits Settlements, and in 1946, it became a separate Crown Colony.[20] Even after its independence from the British to become a sovereign state, Singapore continued to serve the interests of multinational business, and benefited from the relationship in terms of developmental progress. However, with national independence and the changing circumstances, Singapore's development priorities and objectives have changed, and as such, the types of TNCs encouraged to do business in Singapore also have changed over time.[21]

Raffles had always regarded Singapore as a commercial centre. Its convenient location at the southern tip of the Indo-Pacific peninsula and at the cross-roads between eastern and western Asia has been one of its strong points for growth. Its sheltered deep water harbour has for many years become a rendezvous for large European merchant vessels and boats of Chinese and other local owners: the former with goods from India (textiles, arms and opium) for redistribution in the region, and the latter with spices, silks, tropical woods, tea and tin. Of the three British colonies in the strait, Singapore alone had the capacity to receive large ships: Penang had no timber, Malacca was silting up. In 1832 Singapore took the place of Penang as the seat of the governor. [22]

Before 1853 there was no tax levied on commercial transactions. The main aim of the policy was to keep Singapore as a free port and loosen the trading monopoly of Batavia thereby attracting the greatest possible number of traders of all nationalities. The authorities obtained their revenue from trade in opium. However, the free trade policies implemented at the time gave an immediate stimulus to Singapore's mercantile economy, to which the island's demographic evolution bore eloquent witness:[23] from 150 inhabitants (120 Malays and 30 Chinese) in 1819 to 30,000 in 1836 (12,500 Malays and 14,000 Chinese). By 1860 13,000 Indians had been added to the 16,200 Malays, 50,000 Chinese and 2,500 Europeans who shared the island.[24] The first duties based

[20] Chong, Li Choy (1986), "Singapore's Development: Harnessing the Multinationals", *Contemporary Southeast Asia: A Quarterly Journal of International and Strategic Affairs*, 8 (1), pp. 56-69.

[21] Chong, Li Choy (1986), *op. cit.*, p. 59.; Heineberg, Heinz (1988), "Singapore: From the British Colonial Base to the Up-and-Coming 'Chinese' City-State", *Applied Geography and Development*, 31 (1), pp. 15-36.

[22] Regnier, Philippe (1987), *op. cit.*, p. 17.

[23] Ibid.

[24] Hughes, Helen and You, Poh Seng (1969), *op. cit.*, p. 7.

on tonnage and the stamping of harbour documents were introduced in 1853-65, and these have remained very modest since then.

In the 20th century, Singapore's prosperous economy suffered two major setbacks. The first arose because the island's economy depended on the British economy which was severely weakened by four years of conflict in Europe and then by the effects of the economic crisis of 1929-32, which eroded the principles of free trade (through the adoption of the new imperial system of trade preferences). The effect of this was both on the colonial rulers who depended on Britain for shipments to Singapore and the entrepot traders, whose activities were halved during the period. The second setback was as a result of the Japanese occupation, which lasted from 12 February 1942 to 5 September 1945.[25] While the British government had given its assurance of security, the port of Singapore nonetheless was aggressively taken over by the Japanese army.[26] The result was insecurity in the country and a depressed economic condition, which gave rise to acute material shortages and falling living standards. Between 1945-54, the British caretaker government was more concerned with the restoration of the entrepot trade to its full use and the desire to regulate and conserve foreign exchange.

However, in April 1955, the British government decided to introduce limited internal reforms under its policy of decolonisation, namely a democratic constitution with elections, which were won initially by the Labour Front with 27 per cent of the votes, and without interruption from the 1959 onwards by the People's Action Party (PAP)[27] (as it is shown in the appendix). The gaining of self-government, however, marked a new era of disturbance against the backdrop of the anti-Communist state of emergency (in force since 1948) and the riots of 1956, which had seriously threatened the internal security of the island.[28] In 1961, the moderate wing of the PAP faced an onslaught from the left and a split in the party when the left wing Barisan Socialis Party broke away in May of that year and joined the opposition. Fearing that the communists would try to seize power, the Prime Minister of Malaya, Tunku Abdul Rahman, proposed on May 26, with support from London, a grand federation of Malaysia - to include Singapore so that the island should no longer be at the mercy of political developments which could destroy its flourishing economy. In September 1962, a referendum was held and the Singapore electorate decided in favour of unification, and Lee Kuan Yew (the

---

[25] Ibid. p. 11.
[26] Regnier, Philippe (198/), *op. cit.*, p. 21.
[27] Heineberg, Heinz (1988), *op. cit.*, p. 18.
[28] Regnier, Philippe (1987), *op. cit.*, p. 23.

leader of the PAP) proceeded in February 1963 to have the leaders of Barisan Socialis arrested.[29]

In June 1963, Indonesia announced that it did not accept the "neo-colonial" creation of Malaysia. Some months later, for reasons connected with both foreign relations and internal politics, Sukarno (the then President of Indonesia) carried on a semi-armed confrontation consisting of regular attacks and acts of infiltration by Indonesian soldiers and agents directed against Singapore and the west coast of the Malay peninsula. As well as providing undercover support to the communist opposition, and sending commandos to sabotage Singapore's harbour installations, Indonesia declared a commercial boycott, which led to a steep decline in Singapore's entrepot activities and a noticeable falling off in foreign investment.[30] However, two years after unification with Malaysia, Singapore seceded from the Federation and became an independent state, giving itself a new constitution as a Republic: The Republic of Singapore. The question, then, was how was Singapore going to achieve economic development considering its limited geographical size and market, and having relatively little or none of the domestic capital that is necessary for industrialisation.

Existing Literature on Outward Direct Investment in Singapore

Unlike Hong Kong, India and Latin American countries,[31] where considerable research and fieldwork study has been conducted, Singapore's existing literature on outward direct investment is very limited. This is due to the fact that until recently, there was no published data or information on Singapore's direct investment abroad. However, the prevailing argument about

---

[29] Ibid., p. 23.

[30] Ibid.

[31] Diaz-Alejandro, C. F. (1977), "Foreign Direct Investment by Latin Americans", in Agmon,T. and Kindleberger, C. P. (eds.), *Multinationals from Small Countries*, Cambridge, Mass.: MIT Press; Wells, L. T. (1978), "Foreign Investment from the Third World: The Experience of Chinese Firms from Hong Kong", *Columbia Journal of World Business*, pp. 39-49; Kumar, K. and Mcleod, M. G. (1981), *Multinationals from Third World Countries*, Lexington: Heath; Lall, Sanjaya (1982), "Export of Capital from Developing Countries: India", in Black, J. and Dunning, John H. (eds.), *International Capital Movements*, London: Macmillan; Lall, Sanjaya (1983), *The New Multinationals: The Spread of Third World Enterprises*, Singapore: John Wiley.

Singapore's direct investment abroad has proceeded from the premise that location-specific conditions are the main determinants.[32] That is, it is argued that capital flows out of Singapore because of cheap land, labour and raw materials, political stability and favourable investment climate in the neighbouring countries such as Indonesia, Malaysia, Thailand Philippines and even as far as China, Vietnam and Cambodia.

Theoretically, the locational specific hypothesis suffers from three major weaknesses. Firstly, it assumes the motivating pull factors for FDI to be static, where unless a country is endowed with the specified conditions it will forever remain barren or become unattractive. Secondly, it examines partially a country's comparative advantage by concentrating on the pull factors in a recipient country rather than the push factors in the investing country or both. In other words, the locational advantage theory explains the reasons for choosing a particular investment location instead of what actually causes FDI in the donor country. Thirdly, it neglects the macroeconomic determinants of international trade through a country's comparative advantage. For as a country moves from labour intensive industries to capital intensive industries, it loses its comparative advantage as a labour-intensive production to lower income countries who are gaining comparative advantage in labour motivated investment. Given these partial examinations of micro-and macroeconomics explanations of FDI determinants, it has been necessary to reject the locational advantage theory.

Another part of the literature, which has emerged strongly in recent years, claims that Singapore's overseas investment is similar to the pattern of investment undertaken by the present TNCs from the developed countries (DCs).[33] According to the study, Singapore's overseas direct investment is consistent with Vernon's product life cycle, which claims that the internationalisation of firms must pass through three stages from innovation to standardisation and

---

[32] Pang, E. F. and Komaran, R. V. (1985), "Singapore Multinationals", *Columbia Journal of World Business*, 20 (2), pp. 35-42; Lim, M. H. and Teoh, K. F. (1986), "Singapore Corporations go Transnational", *Journal of Southeast Asian Studies*, 17 (2), pp. 336-365; Komaran, R. V. (1986), "Singapore Investment in China", a dissertation submitted to the National University of Singapore, as a partial fulfilment of the Advanced Study Project, for the Master of Business Administration; Ee, Hock Chye (1991), "Foreign Direct Investment from Singapore Manufacturing Sector", a dissertation submitted to the National University of Singapore, as a partial fulfilment of the Advanced Study Project, for the degree of Master of Business Administration.

[33] Aggarwal, Raj (1985), "Emerging Third World Multinationals: A Case Study of the Foreign Operations of Singapore Firms", *Journal of Contemporary Southeast Asia*, 7 (3), pp. 193-208; Lee, Tsao Yuan (1991), *Growth Triangle: The Johor-Singapore-Riau Experience*, Singapore: Institute of Southeast Asian Studies.

maturity.[34] The model was originally developed to explain U.S investment in Europe and also in cheap labour countries. Its relevance arises from the interaction of the evolving forces of demand patterns and production possibilities.

The major problem with the above-mentioned study is that it regards both the determinants of inward and outward direct investment in Singapore to be the same as those of the DCs. Singapore's development was not through technological invention and innovation but through borrowed technology from American and European TNCs. As such, its outward direct investment cannot be compared to those of America or European firms who already possess advantages in invention and innovation of new technology. Above all, Singapore's has no internal market, which is large enough to sustain the innovation of new technology before maturity, standardisation and the ultimate exports. It solely depends on external markets for its own goods and services. However, it is in the light of this lack of market characteristics and the relative capacity to innovate new products that the product life cycle hypothesis has been rejected.

Furthermore, the rejection of the locational approach and the Vernon's product cycle as a theoretical framework for this book is due to the fact that both theories partially examine a firm's FDI from the subjective conditions for capital. Also, they down-play the correspondence between the home and the host countries in international division of labour. For the relationship between the investing and the recipient countries can be competitive and complementary. Complementarity in the sense that labour-demanding firms are relocated abroad to relieve the constraint on resource scarcity. In the case of Singapore, labour shortages have been a growing problem since full employment was achieved in the early 1970s. Limited land size has constrained further development despite reclamation programmes that have increased the island's land area by 8 per cent over the last 30 years. Labour and property costs, labour turnover and congestion have all forced industries to become more capital intensive and/or relocate. Thus both 'moving up' higher value added, technology intensive activities and/or 'moving out' low income assembly work has been the basic objective of the state to position Singapore as the dynamic hub for the growing Southeast Asian economy. However, it is this form of capital movement which constitutes the bulk of outward direct investment from Singapore. Also, it is this unique relationship between the costs of factors of

---

[34] Vernon, Raymond (1966), "International Investment and International Trade in the Product Cycle", *Quarterly Journal of Economics*, 80, pp. 190-207.

production and outward direct investment from Singapore, which forms the central message of this book as briefly, outlined below.

Outline of Kojima's Macroeconomic Theory

The methodology for this book is based on modified Kojima's macroeconomic theory of FDI. According to this theory, there are two types of FDI: macroeconomic FDI, which respond to changes in comparative advantage, and microeconomic FDI, which is contrary to the law of comparative advantage.[35] According to Kojima, the former reflects FDI by small firms, which are undertaken to facilitate transfer of production from high wage to low wage countries. The latter reflects the type of FDI carried out by large firms which is aimed at exploiting oligopolistic factors and product markets.[36] Accordingly, macroeconomic FDI is more dynamic because of its trade-creating effects whereas microeconomic FDI is basically trade-supplanting.[37] Thus, the main distinction between a Japanese and an American FDI is that Japan's FDI is aimed at increasing international trade thus being trade-oriented while American FDI is to serve the recipient country's market as such it is anti-trade-oriented.[38] Kojima's claim is based on the argument that Japanese overseas investments are aimed mostly at exploiting natural resources in resource rich- countries or manufacturing labour intensive products in labour-abundant developing countries.[39] Most output of the first type of investment are shipped back to Japan, while the products from the second type are increasingly exported back to Japan or to third country markets. In contrast, American overseas manufacturing investments are designed mostly to produce highly sophisticated, technology based products for local markets.[40]

---

[35] Kojima, K. (1982), "Macroeconomic Versus International Business Approach to Direct Foreign Investment", *Hitotsubashi Journal of Economic*, 23 (2), pp. 1-19; Kojima, K. and Ozawa, Terutomo (1984), "Micro-and Macro-Economic Models of Direct Foreign Investment: Towards a Synthesis, *Hitotsubashi Journal of Economic*, 25 (2), pp. 1-20; Kojima, K. (1985), "Japanese and American Direct Investment in Asia: A Comparative Analysis", *Hitotsubashi Journal of Economic*, 26 (2), pp. 1-35; Ozawa, Terutomo (1975), "The Emergence of Japan's Multinationalism: Patterns and Competition, *Asian Survey*, 15, pp. 1036-53; Ozawa (1979), "International Investment and Industrial structure: New Theoretical Implications from the Japanese Experience", *Oxford Economic Papers*, 31 (1), pp. 72-92.

[36] Gray, H. P. (1982), "Macroeconomic Theories of Foreign Direct Investment: An Assessment", in Rugman, Alan M. (ed.), *New Theories of the Multinational Enterprise*, London: Croom Helm, Chapter 8.

[37] Ibid., p. 177.

[38] Kojima, K. (1982), *op. cit.*, pp. 1-19.

[39] Ozawa, Terutomo (1979), *op. cit.*, p. 79.

[40] Ozawa, Terutomo (1979), *op. cit.*, p. 79.

Kojima's theory offers the opportunity to examine the fact that FDI by Singapore based firms is determinant by two sets of phenomena. Firstly, the objective conditions of profitability for capital are determined largely by labour costs. That is, Singapore firms in the industries that are losing comparative advantage make FDI because of the relative higher profit potential abroad. Secondly, Singapore firms relocate industrial production because of subjective determinants of FDI.[41]

The modified Kojima's theory incorporates the dynamism of international trade and overseas direct investment carried out to exploit regional economies of scale derived from the region's economic corporations such as growth triangles. However, it would be a pretentious and inflated claim to suggest that the modified Kojima's theory is the best for any country FDI. It only addresses issues which enables better application of the theory for this book. This is important as Kojima's original theory was particularly aimed at explaining outward direct investment from Japan during the 1960s and 70s. Though Japan's FDI is unique in it own way, I have nonetheless modified Kojima's original assertions to reflect three main factors which are fundamental to Singapore's economy: firstly, the role of the state as a special institution responsible for creating the nation's comparative advantage in international division of labour; secondly, the role of regional common markets such as the Association of South East Asian Nations and growth triangles between Singapore-Johor-Riau Islands; and, thirdly, the role of foreign capital in the Singapore economy. Singapore is one of the biggest investors in later economic grouping. For instance, it is the only country in the region with over 80 per cent share of foreign capital in the manufacturing sector.

Therefore, it is argued that FDI is not only aimed at maximising international trade but exploiting economies of scale. The economies of scale may be internal and external to the investing firm; the former normally lead to horizontal investment, and the latter to vertical investment.[42] Foreign investment in vertically related stages of production is common in mainly extracting industries like producing and processing minerals and other raw materials. The main advantage of direct investment here consists in reducing the costs and uncertainties that exist when different producers handle subsequent stages of production by coordinating decisions at various stages within one firm. An increase in production through investment may permit a reduction in the unit

---

[41] Gray, Peter H. (1982), *op. cit.*, Chapter 8.

[42] Ragazzi, Giorgio (1973), "Theories of the Determinants of Direct Foreign Investment", *International Monetary Fund Staff Papers*, 20(2), pp. 471-98.

cost of certain general services, such as financing, marketing or technological research that have the nature of fixed costs. From the country's stand point, the economies of scale can lead to regional economic zones such as the growth triangle.[43] The uniqueness of this form of international division of labour is that it doesn't necessarily need to involve all regions of the participating country but only designated economic zones, which are considered by the investors as potential investment areas. Thus the involvement of large and small firms in FDI from Singapore needs to be distinguished.

Conclusion

The interrelationship between a country's factor prices and FDI as expressed in Kojima's model not only offers a possible explanation of the causes of direct investment abroad, but also the relationship between the investing and the recipient cou.it provides the basis for examining both objective and subjective variables for FDI. These subjective variables or firm's desires to invest abroad are classified here as "push" and "pull" variables for FDI. The variables are tested using data from a fieldwork survey in Singapore. The results show that firms are particularly sensitive to factor prices both in Singapore and other countries.

---

[43] Ibid., p. 488.

2 Determinants of FDI: Review of Theories and Issues

ABSTRACT

This chapter is an attempt to provide a theoretical framework on overseas direct investment from Singapore. Three major theories of FDI are examined: the neoclassical microeconomic theory; the intangible microeconomic theory; and the macroeconomic theory. A modified "Kojima's macroeconomic theory" is proposed to examine the interrelationship between a country's comparative advantage in international division of labour and outward direct investment. It is argued that any change in a country's comparative advantage, which is reflected in its factor costs and intensities would lead to firms substituting capital for labour thus relocating labour-intensive industries.

Introduction

The literature on FDI is vast and any attempt to reference everyone of them will require a life time study. Thus, I have summarised below the work of some of the outstanding authors whom I have quoted extensively, under three main theoretical headings. The first theory reviewed is the neoclassical microeconomic theory, which, until the 1960s was the only established explanation of foreign investment.[44] According to this theory, it is the interest rate difference between countries that causes international capital movements.[45] As pointed out by Aggarwal, this neoclassical theory treats capital just like any other commodity, and its price - the interest rate - thus governs its supply, demand, and allocation.[46] Under perfect competition, capital will flow freely from a country with low rate of return to a country with relative high rate of return.[47] This neoclassical theory, however, does not explain the role of TNCs, since it limits itself to explaining how and where firms decide to obtain the capital needed to finance their global plans and it does not say anything about its investment for the purpose of managerial control of production capabilities. Therefore, its critics[48] argue that its role in modern times is limited primarily to the explanation of portfolio investment rather than FDI.

---

[44] Dunning, John H. (1993), *Multinational Enterprise and the Global Economy*, London: Addison-Wesley.

[45] Stevens, Guy V. (1972), "Capital Mobility and the International Firm", in (ed.) by Machlup, F. et al., *The International Mobility and Movement of Capital*, New York: Columbia University; Stevens (1974), "Determinants of Investment", in (ed.) by John Dunning, *Economic Analysis and the Multinational Enterprise*, London: Allen & Unwin. Also see Ragazzi, Giorgio (1973), *op. cit.*, pp. 471-98.

[46] Aggarwal, Raj (1984), "The Strategic Challenge of Third World Multinationals: A New Stage of the Product Life Cycle of Multinationals?", *Advances in International Comparative Management*, 1, pp. 103-22.

[47] Iverson, Carl (1953), *Aspects of the Theory of International Capital Movements*, London: Oxford University Press.

[48] Hymer, Stephen H. (1976), *The International Operations of National Firms: A Study of Direct Foreign Investment*, Cambridge, Mass.: M.I.T. Press; Kindleberger, Charles P. (1969), *American Business Abroad: Six Lectures on Direct Investment*, New Haven: Yale University Press; Caves, R. E. (1971), "International Corporations: The Industrial Economics of Foreign Investment", *Economica*, 38 (1), pp. 1-27.

The second theory examined is the intangible capital approach, which claims that the possession of firm specific "monopolistic advantages" or "intangible assets" is *sine qua non* for firm's overseas production.[49] The monopolistic advantages may be in the form of production technologies, managerial skills, industrial organisation, knowledge of the product, and factor markets. These firms' specific advantages as pointed out by Lall, must serve three useful purposes.[50] Firstly, it must provide an edge to the firm concerned not only to outweigh its rivals at home but also over potential investors in the host country (both local and from third countries). Secondly, the monopolistic advantage must be transferable overseas and be employed most economically at the foreign location. And, thirdly, it must be more profitably exploited by the firm itself than by licensing it to an independent firm.[51] According to Caves, these firm-specific advantages may be in the form of a unique or differentiated product, which commands revenues superior to competing products in a marketplace.[52]

The third approach reviewed is the macroeconomic theory, which claims that there are two types of FDI: macroeconomic FDI which responses to changes in comparative advantage, and microeconomic FDI which is contrary to the law of comparative advantage.[53] According to Kojima, the former reflects FDI by small firms, which are undertaken to facilitate transfer of production from high wage to low wage countries. The latter reflects the type of FDI

---

[49] Lall, Sanjaya (1980), "Monopolistic Advantages and Foreign Involvement by U.S. Manufacturing Industry", *Oxford Economic Papers*, 32, pp. 102-22.

[50] Lall, Sanjaya and Siddharthan, N. S. (1982), "The Monopolistic Advantages of Multinationals: Lessons from Foreign Investment in the U.S.", *Economic Journal*, 92 (367), pp. 668-83.

[51] Ibid.

[52] Caves, Richard E. (1971), *op. cit.*, p. 1-3.

[53] The main advocates of this approach includes Kojima, K. (1982), *op. cit.*; Kojima, K. and Ozawa, Terutomo (1984), *op. cit.*; Kojima, K. (1985), *op. cit.*; Ozawa, Terutomo *op. cit.*; Ozawa, Terutomo (1979), *op. cit.*

carried out by large firms which is aimed at exploiting oligopolistic factors and product markets.[54] Accordingly, macroeconomic FDI is more dynamic because of its trade-creating effect whereas microeconomic FDI is basically trade-supplanting.[55]

Kojima's theory has been criticised as grossly inaccurate and theoretically misleading because of its rejection of basic microeconomic determinants of FDI.[56] As strongly pointed out by Chung, the microeconomic determinants of FDI are not an alternative to a macroeconomic theory of FDI.[57] Therefore, to argue that microeconomic theory fails to explain phenomena which are essentially macroeconomic is not valid. Which approach one chooses depends on the question one is asking. If one is investigating the causes and patterns of a country's direct foreign investment, one is trying to explain macroeconomic phenomena and identify the factors that account for them. The macroeconomic phenomena cannot be said to have been explained, however, unless it also explained how those factors affect the behaviour of individual decision markers.[58] Whilst the criticism on Kojima's theory may be valid, his theoretical insight of the relationship of a country's comparative advantage and its outward direct investment is useful. The theory offers the opportunity to examine the positive determinants of FDI and the desire of firms from the developing countries and the DCs to invest abroad.

---

[54] Gray, H. P. (1982), *op. cit.*, Chapter 8.

[55] Ibid., p. 177.

[56] Arndt, H. W. (1974), "Professor Kojima on the Macroeconomics of Foreign Direct Investment", *Hitotsubashi Journal of Economics*, 15 (2), pp. 26-35; Gray, H. Peter (1982), *op. cit.*, Chapter 8; Giddy, Ian H. and Stephen Young (1982), "Conventional Theory and Unconventional Multinationals: Do New Forms of Multinational Enterprise Require New Theories?", in Rugman, Alan M. (ed.), *New Theories of the Multinational Enterprise*, London: Croom Helm, Chapter 4; Chou, Tein-Chen (1988), "American and Japanese Direct Foreign Investment in Taiwan: A Comparative Study", *Hitotsubashi Journal of Economics*, 29 (2), pp. 165-79; Lee, Chung. H. (1984), "On Japanese Macroeconomic Theories of Direct Foreign Investment", *Economic Development and Cultural Change*, 32 (4), pp.713-23; Lee Chung H. (1990), "Direct Foreign Investment, Structural Adjustment, and International Division of Labour: A Dynamic Macroeconomic Theory of Direct Foreign Investment", *Hitotsubashi Journal of Economics*, 31 (2), pp. 61-72.

[57] Lee, Chung H. (1984), *op. cit.*, p. 713.

[58] Ibid.

Moreover, the approach offers the opportunity to examine in particular FDI by small firms in developing nations. Since the approach was originally formulated to examine outward direct investment by Japanese firms, it needs to be modified for application to this book in three respects. Firstly, Japan as a nation has a distinct institutional set-up, which although does not on its own cause firms to invest abroad could be significant as a push for FDI.[59] By institution I imply the "collective action in the control, liberation, and expansion of individual action".[60] Thus, the role of the state, courts, corporations, and trade unions is fundamental in the economic negotiations between individuals.[61] This is important as the collective action of the state, individuals and firms in Japan is fundamental to outward direct investment. Secondly, Kojima's theory of comparative advantage is based on the neoclassical static two-country model, which examines a country's international trade and factor endowments from a general equilibrium position. The modified theory however incorporates a more dynamic model, which accounts for more than two nations in the international division of labour. This is discussed in the light of recent growth triangles in the Asia region where more than two economic zones are concerned. Thirdly, Kojima's assumption of stable labour conditions in recipient countries is far from real in most of the Asian countries. The proposed modification argues that the state and the trade unions can influence labour costs and consequently foreign investment conditions. Fourthly, Kojima's distinction of "small" and "large" firms which is represented here as "foreign" and "local" firms is based on total assets. However, firm size can be measured by book value of net assets, book value of total assets, sales, stock-market valuation and/or employment. Thus the book uses employment criteria to define the size of firm. In view of these changes, it has been necessary to modify Kojima's theory to explain the dynamism of a country's comparative advantage and FDI outflow on the one hand, and the international division of labour between countries on the other.

---

[59] Buckley, Peter J. and Mirza, Hafiz (1985), "The Wit and Wisdom of Japanese Management: An Iconoclastic Analysis", *Management International Review*, 25, pp. 16-32.

[60] Commons, John R. (1959), *Institutional Economics*, Madison: University of Wisconsin Press, p. 901.

[61] McClintock, Brent (1989), "Direct Foreign Investment: A Reply", *Journal of Economic Issues*, 23 (3), pp. 885-89. Also, see McClintock (1988), "Recent Theories of Direct Foreign Investment: An Institutionalist Perspective", *Journal of Economic Issues*, XXII 22 (2), pp. 477-84.

The Neoclassical Microeconomic Theory

Central to the neoclassical capital theory is the argument that the flow of FDI is largely determined by the objective factor of capital for profitability which depends mainly on factor prices. By profit, neoclassical theory means the difference between a firm's total revenue and its total costs. However, the theory owes much of its argument to the classical economists, who argue that the sole objective of a firm is to maximise profits under the assumptions of perfect competition, perfect flow of information, and equal exchange between countries. Accordingly, it is the search for locations with relatively higher profits which causes overseas investment. In other words, out of profit maximisation comes, the firms' optimal plan for foreign investment.[62] As argued by Stevens, the firm's investment policy is assumed to respond to all product prices, factor prices, interest rates, and tax rates that affect profits.[63] Through competition in product markets, prices will be forced down to the level of long-run average costs, where the firm will have to maximise profits if it is to break even. Therefore, it is the maximisation of profits in relation to the capital invested which is the driving force for the establishment of the firm.

As pointed out by Stevens, the neoclassical view of foreign investment is a gradual adjustment of actual to desired capital. That is, given the desired stock of capital, a fall in the rate of return in either 'home' or 'host' country would lead to the fall in rate of profit. In other words, FDI responds to the falling rate of profit. To be specific, FDI flows out of countries with low returns to those expected to yield higher returns.[64]

According to Horst, the choice between exporting and carrying out FDI, depends on whether marginal revenue from foreign sales is greater or less than marginal cost of foreign production.[65] Even if the firm initially finds exporting to be more profitable than producing abroad, the time may come when there is a balance between the fixed-cost savings of exporting and the variable-cost saving of foreign production. If this happens, modern firms would prefer to produce abroad.

In the 1950s, the theory gained strong popularity when American firms' FDI increased very quickly, especially in Western Europe where the profits earned by American firms were considerably higher than those accruing in the

---

[62] Stevens, Guy V. G. (1974), *op. cit.*, Chapter 3.

[63] Ibid. p. 49.

[64] Ibid.

[65] Horst, Thomas O. (1974), "Theory of the Firm", in Dunning, John H. (ed.), Economic Analysis and the Multinational Enterprise, London: Allen & Unwin, Chapter 2.

US.[66] Furthermore, in the late 1960s and early 1970s, the new international division of labour theorists used a similar form of analysis to justify the claim that outward manufacturing investment from the DCs to LDCs was due to profitability.[67]

Empirically, evidence collected and statistical tests conducted over the last thirty years have failed to produce conclusive results. Whereas a few studies have either partially or wholly supported neoclassical theory, many others have not been able to find any association between the flow of FDI and international differences in rate of return.[68] An OLS regression analysis of firms' FDI outflow and profitability in Singapore indicated positive correlation. This is very much in line with the neoclassical microeconomic theory, which claims that capital moves from a country with relatively low rate of return to a country with higher rate of return. However, the result does not suggest that FDI is only responsive to profitability for capital. In the case of Indonesia and other statistically-insignificant countries, it is evident that other factors may have affected the decisions of firms to invest in these countries. The results are also in line with Kojima's theory, which claims that firms in labour-intensive industries, which are losing comparative advantage in the domestic economy, will relocate to countries which are gaining comparative advantage and whose profitability is relatively higher. Thus, it is reasonable to conclude that a firm's objective profitability for capital is a major but not the sole determinant of FDI.

Evidence presented by Agodo strongly supports the "rates of returns" motive as a fundamental determinant of U.S. private manufacturing direct investment in Africa during the 1970s.[69] The study, which involved 33 U.S. firms having, 46 manufacturing investments in 20 African countries argued that there was a strong correlation between U.S. FDI in Africa and the expected premium. According to Agodo, four main factors explain why U.S. firms' managers insist on a higher rate of return as a motivation. Firstly, that the move to Africa entails new risks and problems beyond what the U.S.

---

[66] Argawal, A. P. (1980), "Determinants of Foreign Direct Investment: A Survey", *Weltwirtschaftliches Archive*, Band 116, pp. 739-773.

[67] Arrighi, G. (1978), "Towards a Theory of Capitalist Crisis", *New Left Review*, 111 (3), pp. 3-24; Landsberg, M. (1979), "Export-led Industrialisation in the Third World: Manufacturing Imperialism", *The Review of Radical Political Economy*, 11 (4), pp. 1-29; Frobel et al (1980), *The New International Division of Labour*, Cambridge: Cambridge University Press.

[68] Argawal, A. P. (1980), *op. cit.*, p. 741.

[69] Agodo, Oriye (1978), "The Determinants of U.S. Private Manufacturing Investments in Africa", *Journal of International Business Studies*, 9 (3), pp. 95-107.

investor will ordinarily encounter in the domestic market. Secondly, that the higher rate of return in Africa is thus intended to compensate for the new risks and problems and its size is determined by, and varies in accordance with, the risk factor and other pertinent circumstances confronting the U.S. investor in the host country. Thirdly, the expected premium is intended to provide a sound independent basis for the long-term growth of the new venture without continued financial reliance on the parent firm. Finally, the expected premium also provides a modest reward for the parent's invested capital. The major problem with Agodo's research is that he did not specify whether the U.S. investors were more interested in short or long-term expected profits. A business survey, conducted by Barlow and Wender, found that while investors are generally influenced by profitability motives they are guided more by longer-term prospects than by immediate short-term profits.[70]

Regression analysis (based on cross section data mainly from company reports) by Popkins in 1965 also supported the view that there is a special relationship between FDI and domestic investment profitability level.[71] Stevens in a regional study of Latin American countries found evidence to support the hypothesis that the rates of return are significant for investment flows. However, on an individual country basis, with the exception of Brazil, the data used for investigation could not prove a positive result as was the case for regional study.[72]

A simple regression analysis by Reuber for the period 1956-69 showed that US manufacturing investment in Argentina, Brazil, Chile, India, Indonesia, Mexico and the Philippines was positively correlated with yearly rates of return. He concluded that both quantitative and qualitative evidence emanating from his survey supported the proposition that profitability is a

---

[70] Barlow, E. R. and Wender, Ira T. (1955), *Foreign Investment and Taxation*, Englewood Cliffs: Prentice-Hall Inc., Chapter 11.

[71] Popkin, J. (1965), *Interfirm Differences in Direct Investment Behaviour of US Manufacturers* (Ph.D Dissertation, University of Pennsylvania).

[72] Stevens, Guy V. G. (1969), "Fixed Investment Expenditure of Foreign Manufacturing Affiliates of US Firms: Theoretical Models and Empirical Evidence", *Yale Economic Essays*, 9 (1), pp. 137-200.

fundamental determinant of direct investment.[73] Furthermore, the survey carried out by Blais indicated that during the period 1950-71, the stock of manufacturing FDI from UK and Canada in the US was sensitive to expected rate of return.[74]

The test by Weintraub on US data however could not find any correlation between intercountry differences in the rates of return and the flow of US capital.[75] In another empirical examination, Bandera and White tested a number of data on American investments in Europe between the period 1953-62.[76] They, too, could not find any relationship between rate of return and the movement of investment capital. Also, studies carried out by Hufbauer and Walia conclude that there was insufficient evidence to support the hypothesis that US capital has 'migrated' in search for higher returns.[77]

The managerial theory of the firm developed by Cyert and March, Berle and Means, Marris, Williamson, and Baumol has questioned the neo-classical assumption of profit maximisation. According to Marris, the environment in which modern firms operate though competitive is surrounded by risks and uncertainty. As such, it is not possible for firms to "maximise" profit but rather to earn "satisfactory" profits. For satisfying profits is an approximation to maximising profits. By implication, a target rate of return is consistent with both satisfying and maximising profits.[78] Berle and Means on the other hand, have argued that shareholder ownership and managerial

---

[73] Reuber, G. L. et al (1973), *Private Foreign Investment in Development*, Oxford: Clarendon Press, p. 109.

[74] Blais, Jeffery P. (1975), *A Theoretical and Empirical Investigation of Canadian and British Direct Foreign Investment in Manufacturing in the United States* (Ph.D Dissertation, University of Pittsburgh).

[75] Weintraub, Robert (1967), "Studio empirico sulle relazioni di lungo andare tra movimenti di capitali e rendimenti differenziali", *Rivista Internazionale di Scienze Economiche e Commerciali*, 14 (2), pp. 401-15.

[76] Bandera, Valdimir N. and White, Joseph T. (1968), "U. S. Direct Investments and Domestic Markets in Europe", *Economia Internazionale*, 21 (3), pp. 117-33. See also Bandera, V. N. and Lucken, J. A. (1972), "Has U.S. Capital Differentiated between EEC and EFTA?", *Kyklos*, 25 (1), pp. 306-14.

[77] Hufbauer, G. C. (1966), *Synthetic Materials and the Theory of International Trade*, London: Gerald Duckworth; Walia, Tirlochan S. (1976), *An Empirical Evaluation of Selected Theories of Foreign Direct Investment by U.S. Based Multinational Corporations* (Ph.D Dissertation, New York University, Graduate School of Business Administration).

[78] Marris, Robin (1964), *The Economic Theory of "Managerial" Capitalism*, London: MacMillan Press, p. 276.

control were separate from one another in most large corporations.[79] According to both authors, the management might have an interest in motives other than that of profit maximisation. For instance, the management may want to maximise growth rather than profit. However, as noted by Wildsmith, there is a significant relationship between growth and profitability, and that this relationship possesses elements of dual causation.[80] Firstly, profitability is one of the vital contributions toward the ability of the firm to grow. Secondly, at any one time the rate of growth of the firm will determine the level of profitability attainable commensurate with that rate of expansion. Thus, growth maximisation is consistent with profit maximisation.

Another major criticism of the neoclassical theory of the firm is that the approach is inconsistent and unrealistic in the modern world. Their assumptions are said to be too abstract and as such their predictions are unreal in two respects. Firstly, that firms are regarded as primitive with no distinction between complex conglomerates on the one hand, and a sole trader on the other. What matters are the fact that they transform input to output for profit maximisation.[81] Secondly, the approach neglects the fundamental importance of technology by TNCs as a major determinant of FDI.

Caves and Rieldel[82] have separately attempted to provide a solution to the first criticism by incorporating the neoclassical general-equilibrium model developed by Heckscher-Ohlin (H-O). Essentially, the theory posits that comparative advantage derives from differences among countries in relative endowment of resources. The theorem as it is generally formulated rests on several key assumptions: constant returns to scale, a common worldwide stock of technological knowledge, common tastes and preferences among countries, and no country specific resources or factors of production. Under these assumptions it follows that a country will find a comparative advantage in those goods which use the relative abundant factor of production relatively intensively. In other words, relatively labour-abundant (developing) countries

---

[79] Berle, A. and Means, G. (1968), *The Modern Corporation and Private Property*, New York: Transaction Publishers; Cyert R. M. and March, J. G. (1963), *A Behaviourial Theory of the Firm*, New York: Prentice Hall; Marris, Robin (1964), *op. cit.*

[80] Wildsmith, J. R. (1973), *Managerial Theories of the Firm*, New York: Dunellen, p. 409.

[81] Crew, Michael A. (1975), *Theory of the Firm*, London: Longman, p. 2.

[82] Caves, Richard E. (1982), *Multinational Enterprise and Economic Analysis*, Cambridge: Cambridge University Press; Riedel, James (1991), "Intra-Asian Trade and Foreign Direct Investment", *Asian Development Review*, 9 (1), pp. 111-46.

are predicted by the theory to have a comparative advantage in relatively labour-intensive goods, while relatively capital-intensive (developed) countries find a comparative advantage in capital-intensive goods.[83]

The H-O hypothesis has been tested empirically for many countries and found generally to hold, especially for trade in manufactures between countries at different per capita income levels. The hypothesis however, fails when its key underlying assumptions are seriously at odds with reality. For instance, the assumption of no country specific resources clearly does not apply to natural resources, which are distributed very unevenly around the world. The second problem with the theory is that it assumes a common worldwide stock of technological knowledge to which every country should have equal access. Even if technology is ultimately diffused around the world, it takes time for this to happen. Therefore, countries, which are better able to generate new technologies, gain a comparative advantage, albeit a temporary one, in producing new goods which use newly minted technology, which the intangible microeconomic theory examined below call ownership advantages.

The Intangible Microeconomic Theories of FDI

The main argument of this approach is that FDI is determined by intangible assets (monopolistic advantages) possessed by firms. These assets are very similar to barriers to entry of new competition which are believed to lead to increased concentration at industrial level and to the forces making for growth and diversification at the level of the firm.[84] However, this approach owes much of its theoretical framework to the pioneering work of Hymer, who questioned the fundamental assumption of the neoclassical international capital theory, mainly perfect competition, and paved the way for the work of Charles Kindleberger, Raymond Vernon, Richard Caves, John Dunning, Alan Rugman, Peter Buckley, Mark Casson and others.[85] However, the various theoretical interpretations of intangible capital theories are examined through the theory of ownership advantage, the theory of internalization, and the theory of location advantage.

---

[83] Riedel, James (1991), *op. cit.*, p. 112.

[84] Lall, Sanjaya (1983), *op. cit.*, p. 2.

[85] Hymer, Stephen (1976), *op. cit.*; Vernon, Raymond (1966), "International Investment and International Trade in the Product Cycle", *Quarterly Journal of Economics*, 80, pp. 190-207; Vernon, Raymond (1971), "The Multinational Enterprise: Power vs. Sovereignty, *Foreign Affairs*, 49, pp. 736-51; Caves, Richard (1971), *op. cit.*, Caves (1974), Multinational Firms, Competition and Productivity in Host Country Markets, *Economica*, 41, pp. 176-93.

FDI Theory of Ownership Specific Advantage

Originally developed to explain post-war U.S. corporate investment in Western Europe, the *ownership theory* has been extended to cover all TNCs direct investment. Initially, three main analytical questions were posed.[86] Firstly, why do the investing firms produce in Europe rather than in the U.S.? Secondly, how can they compete with indigenous producers, given the additional costs of doing business abroad? Thirdly, why do U.S. firms not license their ownership advantages to European firms?

The answer to the first question according to Casson, is that direct investment was largely import-substituting at the time. In some cases, it provided access to cheaper labour.[87] Although labour productivity may have been lower in Europe - due partly to the lower scale of production - labour was relatively cheap in Europe, because the combination of the dollar shortage and nominal wage stickiness in the U.S. made the U.S. own-product wage very high. For the second question, the answer lies in the technology gap: this ensured that the cost to U.S. firms of doing business abroad was offset by lower production costs and better product quality achieved through superior technology and professional management practices. Considering the third question it was believed that if advantage was advertised for sale, it would attract attention: and encourage imitation, and make the appropriation of monopoly rents that much difficult.[88] Also, buyers will be reluctant to pay the full value for the advantage as they will be uncertain of exactly what is on offer, or what its quality is. Finally, transfers of technology between employees of the same firm may be less costly than transfers of technology between different firms, because the employees share a common corporate culture, and this makes it easy for them to learn from one another. However, the solution to question two became the focus of Hymer's research of the ownership specific advantage.

According to Hymer and others,[89] firms operating across national boundaries and over long distance suffer an intrinsic disadvantage - caused by difficulties of communication, linguistic and cultural differences, lack of knowledge of local market conditions and so on - which, for FDI to take place,

---

[86] Casson, Mark (1991), "General Theories of the Multinational Enterprise: Their Relevance to Business History", in Mira Wilkins (ed.), *The Growth of Multinationals*, London: Elgar Reference Collection, Chapter 3.

[87] Ibid.

[88] Ibid.

[89] Hymer, Stephen (1976), *op. cit.*; Vernon, Raymond (1966), *op. cit.*; Caves, Richard (1971), *op. cit.*; Dunning, John (1970), *op. cit.*

foreign investors must be able to offset by some sort of special advantages over potential local investors.[90] These special advantages may vary between firms, and could be industry and/or country specific. For instance, in capital goods industries, the advantage may be in the nature of products supplied and the firm's ability to produce at lower cost or take advantage of the economies of large scale production. In consumer goods sectors, the possession of branded products, and trademarks together with the ability to offer a reliable product may be customized to the needs of the local market.[91] In general, the special advantage must outweigh the disadvantage of being foreign if FDI is to take place.[92]

According to Lall, the bulk of the empirical studies in support of the ownership advantages theory has been from the experience of American and European firms.[93] For instance, Pearce, in the study of the world's largest industrial enterprises, found R&D expenditure of U.S. firms to be positively correlated to their foreign production. However, in U.K. firms, Pearce's correlation was negative as most of U.K. overseas investment is found to be in resource intensive sectors. For Japanese firms, Pearce's conclusion was that their propensity to engage in FDI was positively correlated to the average research intensity of industries, but that within industries there seemed to be some tendency for the less R&D intensive firms to follow suit.[94] A more recent study by Kogut and Chang, and Euro-Asia Centre of INSEAD, argued that Japanese investment in the U.S. and Europe is to acquire access to technology.[95] Similarly, the study by the World Bank has reported Third World TNCs as increasingly penetrating U.S. and European markets to gain access to technology and market information.[96]

[90] Lall, Sanjaya and Streeten, Paul (1980), *Foreign Investment, Transnational and Developing Countries*, London: The Macmillan Press, p. 18.
[91] Dunning, John (1993), *op. cit.*, p. 142.
[92] Riedel, James (1991), "Intra-Asian Trade and Foreign Direct Investment", *Asian Development Review*, 9 (1), pp. 1-30.
[93] Lall, Sanjaya and Siddharthan, N. S. (1982), *op. cit.*, pp. 668-83.
[94] Pearce, R. D. (1989), *The Internationalisation of Sales by Leading Enterprises: Some Firm, Industry and Country Determinants*, University of Reading, Discussion Papers in International Investment and Business Studies, Series B, no. 135. Summary of Pearce's paper can also be found in Dunning (1993), *op. cit.*, p. 149.
[95] Kogut, B. and Chang, S. J. (1991), "Technological Capabilities and Japanese Direct Investment in the United States", *Review of Economics and Statistics*, LXXIII, pp. 401-13; Jocelyn, Probert (1991), *Asian Direct Investment in Europe*, a research carried out for Euro-Asia Centre, INSEAD.
[96] World Bank, *World Development Report 1989*, Oxford: Oxford University Press, 1989.

Though the ownership specific hypothesis represents a unique microeconomic theory for explaining FDI flows from America and Europe, there are problems with respect to its methodology. Firstly, the theory suggests that foreign firms must possess some type of firm specific, rent-yielding advantages and that these advantages be sufficiently great to offset the cost of being foreign. It then follows that the investing firms are exclusively in oligopolistic markets in which some firm's specific advantages are necessary. This also means that until a firm reaches a relatively large scale of operation at home, it is likely to put off foreign investment.[97] As pointed out by Dunning, Buckley and Casson, the weakness of the ownership specific advantage theory is that it ignores the importance of transport costs, which are borne by large firms, which participate in international production.[98]

Apart from the above mentioned weakness of the ownership advantage theory, it does provide a framework for the discussion of outward direct investment by large TNCs. The ownership advantage theory also concentrates on technology as a major criteria for FDI. However, its usefulness here is that it provides a contrast in the argument between micro and macroeconomic determinants of FDI.

FDI Theory of Internalisation

This approach has its roots from early work of Ronald Coase, Oliver Williamson and others that claim that firms internalise their economic activities to minimize transaction costs so as to provide more efficient outcomes.[99] In recent years this analysis has been applied to TNCs by a number of modern

---

[97] Ozawa, T. (1979), *op. cit.*

[98] Argawal, A. P. (1980), *op. cit.*, p. 749.

[99] Coase, R. II. (1937), "The Nature of the Firm", *Economica*, 4 (1), pp. 386-405; Williamson, O. E. (1971), "The Vertical Integration of Production: Market Failure Considerations", *American Economic Review*, 61 (2), pp. 112-27; Williamson (1975), *Markets and Hierarchies: Analysis and Anti-Trust Implications: A Study in the Economics of Internal Organisation*, New York: Free Press; Williamson (1979), "Transaction-cost Economics: The Governance of Contractual Relations", *Journal of Law and Economics*, 22 (2), pp. 233-61; Williamson (1981), "The Modern Corporation: Origins, Evolution, Attributes", *Journal of Economic Literature*, 19 (4), pp. 1537-68; Arrow, K. J. (1969), *The Organisation of Economic Activity: Issues Pertinent to the Choice of Market Versus Nonmarket Allocation*, United States Congress, Joint Economic Committee, pp. 47-64; Arrow (1974), *The Limits of Organisation*, New York: W. W. Norton & Company.

theorists.[100] According to these theorists, firms will only engage in FDI if they perceive the net benefits of their joint ownership of domestic and foreign activities, and transactions arising from them, to exceed those offered by external trading relationships.[101] Thus, the internalisation of FDI occurs as a consequence of transactions costs, risks and uncertainties in arm's-length markets, and the potential for increased control, improved deployment of market power, reduced uncertainty, scale and scope economies, and advantageous transfer pricing in internalised systems.[102] In other words, market failure causes firms to internalise transactions in intangible assets which otherwise would be externalised. As such, internalisation is a means of overcoming market imperfections - generated by national boundaries, informational deficiencies, and the like via the creation of 'internal markets'.[103] For instance, government intervention in the form of tariff, taxation, dividend remittance and exchange rate policies provides a rationale for internalisation, since in this way the firm has the opportunity, through transfer pricing, to minimise tax payments.

The incentive to internalise depends on the relationship between four groups of factors: (i) industry-specific factors, such as the nature of the product, external market structure and economies of scale; (ii) region-specific factors, such as geographical distance, and cultural differences; (iii) nation-specific factors, for example, political and fiscal factors and (iv) firm-specific factors, for example, management expertise; with the main emphasis being on industry-specific factors.[104] Although this approach is different from the ownership-specific hypothesis, it owes much of its theoretical framework to the theory of choice and markets.

---

[100] Buckley, P. J. and Casson, M. C. (1976), *The Future of the Multinational Enterprise*, London: The MacMillan Press; Giddy, Ian H. and Young, Stephen (1982), "Conventional Theory and Unconventional Multinationals: Do New Forms of Multinational Enterprise Require New Theories?", in Rugman, Alan M. (ed.), *New Theories of the Multinational Enterprise*, London: Croom Helm; Lundgren, N. (1977), "Comment" (on a chapter by J. H. Dunning), in *The International Allocation of Economic Activity*, Ohlin, B., Hesselborn, P.O. and Wijikman, P.M. (eds.), London: MacMillan; Swedenborg, B. (1979), *The Multinational Operations of Swedish Firms: An Analysis of Determinants and Effects*, Stockholm: Industrial Utrednings-institut; McManus, J. C. (1972), *The Theory of the Multinational Firm and the Nation State*, Toronto: Collier, MacMillan.

[101] Dunning, J. H. (1993), *op. cit.*, p. 75.

[102] Helleiner, G. K. (1989), "Transnational Corporations and Direct Foreign Investment", in Chenery, Hollis and Srinivasan,T. N. (eds.), *Handbook of Development Economics*, Oxford: Elsevier Press, pp. 1441-80.

[103] Ibid., p. 1452.

[104] Buckley, P. and Casson, M. (1976), *op. cit.*, p. 33. Also see Jeremy Clegg (1987), *op. cit.*, p. 20.

Nonetheless, the attempt by Buckley and Casson to explain outward investment is valuable as it stresses the need for a systematic general theory of FDI and multinational enterprise. The theoretical interpretation given by them, however, does not apply in the short run and especially to FDI by smaller firms operating in one or two foreign countries. The results of the statistical tests done by them under very simplified assumptions boil down to the conclusion that the process of internalisation is concentrated in industries with relatively high incidence of Research and Development (R & D) expenditure. This is a conclusion reached in many other studies.[105] However, the internalisation theorists still do not answer the question why firms choose a particular country instead of the other. This is the question that the locational theorists attempt to answer as is outlined below.

FDI Theory of Locational Specific Advantage

Among the modern theorists, John Dunning has been the most eloquent contributor to the locational specific advantage theory of FDI. Central to this hypothesis is the argument that though the possession of monopolistic advantages, and the internalisation process by foreign investors, are a necessary condition they do not satisfy investors' decision to invest abroad. The 'rational investor' is deemed to calculate location costs, including trade barriers, political stability, government policies towards foreign investments, labour and costs, market characteristics and productivity, and on a comparative cost basis, select the optimal location strategy. Where such factors favour a foreign rather than a domestic location, the direct investment route will be chosen in place of exports.[106]

In other words, the potential host country possesses specific resource, cultural and institutional characteristics. Whether a firm exploits its advantages through overseas production or through exports depends on whether a foreign country offers an environment, which is particularly favourable to its activities. Lower factor prices for example, lower wages or rents, cannot explain the particular phenomenon of direct investment, for, where these exist, foreign capital will tend to flow in until returns are equalised across countries. It is the additional return that is generated from the exploitation of the firm's

---

[105] Argawal, A. P. (1980), *op. cit.*, p. 754.
[106] Giddy, Ian H. and Young, Stephen (1982), "Conventional Theory and Unconventional Multinationals: Do New Forms of Multinational Enterprise Require New Theories?", in Alan Rugman, M. (ed.), *New Theories of the Multinational Enterprise*, London: Croom Helm, p. 57; Buckley, Peter J. (1989), *The Multinational Enterprise: Theory and Applications*, London: The Macmillan Press, p. 20.

31

monopolistic advantages in the foreign environment that provides the incentive for the firm to accept the higher costs and risks associated with an overseas venture.[107]

By explaining outward FDI in this way, this hypothesis has provided partial answers to the questions why firms invest overseas and why firms choose foreign investments rather than exports. According to locational theorists, foreign investments cannot be explained by just one factor such as the rate of return, output size or ownership advantage but through the combination of locational pull factors which may differ in terms of ranking from one firm to another. Only on comparative basis would a firm decide whether to invest overseas or not. For example, countries such as United Kingdom, Germany and France offer well endowed and comprehensive research and development, infrastructure, relatively low-cost technical expertise, access to a large, high-income market in the European Union (EU), and a mature and independent legal system. Such advantages tend to create a particularly attractive location for the production of high technology products.[108] On the other hand, the location attractiveness of the many Third World countries lies in their abundant and cheap labour, markets and natural resources.

However, one of the main drawbacks of the locational theory of FDI is it static assumption of a country's specific advantage. Though a country may possess locational advantages, the reason for TNCs to exploit these factors depends on the extent to which that country is willing to liberalise. Many of the Eastern Europe countries such as Russia, Poland and Hungary have more location advantages than China and yet the flow of FDI into China is more than that of all the Eastern Europe countries put together.[109] Likewise, Latin American countries have more locational advantages than East Asian countries, but investors prefer Asian countries to Latin America.[110] The point is that

---

[107] Brech, Michael and Sharp, Margaret (1984), *Inward Investment: Policy Options for the United Kingdom*, London: The Royal Institute of International Affairs and Routledge & Kegan Paul, p. 28.

[108] Ibid. p. 28.

[109] For more information on the FDI climate in the former Soviet Union see Zhuravlev, S. N. (1992), "Foreign Investments in the Economy: Methods for Regulating Their Volume and Structure", *Matekon*, 28 (2), pp. 45-63; Langhammer, Rolf J. (1992), "Salient Features of Trade Among Former Soviet Union Republics: Facts, Flaws and Findings", *Aussenwirtschaft*, Band 47, pp. 253-77; Klodt, Henning (1991), "Comparative Advantage and Prospective Structural Adjustment in Eastern Europe", *Economic Systems*, 15 (2), pp. 265-81.

[110] Birch, Melissa H. (1991), "Change Patterns of Foreign Investment in Latin America", *Quarterly Review of Economics and Business*, 31 (3), pp. 141-58.

locational advantages depend on state policies, where the state has the capability to create and shape the country's comparative advantage by controlling factor prices. Also, if the state investment policy is seen by the investor as liberal, then it may consider such a location as suitable. But if the state policy is seen as hostile then country locational advantages become no more than a monument. Thus it is the heavy hand of the Asian governments which controls the labour force and creates a favourable investment climate plus political stability which explains why Asian economies are more successful in attracting FDI than either Eastern European or Latin American countries.

An attempt has been made by the "Reading School" led by Dunning to establish a general consensus known as the eclectic theory of FDI. According to this theory, all firms will invest overseas if three monopolistic advantages are present.

(i) The extent to which firms possess sustainable ownership specific advantage *vis-á-vis* firms of other nationalities in the particular markets they serve or are contemplating serving. These ownership advantages can take the form of privileged possession of intangible assets as well as those which arise as a result of the common governance of cross-border value added activities.

(ii) The extent to which firms perceive ownership advantages to be in their best interest rather than to sell them, or their right of use, to foreign firms. For these advantages may reflect either the greater organisational efficiency of hierarchies or their ability to exercise monopoly power over the assets under their governance.

(iii) The extent to which the global interests of firms are served by creating, or utilising their ownership advantages in a foreign location.[111]

It is the interaction of these three advantages which provides the necessary conditions for firms to invest overseas. The implication of this is that neither ownership nor locational advantages nor internalisation theories on their own can provide a general theory of FDI. The major problem with the eclectic theory is that it is too general an approach so that even its explanation of FDI is vague. By grouping together under one heading three diversified established theories of FDI, the eclectic approach is in danger of obscuring the crucial analytical issues of these hypotheses. Also, it could then be argued that the eclectic theory is less of an alternative theory of international production since the theories of ownership, internalisation and location explain different types of FDI. However, since the eclectic theory does not offer any alternative

---

[111] Dunning, J. H. (1993), *op. cit.*, p. 79.

explanation to the already discussed ownership, internalisation and locational advantages, I will now examine the macroeconomic determinants of FDI.

Macroeconomic Theories of FDI

Vernon's Product Life Cycle Theory

The theory of product cycle offers an explanation of FDI from both microeconomic and macroeconomic perspectives. From the microeconomic perspective, it combines and assigns varying roles to technology, production costs and marketing factors[112] (all considered as ownership advantages). However, Vernon's approach differs considerably from Hymer's ownership advantage hypothesis examined earlier, in the sense that the latter gives priority to oligopolistic elements, while the former underlines the significance of new products in the overseas expansion of U.S. firms.[113] From the macroeconomic perspective, the theory explains a country's pattern of international trade and investment. In other words, it is the high average income and the high unit cost of labour relative to the cost of capital in the U.S. that accounts for its high rate of expenditure on product development and the introduction of new products. These products go through the cycle of birth, maturation, and standardisation, and this cycle accounts for the pattern of FDI as well as the pattern of international trade.[114]

According to Vernon, in the first stage, when the product is new, it is produced by the innovating firm in its home market. This is due to the fact that the absolute advantage in financial, organisational and intellectual resources to undertake the requisite research and development can only be met at home. This then means that the home market plays a dual role of not only acting as the source of stimulus for the innovating firm, but also the preferred location for the actual development of the innovation.[115] Thus, because of high per capita income and high labour costs in the U.S., there is a particular incentive to develop new products which are technology intensive. Given this absolute advantage, the innovating firm serves foreign markets by exports instead of FDI.

The second stage is that of the maturing product. Some element of

---

[112] Lall, Sanjaya and Streeten, Paul (1980), *Foreign Investment, Transnational and Developing Countries*, London: The Macmillan Press, p. 32.

[113] Adam, Gy (1974), "Some Reasons for Foreign Investment", *Acta Oeconomica*, 13 (3-4), pp. 323-37.

[114] Chung, H. Lee (1984), *op. cit.*, p. 720.

[115] Vernon, Raymond (1979), "The Product Cycle Hypothesis in a New International Environment", *Oxford Bulletin of Economics and Statistics*, 41 (4), pp. 255-67.

standardisation is introduced in design and production. In general there is less need for the flexibility that goes with experimentation and product development, and long-run production with established technology becomes possible. New competitors are introduced in the market either by producing exactly the same product or imitation. But in as much as the marginal production costs plus the transport costs of the goods exported by the 'original investor' are lower than the average costs of prospective production in the marketing, the investors would export and avoid FDI.[116]

In the final stage, namely the standardised product, the priority is for the lowest cost supply point. The innovating firm seeks to maintain its profits by making more intense marketing efforts and by investing abroad in cheaper locations and nearer foreign markets, so exploiting its technological quasi-rent to the utmost. Production shifts in location down the income scale, say from the USA to Europe, and from Europe to LDCs. This implies that overseas production of new products is essentially of a defensive nature; it is an alternative to the export of a new product.

However, the scope of the product cycle hypothesis has been widened several times so that it now takes into account not only labour costs but also other factor costs such as land and raw materials,[117] and its applicability to U.S TNCs only has been changed to include all developed countries.[118] Nonetheless, the product cycle hypothesis is still restricted to highly innovative industries and is thus unable to explain other forms of FDI particularly those from LDCs, who are not as innovative as the DC's firms.

Kojima's Comparative Advantage Theory

Unlike Vernon's macroeconomic theory which sees all products as going through the cycle of new, maturity and standard, and the cycle accounting for the pattern of international trade and FDI, Kojima's macroeconomic theory sees FDI as evolving around four major orientations: natural resource oriented, labour oriented, trade-barrier-induced market oriented, and oligopolistic market oriented. The first two according to Kojima are trade-oriented, the third can only be considered trade-oriented only if it has the initial potential of transforming import-substitution to export-led, but the fourth is anti-trade-oriented.[119]

---

[116] Hood, Neil and Young, Stephen (1979), *The Economics of Multinational Enterprise*, London: Longman, p. 60.

[117] Vernon, Raymond (1971), *Sovereignty at Bay: The Multinational Spread of U.S. Enterprise*; Vernon, R. "Competition Policy Toward Multinational Corporations", *The American Economic Review*, 64 (2), 1974, pp. 276-82.

[118] Argawal, A. P. (1980), *op. cit.*, pp. 751-2.

[119] Arndt, H. W. (1974), "Professor Kojima on the Macroeconomic of Foreign Direct Investment", *Hitotsubashi Journal of Economics*, 15 (2), pp. 26-35.

According to Kojima, the last is a true description of the American type of FDI and the first three, and in particular, the first two are a picture of Japan's FDI. Accordingly, the main distinction between a Japanese and an American FDI is that Japan's FDI is aimed at increasing international trade and is thus trade-oriented while American FDI is to serve the recipient country's market as such and is anti-trade-oriented.[120] Kojima argued that Japanese overseas investments are aimed mostly at exploiting natural resources in resource rich- countries or manufacturing labour intensive products in labour-abundant developing countries.[121] Most output of the first type of investment are shipped back to Japan, while the products from the second type are increasingly exported back to Japan or to third country markets. In contrast, American overseas manufacturing investments are designed mostly to produce highly sophisticated, technology based products for local markets, as envisaged in Vernon's product life cycle.[122]

Vernon's theory assumes investing firms to be large and to continue the production of new products in order to stay competitive. Such a view, according to Kojima, cannot explain why small labour-intensive Japanese firms invest overseas. For FDI by Japanese firms needs to be understood in the context of two phenomena. Firstly, the objective conditions of profitability for capital as determined largely by factor prices. That is, firms in the industries that are losing comparative advantage make FDI because of the relative higher profit potential abroad. Kojima attempts to prove this by assuming that if I take x and x as the rates of profit in x industry at home and abroad, respectively, and y and y as the rates of profit for the y industry at home and abroad, respectively: then, if $x = 12$ per cent, $y = 5$ per cent, and $x = y = 10$ per cent, the home country has a comparative advantage in the y industry. It will increase domestic investment in the y industry and will invest abroad in the x industry. Furthermore, the home country will be better off with this pattern of investment since it is more profitable.[123] Thus, local firms will be guided by this comparative profitability analogy. Secondly, Japanese firms relocate industrial production because of subjective determinants of FDI. According to Kojima, the desire of firms to invest in countries other than Japan may include labour shortage, appreciating yen, government industrial restructuring from labour-intensive to capital-intensive, domestic labour costs and the erosion of

---

[120] Kojima, K. (1982), *op. cit.*, pp. 1-19.
[121] Ozawa, Terutomo (1979), *op. cit.*, p. 79.
[122] Ibid.
[123] Lee, Chung. H. (1984), *op. cit.*, p. 717.

Japan as a low cost production site.[124]

So far, Kojima's analysis tends to suggests that there are two types of FDI. The first is the American and European type of FDI which is characterised by an oligopolistic structure, and the second, being the macroeconomic type of FDI which consists of small and medium sized Japanese firms. Furthermore, the argument is that American FDI is consistent with Vernon's product life cycle and as such is anti-trade for three main reasons. Firstly, that the product life cycle type of FDI cuts-off the investing country's own comparative advantage.[125] That is, where the U.S economy is claimed to have a dualistic structure consisting of oligopolistic, technologically advanced industries alongside a traditional, stagnant, price competitive sector (textiles, steel, agriculture), FDI takes place only within the former sector as firms attempt to defend markets and maintain oligopolistic position. By contrast, marginally efficient firms within the declining sectors in Japan are considered to find it profitable to establish operations overseas because of domestic constraints on factors of production.[126] Secondly, instead of transferring whole industries from the investing to the host countries, it leaves a tail of high cost industries in the investing country which then require protection from foreign competition. Thirdly, the new industries, which it establishes in the host countries, are unsuited to their factor proportions and therefore unlikely either to become internationally competitive or to have favourable spillover effects or leakage.[127]

Comparatively, Japan's FDI plays two important roles. Firstly, it creates manufacturing capacity in developing countries; and secondly, it plays a harmonious role for both sides because of the industries chosen, such as textiles and other labour intensive consumer goods industries, in which the investing country is losing comparative advantage while developing countries are gaining in it.[128] Furthermore, Japan's FDI success has been a result of the type of technology that is transferred from Japan to the developing countries. According to Kojima, the type of technology that is transferred from the developed countries to developing countries is usually inappropriate because of its capital-intensive and labour-intensive nature. Because of factor availabilities in developing countries, the type of technology required should be of adaptable nature to the local economy. In other words, the type of industries transferred should be of a conventional nature where benefits are appropriate to the developing country's factor endowments.[129]

---

[124] Gray, Peter, H. (1982), *op. cit.*, Chapter 8.

[125] Arndt, H. W. (1974), *op. cit.*, p. 28.

[126] Giddy, Ian H. and Young, Stephen (1982), *op. cit.*, pp. 64-65.

[127] Arndt, H. W. (1974), *op. cit.*, p. 28.

[128] Kojima, K. (1973), *op. cit.*, pp. 1-12.

[129] Ozawa, Terutomo (1979), *op. cit.*, p. 83.

The type of technology transfer should play the role of a "tutor" in the words of Kojima, or "midwife" as suggested by Findlay. That is, the main role of FDI should be to transplant superior production technology through training of labour, management, and marketing, from advanced industrial countries to LDCs, or it should transfer technology which will replace the inferior ones in the host country. Thus, FDI should be an initiator and tutor of industrialisation in LDCs. For this type of industrial transplant will help to reorganise the "old" international division of labour, thus increasing production and consumption gains from trade for both countries.[130] This welfare aspect of Kojima's macroeconomic theory contribution is undoubtedly an important feature, and is not found in the traditional and monopolistic microeconomic theories of FDI. Monopolistic microeconomic approaches justify a giant multinational enterprise that pursues profit maximisation on a global scale so that it may grow and survive, ignoring the interests of the developing host countries.[131] The fact that Japan's type of FDI contributes to local development explains why many developing host countries encourage this type of industrial transplant by offering various incentives, since their factor endowments are more suitable to it.

Kojima's macroeconomic theory has been extended by Ozawa to incorporate elements of a classical growth model - the Ricardo-Hicksian trap of industrial stagnation.[132] Central to the Ricardo-Hicksian industrial stagnation theorem is that an economy cannot expand indefinitely as sooner or later it must encounter "irremovable scarcities" of key factors such as land and labour.[133] Such an economy will be in a trap as labour costs continue to increase the potential for profitability decline. According to Hicks, it is the impulse of invention, which will rescue the economy from stagnation.[134] Ozawa has compared the classical model to Japan's industrialisation during the 1960s and 1970s. Japan's economy, he argued, was inescapably headed for a slow-down due to intense labour shortages and rising wage costs. As such, outward direct investment, strong government support and intense industrial restructuring were the only escape routes from industrial stagnation. This then implies that Japan's FDI is due mainly to scarcities of natural resources and increasing labour shortages.

---

[130] Kojima (1982), *op. cit.*, pp. 3-5.
[131] Ibid., p. 14.
[132] Ibid.
[133] Lee, Chung H. (1984), *op. cit.*, p. 719.
[134] Hicks, John (1974), "The Future of Industrialism", *International Affairs*, 50 (2), pp. 218-29.

The above-mentioned Kojima and Ozawa's "sweeping dichotomy" of microeconomic and macroeconomic theories of FDI has been criticised by some authors. According, to Arndt, Kojima's contrast of "large microeconomic FDI" and "small macroeconomic FDI" determinants is theoretically and empirically unfounded. Theoretically, firms whether large or small, carry out FDI to overcome competition at home and abroad.[135] Moreover, Kojima's definition of Japanese firms as small and American firms as large is absolute tautology. Japanese firms such as Nissan and Fuji were already conglomerates before the 1970s. Also, Chung has criticised the Kojima's approach as a narrow examination of FDI. For the economic theory of FDI is macroeconomic in the question asked but microeconomic in the choice of logistic. In other words, to understand things of the large one must begin with things in the small.[136] However, it is this linkage of microeconomic and macroeconomic determinants that leads to the comparison of Kojima and Vernon in the next section.

Vernon and Kojima Theories of FDI Compared

In this section, I compare Kojima and Vernon's macroeconomic theories of FDI. However, it will be easier to start with the authors' similarities than their differences. But first, it is important to point out that Kojima wrote most of his masterpiece in the early 1970s, and even at that time, Japanese firms were already large enough to compete with the American firms.[137] Secondly, Japanese TNCs in recent years are as oligopolistic as American firms.[138] However, the similarities between American and Japanese are also reflected in the similitude of Kojima and Vernon's theories of FDI. In both theories, FDI is motivated by comparative advantage. Both authors regard labour costs to be fundamental for outward direct investment and argue that the firm's cost of labour is determined by wage rate and productivity of the work force.

According to Arndt, the similarity between American and Japanese FDI motives can be deceptive.[139] Because American manufacturing exports have been very different from Japanese, so have FDI projects designed to pro-

---

[135] Arndt, H. W. (1974), *op. cit.*

[136] Lee, Chung H. (1984), *op. cit.*, p. 714.

[137] Hymer, Stephen H. (1971), "The Multinational Enterprise and the Law of Uneven Development", in Bhagwati, J. (ed.), *Economics and the World Order*, New York: World Law Fund.

[138] Chou, Tein-Chen (1988), "American and Japanese Direct Foreign Investment in Taiwan: A Comparative Study", *Hitotsubashi Journal of Economics*, 29 (2), pp. 165-179.

[139] Arndt, H. W. (1974), *op. cit.*, p.32.

tect established or potential export markets. The difference, in fact, illustrates the importance of the width of the technology gap between home and host countries. American manufacturing exports have for long depended on comparative advantage in the most technology intensive industries, while Japanese manufacturing exports before the 1960s and 1970s consisted predominantly of products of relatively labour intensive consumer goods industries. Accordingly, this gives Japanese FDI two important potential advantages over American in LDCs: greater ease of transmission of technology and business know-how and greater likelihood that new industries will be international competitive. On the other hand, the technology gap between American firms and their subsidiaries abroad has constituted a major obstacle for the transmission of technical and business know-how conducive for economic development.[140]

However, the difference between the choice of American and Japanese technology has been diminishing. An empirical study by Tein-Chen in Taiwan shows that there were no differences between American and Japanese ownership specific advantage in that country.[141] Both groups of investors possessed ownership advantage and their investments were designed to defend exports. Also, current studies indicate that Japan's FDI in Europe and Mexico is a result of the fear of tariff and fortress markets.[142]

Thus, the internationalization of Japanese firms can be said to have undergone a gradual process from small-size firms to large conglomerates which entails the possession of ownership-specific advantages as a necessary condition for the stages of the product cycle. Therefore, its resemblance with the American FDI, which underwent all stages of the product cycle, is not surprising. The American experience reflected an economy which has not lacked natural resources and which has been a leader in technological innovations. The Japanese experience shows an economy, which lacks natural resources and has been a net importer of technology[143] but still completed the product cycle in a different way. However, in recent years the experience of both

---

[140] Ibid.

[141] Chou, Tein-Chen (1988), "American and Japanese Direct Foreign Investment in Taiwan: A Comparative Study", *Hitotsubashi Journal of Economics*, 29 (2), pp. 165-179.

[142] Probert, Jocelyn (1991), *op. cit.*; Ozawa, T. (1991), "Japanese Multinationals and 1992", in Burgenmeier, B. and L. J. Mucchielli (eds.), *Multinationals and Europe 1992*, London: Routledge; Ozawa, T. (1991), "The Dynamics of Pacific Rim Industrialisation: How Mexico can join the Flock of Flying Geese" in Roett, R. (ed.), *Mexico's External Relations in the 1990's*, London: Lynne Rienner.

[143] Lee, Chung H. (1984), "On Japanese Macroeconomic Theories of Direct Foreign Investment", *Economic Development and Cultural Change*, 32 (4), pp. 713-23.

countries has become similar. The USA for instance, has now emerged along with Japan as the world's largest importer of raw materials. However, the issue here is to establish the fact that what determines a large firm to invest abroad is not necessarily the same for small firms. As is examined below the determinants of FDI by small firms need to be distinguished from those of large firms.

Modified Kojima's Macroeconomic Theory of FDI

The main purpose for the modification of Kojima's macroeconomic theory of FDI is to enable better use and application of the theory for this book. This is important as Kojima's original theory was particularly aimed at explaining outward direct investment from Japan. Though Japan's FDI is unique in it own way, it nonetheless needs to be modified to reflect three main factors which are common in the Third World: firstly, the role of the state as a special institution responsible for creating the nation's comparative advantage in international division of labour; secondly, the role of regional common markets and the benefits of economies of scale; thirdly, the role of foreign capital in the local economy and the "crowding-out effect" of indigenous entrepreneurs. Thus the modified theory states that there is correspondence between a country's comparative advantage and outward direct investment on the one hand, and the international division of labour between the investing and the recipient countries on the other. That is, firms in labour-intensive industries, which are losing comparative advantage, will invest in countries that are gaining comparative advantage in that industry. Therefore, FDI is aimed at maximising international trade and economies of scale. The main reason for this is because of the factor price differentials between the participating countries and/or economic zones. If all countries were "borderless" mobile factors would maintain their value. But, since borders exist capital migrates across national boundaries to take advantage of the factor price differences.[144]

However, it is apparent that the definitions of "small firm" vary according to research and context. Definitions are not right or wrong, just more or less useful.[145] For the purpose of this book, I shall classify small and medium sized firms as employing less than 100 workers. To this end, small firms are constrained by the availability of capital, labour, management exper-

---

[144] Lee, Tsao Yuan (1992), *op. cit.*, p. 8.
[145] Buckley, Peter J. (1989), *The Multinational Enterprise: Theory and Applications*, London: MacMillan, Chapter 2.

tise and technology. This is important as the availability of managerial skills may for instance constrain the growth of local entrepreneurship. Thus the faster the rate of economic development in the local economy, the higher the demand for these factors. By this, I am not suggesting that small firms possess ownership advantages as argued by Lall.[146] Instead, I am arguing that because of the faster rate of change in the local economy, smaller firms are unable to continue production as factor costs are becoming more and more expensive. Thus it is the loss of comparative advantage of these firms plus the industrial policy of the state, which is forcing small firms to relocate.

As argued by Lall, some small firms do possess firm specific advantages, which they try to exploit abroad.[147] Although the advantages are not exactly the same as those of large firms, they are enough to give the small firms competitive edge over the local firms in the recipient country. However, the problem with the ownership advantage theory is that the possession of firm specific advantages is seen as the basis for competition and the classification of large and small firms.

The modified theory claims that FDI by developing countries are, in general, to take the opportunity of economies of scale rather than to exploit ownership advantage. From the firm's point of view, this sort of economy of scale may be internal and external to the investing firm; the former normally lead to horizontal investment, and the latter to vertical investment.[148] Foreign investment in vertically related stages of production is common in mainly extracting industries producing and processing minerals and other raw materials. The main advantage of direct investment here consists in reducing the costs and uncertainties that exist when subsequent stages of production are handled by different producers by coordinating decisions at various stages within one firm. An increase in production through investment may permit a reduction in the unit cost of certain general services, such as financing, marketing or technological research that have the nature of fixed costs. From the country's stand point, the economies of scale can lead to regional common markets such as the growth triangle.[149] The uniqueness of this form of international division of labour is that it doesn't necessarily need to involve all regions of the participating country but only designated economic zones, which are considered by the investors as potential investment areas. However, the participating countries or economic zones benefit from four economies of scale:

---

[146] Lall, Sanjaya (1983), *op. cit.*, Chapter 1.
[147] Ibid.
[148] Ragazzi, Giorgio (1973), *op. cit.*, p. 488.
[149] Ibid.

firstly, economies of agglomeration, achieved through locating different parts of a value chain, which often require different mixes of factors, in different locations which have the appropriate factor endowments; secondly, economies of scale in distribution and financial and business services; thirdly, economies of scale of consumer and market diversity; and fourthly, economies of scale of public infrastructure networks, such as telecommunications and utilities.

The modified economic complementarity concept is based on a three-country model as follows: a developed country, a developing country and a less developed country[150] differing from Kojima's static comparative advantage theory, where only two countries are used. The developed country gains comparative advantage in technology intensive production due to R & D, while the developing country undergoes structural transformation from labour intensive to capital intensive production methods. The developing countries lose comparative advantage in labour-intensive production, and the less developed country gains comparative advantage in labour-intensive industries because of the availability of labour. In both the developed and developing countries the general characteristics will include a well-developed manufacturing sector, financial, commercial and transportation capabilities, including infrastructure and skilled personnel. The achievement of economic growth, full employment and strong labour unions in the developed country will lead to high labour costs, limited supply of unskilled labour, and high operational costs. On the other hand, the less developed country will have abundant and cheap labour, land and raw material. This then implies that there is complementarity with regards to land, natural resources, labour, transportation and communications, infrastructure, and financial facilities.[151] The division of labour between the three countries will start when the developed country relocates labour intensive and capital-intensive industries to developing and less developed countries. The developing country in turn will relocate labour-intensive production facilities to the less developed country since it no longer has comparative advantage in such industries.

This type of investment is currently evident in some of the world regional groupings. For instance, the Johor-Singapore-Riau growth triangle,

---

[150] Lee, Chung H. (1990), "Direct Foreign Investment, Structural Adjustment, and International Division of Labour: A Dynamic Macroeconomic Theory of Direct Foreign Investment", *Hitotsubashi Journal of Economics*, 31 (2), pp. 61-72.

[151] Lee, Tsao Yuan (1992), "Regional Economic Zones in the Asia-Pacific: A Conceptual Overview", Paper presented at the conference on *Regional Cooperation and Growth Triangles in ASEAN*, jointly organised by Centre for Business Research & Development, and Centre for Advanced Studies, National University of Singapore, 23-24 April, p. 6.

which consists of Singapore as the "developed country", Malaysia the "developing country" and Indonesia, the "less developed country". The determinant of FDI in the region is not only large internal markets, but also the differences in resource availability between the three countries involved and hence economic complementarity and integration.

In Kojima's theory, the labour market is assumed to be competitive such that workers are easily hired and laid off. Consequently, only the effect of the decision either to invest abroad or to invest at home on the basis of industry specific capital is considered. But, clearly such labour market conditions cannot be assumed for all countries. Being largely immobile between countries because of national boundaries, labour cannot preserve the value of its industry specific skills by moving abroad and has therefore a greater incentive to protect its value through other measures. The labour union is certainly one of these.[152] In many of the developing and the less developed countries, there are strong union movements to protect the interests of their members. The strong presence of trade unions can affect the costs of labour. So that countries with strong union powers will be in the position to negotiate for higher wages, which may in turn lead to the loss of comparative advantage. It is also assumed that the government can affect labour costs through its industrial policy, where domestic firms may be encouraged to use more capital for their production, with the importation of foreign labour to ease the pressure on wages, and the introduction of wage councils. Also, it is assumed that other factors such as geographical proximity, political stability, availability of cheap labour, cultural similarities and incentives are important as determinants in the modified theory.

Finally, Japan's industrialisation, as is well documented in Ozawa's work,[153] has been developed with indigenous capital rather than foreign capital by TNCs. Japan has never experienced a high level of foreign capital domination in its economy. While in most parts of Asia, foreign capital and trade has been the main engine for economic growth. With the exception of Taiwan and Korea where government policies have been designed deliberately to discourage wholly foreign owned firms,[154] places such as Singapore and Hong Kong have depended heavily on foreign capital. As such, the economic policy investment incentive and the role of the state tend to favour foreign investors rather than local firms. As will be noted in the next

---

[152] Lee, Chung H. (1990), op. cit., pp. 61-72.

[153] Ozawa, T. (1979), "International Investment and Industrial Structure: New Theoretical Implications from the Japanese Experience", *Oxford Economic Papers*, 31 (1), pp. 72-92.

[154] Amsden, Alice H. (1989), *Asian's Next Giant: South Korea and Late Industrialisation*, Oxford: Oxford University Press.

chapter, such dependence on foreign capital has led to a discriminating industrial policy in Singapore, where foreign investors have been given greater incentives than local entrepreneurs. This has in effect led to the "crowding out" of local firms. The role of the state is also different between Japan and Singapore. For instance, in Singapore, the success of the state is closely tied to foreign capital whereas in Japan, the popularity and power of the state is closely linked to indigenous firms. Moreover, if the level of foreign dominance in Singapore were to be allowed in Japan, the state would be seen by the electorate as weak. So that for Kojima's theory to be applicable to other countries, with different experience of industrialisation and institutional set up, the earlier-mentioned modifications are necessary.

Conclusion

Having reviewed the three major theories of FDI, it is clear that any approach which plays down or obscures the interrelationship between a country's comparative advantage and its FDI is limited as an adequate framework for the research. As noted, the neoclassical theory claimed that firms pursue profits by moving capital from countries where its return is low to countries where it is high. Theoretically, the approach serves to tie together a considerable body of literature on the general-equilibrium theory about international trade and international movements of factors of production. That is, where firms are expected based in countries best endowed with capital will relocate because of the low marginal productivity, to countries least well endowed with capital because of their high marginal products of capital.[155] However, the capital arbitrage theory on it own is not sufficient as an inducement, except that it provides the vital link between the motivating push and pull factors for FDI.

The intangible microeconomic theory on the other hand, although accepting profitability as a motive for investment by TNCs, argues that firm-specific advantages are the necessary requirements for outward direct investment. By implication, the investing firm must be oligopolistic in structure and must posses intangible assets such as technology. The usefulness of the intangible microeconomic theory, however, is to firms from developed nations who are constantly involved in invention and innovation of new technology and not to developing country firms which, because of the nature of the growth, had depended on borrowed technology from the DCs.

The macroeconomic theory provides a framework, which is not only consistent with a country's comparative advantage but also FDI by small and large firms. In the case of Vernon's theory, it bridges the gap between

---

[155] Caves, Richard E. (1982), *op. cit.*, p.31.

45

monopolistic and macroeconomic FDI determinants by the use of microeconomic theory of industrial organisation and macroeconomic theory of traditional trade. On the other hand, Kojima's macroeconomic theory provides a framework, which is suitable for explaining FDI by small and large sized firms. However, it fails to capture the institutional differences between Japan and other developing countries and in particular, Singapore. Also, it fails to incorporate the growing importance of the economies of scale which firms derive when they invest in common markets such as a growth triangle. However, the main purpose of the modified theory has been to incorporate Kojima's model of FDI to the changing international division of labour and to be able to employ the approach for the book. However, it would be a pretentious and inflated claim to suggest that the modified Kojima's theory is the best for any country FDI. Its value to us is that it addresses issues, which are useful for this book. This is important as the modification is to reflect Singapore's economic development, which is unique as compared to some of the Southeast Asian countries. For instance, it is the only country in the region with over a 90 per cent share of foreign capital in the manufacturing sector. Thus, it is important to examine separately the determinants of FDI by indigenous firms and TNC subsidiaries in Singapore. Therefore, from now on I shall substitute Kojima's large and small firms for foreign and local firms. A clear distinction of these two groups of investors is given in chapters 4 and 5. For now, the next chapter examines Singapore's comparative advantage and government's industrial policies since independence.

3 Singapore's Economic Policy and FDI Inflow

ABSTRACT

The main argument of this chapter is that the role of the state is fundamental to any country's comparative advantage and economic growth. Thus, Singapore's economic success is a manifestation of active participation by the state. By contrast, the neoclassical theory argues that government intervention distorts a country's comparative advantage and therefore, contradicts economic rationality. Thus a country's "openness" is equated with economic success and an unsuccessful economy is regarded as "closed" to international market forces. However, it is concluded that the active role of the state in Singapore's economy has a major significance for other developing countries.

Introduction

With a total land area of only 639.2 square kilometres and a population of 3 million[156] [see table 3.1], Singapore is recorded as one of the smallest nation-states in the world by the World Bank's "World Development Report 1992". As pointed out by Mirza, the city-state is about half the size of Hong Kong and a third of Greater London.[157] Its physical constraints, limited domestic market, and lack of natural resources have meant that the country needed to attract FDI and thus specialise in economies of scale and exports.[158]

Once described by an analyst as fantasy island comprising of shopping centres, companies and people, Singapore's economic miracle over the last three decades is undoubtedly one of "the world's big success stories".[159] According to the World Bank's "World Development Report 1986", Singapore's real per capita GNP between 1965 to 1985 grew at the average rate of 8 per cent per annum. This was nearly 62 per cent above the corresponding rate of 5 per cent for Japan, and Japan was well known to have a high rate of growth among the industrialised economies. Moreover, in 1985, Singapore's GNP per capita at current prices of US$7,420 was higher than those of Italy, Ireland, Spain, Greece, Portugal and New Zealand. Furthermore, its average growth rate of 7 per cent between 1980-90 was competitive with other East Asia NIEs (South Korea, Taiwan and Hong Kong), and the ASEAN countries[160] (see table 3.2). As at 1996, its per capita GNP of S$ 37,035 was sufficient for the OECD to upgrade Singapore from a developing nation to a developed country status.

Even more remarkable about its growth is the fact that it has been managed with relative price stability compared to its neighbours. Increases in average per capita money incomes have not been eroded by high inflation. As is indicated in table 3.2, Singapore's Consumer Price Index (CPI) between 1965-80 rose on an annual average rate of just over 5 per cent and 1.4 per cent in 1996. This was slightly higher than that of Malaysia (5 per cent), but much lower than that of Indonesia (36 percent), Korea (18 per cent), Taiwan (11 per cent) and Philippines (12 per cent) (see table 3.2). Most of Singapore's

---

[156] Ministry of Information and the Arts (1991), *Singapore 1991*, p. 33; The International Bank for Reconstruction and Development/ The World Bank (1992), *World Development Report 1992*, Oxford: Oxford University Press.

[157] Mirza, Hafiz (1986), *Multinationals and the Growth of the Singapore Economy*, London: Croom Helm, p. 1.

[158] Lim, Chong Yah (1988), *Policy Options for the Singapore Economy*, London: McGraw-Hill Company.

[159] See Lim, Linda Y. C. (1983), "Singapore's Success: The Myth of the Free Market Economy", *Asian Survey*, 23 (6), p. 753.

[160] Lim, Chong Yah (1988), *op. cit.*, p. xi.

inflation occurred during the 1970s when inflation was both imported and domestically generated. Import prices were higher due to inflationary conditions abroad; in particular, prices of imported food rose sharply during 1973-74 and oil because of the shortage between 1973-74 and 1979, giving rise to double digit inflation in 1973-74. Domestically, the economic boom and full employment generated inflationary pressures in the labour and real estate markets.[161]

Rapid economic growth and relative price stability was accompanied by structural transformation of economic activities. Between the late 1950s and early 1960s, Singapore's early production structure reflected its geographical location as an entrepot trading nation. Entrepot trade has over the years declined considerably from 32 per cent share of the GDP in 1960 to just 17 per cent in 1990 (see table 3.1). Manufacturing activity on other hand, has substantially increased its share of GDP from 11 per cent in 1960 to 29 per cent in 1990, thus becoming one of the leading growth sectors since the introduction of export-led industrialisation. This successful transformation has also led to employment growth which averaged 6 per cent per annum during 1966-73, 4 per cent during 1973-79, and 3 per cent 1996.

The above mentioned transformation depended on the constant flow of FDI actively pursued by the government. In fact, the success of the export-led development would not have been possible if FDI in the manufacturing sector had not increased dramatically since 1966. At the end of 1986, wholly-owned foreign subsidiaries and majority-foreign owned joint ventures accounted for over half of manufacturing employment, two-thirds of manufacturing output and value added, and over four-fifths of direct exports in manufacturing. Presently, FDI accounts for over 80 per cent of manufacturing direct investment, indicating that Singapore has probably the most heavily foreign dominated export-led manufacturing activity in the world. The high foreign share of manufacturing activities in the Singapore economy is however, not resented by most Singaporeans, since local workers have benefited from extensive job creation and high wages in the foreign sector, which has also created many business opportunities for local firms.[162] However, if such a high levels of foreign domination were to exist in countries such as Japan, Taiwan and South Korea, the state would have been heavily criticised by the electorate as being weak and incompetent. It has been a tradition in these countries that the state should protect local entrepreneurs rather than discriminate against them.

---

[161] Lim, Chong Yah (1988), *op. cit.*, p. xi.
[162] Lim, Linda Y. C. and Pang, Eng Fong (1991), *op. cit.*, p.52.

Table 3.1 Singapore: Major Indicators of Economic Growth and Structural Change, 1960-96

INDICATOR	1960[1]	1970[1]	1980[1]	1990[1]	1995[1]	1996[1]
1 GDP[2] (S$M)	2,149.6	5,804.9	25,090.7	63,672.9	102,625.0	109,787.1
Growth Rate	8.7	9.4	10.2	8.3	8.8	7.0
Percentage share of:						
Agriculture & Fishing	3.5	2.3	1.2	0.2	0.2	0.2
Quarrying	0.2	0.3	0.3	0.1	0.0	0.0
Manufacturing	11.3	20.0	29.1	29.4	26.3	26.1
Utilities	2.3	2.5	2.2	1.9	1.6	1.6
Construction	3.3	6.8	6.4	5.6	7.1	7.9
Trade	32.0	27.0	21.6	17.2	19.4	18.6
Transport & Communications	13.2	10.5	14.0	13.3	11.6	11.1
Finance & Business	13.9	16.4	19.7	28.0	29.6	30.5
Other Services	17.0	12.7	9.1	9.9	10.6	10.7
Less: Imputed Bank Service Charge	1.5	1.8	5.6	7.0	7.1	7.2
2 Gross National Product (GNP)[3]	2,189.0	5,861.1	188.5	64,467.4	121,381.2	133,772.4
Annual Change (%)	9.9	14.9	10.9	12.6	10.7	10.2
Per Capita GNP ($)	1,329.6	2,825.3	9,940.6	21,372.3	35,005.4	37,035.5
Per Capita Indigenous GNP ($)[4]	na	2,478.1	8,342.8	18,864.8	32,146.0	34,220.4
3 Employment						
Employed ('000)	448.6[5]	644.2	1,073.4	14,629.2	1,702.1	1,748.1
Unemployment Rate (%)	4.9[5]	6.0	3.0	1.7	2.7	3.0
4 Population	1,646.4	2,074.5	2,413.9	2,705.1	2,986.5	3,044.3
Annual percent growth	2.4	1.5	1.2	1.8	1.9	1.9
5 Trade (%)						
Total Trade	4.2	20.2	10.3	11.4	13.2	5.1
Imports	4.8	19.9	9.7	13.4	12.7	5.0
Exports	3.5	20.6	10.9	9.3	13.7	5.2
Domestic Exports	25.5	26.9	11.7	13.6	11.2	5.2
Re-exports	-0.7	15.3	9.6	1.8	17.4	5.3

Notes:
1. Annual Changes refer to averages for the decade.
2. GDP at current prices.
3. GNP at market prices.
4. Based on resident populations.
5. Census of Population 1957.

Source: *Economic Survey of Singapore*, Singapore: Minister of Trade and Industry, 1997.

Some academics[163] have however argued that the large number of foreign firms in Singapore not only "squeezes out" local firms but also undermines potential local talents that would otherwise go into risk taking entrepreneurial ventures. However, the state has strongly been in favour of foreign investors as its success and power is closely tied to foreign capital.[164]

---

[163] These includes Lim, Linda Y. C. and Pang, Eng Fong (1991), *op. cit.*; Mirza, Hafiz (1986), *op. cit.*; Rodan, Garry (1989), *The Political Economy of Singapore's Industrialisation: National State and International Capital*, London: MacMillan.

[164] Lim, Linda Y. C. and Pang, Eng Fong (1991), *op. cit.*

Table 3.2 Comparative Growth and Inflation Rates for ASEAN Countries, 1965-96

Country	Average Annual Growth Rate of GDP				Average Annual Growth Rate of Inflation (%)			
	1965-1980	1980-1989	1990	1996	1965-1980	1980-1989	1990	1996
Singapore	10.0	6.1	8.5	7.0	5.1	1.5	8.5	7.0
ASEAN								
Indonesia	7.0	5.3	7.0	7.8	35.5	8.3	7.0	7.8
Malaysia	7.4	4.9	9.5	8.2	4.9	1.5	9.5	8.2
Philippines	5.9	0.7	3.1	5.7	11.7	14.8	3.1	5.7
Thailand	7.3	7.0	10.9	6.4	6.2	3.2	10.9	6.4

Sources: The World Bank, World Development Outlook 1991. Asian Development Bank, Asian Development Outlook 1991. Crosby Research, Quarterly Economic Review, No. 1, 1997.

The state's role in the economy is by far one of the most prominent in southeast Asia. In fact, many have described Singapore's economic success as a "miracle by design" which in effect is contrary to the neoclassical economists who argue the case of the minimalist role of the state in Singapore.[165]

Micro and Macroeconomic Industrial and FDI Policies

A cursory review of Singapore's development since the 1950s indicate that the economy has evolved through five interesting phases: the pre-industrial phase (1955-1960); the import - substitution phase (1960-65); the export-led phase (1966-73); the initial shift towards high-technology phase (1973-78); and the high wage phase (1979-84 & 1985-96). Though my analysis will proceed in the above order of Singapore's development, the documentation of each phase is however arbitrary, descriptive and based on common knowledge.

The Pre-industrial Phase (1955-60)

In 1965, Singapore's economy was sustained by two pillars: its entrepot activities and rising population. Its population growth, which was one of the highest in the world between 1947-57 period, averaged 4 per cent per annum.[166] The rapid population imposed its burdens on the economy in the form of a high

---

[165] See the section on the role of the state in Singapore's economy.
[166] Lim, Chong Yah (1988), *op. cit.*, p. 6.

dependency ratio, heavy social service requirements such as housing, and a subsequent employment creation problem. In 1957 there were only about 24,000 people classified as unemployed. By the end of 1958, the unemployment rate estimate had reached 11 per cent and increased to 15.2 per cent in 1962. The employment opportunities between 1955 to 1959 were limited mostly to three sectors of the economy (entrepot, manufacturing and agriculture),which were in decline.

The government responded to this economic problem by introducing an industrial policy which shifted the economy from entrepot-based to manufacturing activities - because of the multiplier effects it would have on other sectors, mainly building and construction and trade and services - creating sufficient jobs to absorb the unemployed.[167] The policy was also echoed in the two independent reports that were produced between 1955-63.[168] According to the reports, Singapore's future existence with entrepot activities was bleak.[169] The report pointed out the need for state assistance for feasibility investigations and the promotion of industrial activities, in helping to provide industrial finance, and, to a carefully limited extent, in introducing tariffs to protect infant industries.[170]

To implement the above mentioned recommendations by the two independent reports, the newly elected PAP government immediately introduced three major incentives to attract FDI.[171] These were the Pioneer Industries (Relief from Income Tax) Ordinance, the Industrial Expansion (Relief from Income Tax) Ordinance, and the Control of Manufacture Ordinance, all enacted in 1959. Under the Pioneer Ordinance, pioneer status was granted to

---

[167] Economic Development Board (1965), *Annual Report*, pp. 5-6.

[168] International Bank for Reconstruction and Development (1955), *The Economic Development of Malaya*, Chapter 6, pp. 84-95, and Technical Report 8, pp. 301-16; United Nations (1963), *A Proposed Industrialisation Programme for the State of Singapore*, New York: UN Industrial Survey Mission.

[169] Hughes, Helen and You, Poh Seng (1969), *op. cit.*, p. 20.

[170] Wong, K. P. (1980), *The Cultural Impact of Multinational Corporations in Singapore*, Paris: United Nations Educational, Scientific and Cultural Organization, p. 1.

[171] Yoshihara, Kunio (1976), *Foreign Investment and Domestic Response: A Study of Singapore's Industrialisation*, Singapore: Eastern Universities Press; Wain, Barry (1979), "The ASEAN Report", *The Asian Wall Street Journal*, 1, pp. 1-5; Mirza, Hafiz (1986), *Multinationals and the Growth of the Singapore Economy*, London: Croom Helm; Chong, Li Choy (1986), "Singapore's Development: Harnessing the Multinationals", *Contemporary Southeast Asia: A Quarterly Journal of International and Strategic Affairs*, 8 (1), pp. 56-69; Lim, Chong Yah (1988), *Policy Options for Singapore Economy*, London: McGraw-Hill Company; Chng, Meng Kng, Low, Linda and Toh, Mun Heng (1988), *Industrial Restructuring in Singapore: For ASEAN-Japan Investment and Trade Expansion*, Singapore: Chopmen.

industries which carried out economic activities in Singapore on a scale compatible with the economic needs of the country. The basic strategy was to provide foreign capital with the incentives to establish manufacturing industries in Singapore. The ultimate goal was to promote the establishment of new industries to produce manufactured goods for domestic and export markets. The major benefit of a pioneer firm was tax relief from the prevailing 40 percent company profit tax for a maximum of five years. Losses during the exemption period were carried over, to be set against profits in later years. In addition, depreciation allowances were written-off against profits in succeeding years.[172]

The Industrial Expansion (Relief from Income Tax) Ordinance on the other hand, granted tax relief to firms on their expansion in capital investment for a maximum of five years. However, the aims of both ordinances were to create a suitable investment climate for foreign investors. The Control of Manufacture Ordinance limited the number of industries involved in producing certain goods. This action was designed to avoid excessive competition and duplication in production for domestic markets, but later became unnecessary when an export-led strategy was adopted.[173] However, the success of these incentives is not altogether clear as there is inadequate data to accurately examine its success. According to Hughes and You, the response of foreign investors to these incentives was slow.[174] For instance, between 1959 and 1962, 24 pioneer certificates were granted, followed by 95 in 1963. Out of this 14 firms were engaged in production in 1962, 29 in 1963 and 95 in 1965. Employment in the whole manufacturing sector virtually stagnated between 1959 and 1962, and showed some increase only in 1963.

The lack of interest by foreign investors to invest in the way the Singapore government had hoped for was partly as a result of the increasing violent and political instability. There was intense hostility between the PAP government and the trade unions. The hostility also caused direct confrontation and violent conflict between the left wing Barisan Socialise unions and the PAP supporters, which rendered the country uncontrollable, and as such unsuitable for foreign investment. To overcome this drawback, the PAP government used drastic measures such as arrests of leaders of the Barisan Socialise

---

[172] Tan, Augustine H. H. and Hock, Ow Chin (1982), "Singapore", in Bela Belassa and Associates, *Development Strategies in Semi-Industrial Countries*, World Bank: The John Hopkins University Press.

[173] Ibid., p. 281.

[174] Hughes, Helen and You, Poh Seng (1969), *op. cit.*, p. 34.

unions to maintain stability.[175] Such action, though not necessary, was seen as significant for improving the country's chance of attracting FDI. To this effect, the economic planners offered economic unification with Malaysia in order to pursue its new industrialisation policy.

Import-Substitution Phase (1960-65)

Even under the federation with Malaysia, Singapore's internal political and economic climate was still characterised by uncertainty. Internally, the political struggle between the PAP government and Barisan Socialise shifted to the labour movement, with serious confrontations between the government and the left-wing Singapore Trade Unions Council (STUC), eventually leading to detention of labour leaders and de-registration of the entire STUC.[176] Above all, the period between 1960-65 witnessed the most severe industrial relations disturbance in Singapore's history. As is shown in figure 3.4, man-days lost in strikes between 1960-65 was at its highest level. Within a space of twelve months, man-days lost due to stoppages increased from 152,000 to over 410,000. The membership of the unions also increased from 145,000 in 1960 to over 190,000 in 1962. The number of workers involved in union stoppages increased from 6,000 in 1960 to over 66,000 in 1963 (see appendix for more detail). Furthermore, the internal racial riots between Chinese and Malays, and the threatening attitude of Malaysia and Indonesia towards their Chinese minorities provided another platform for tension. Even the Chinese which makes up about 75 per cent of the total population in Singapore were themselves fragmented in a variety of dialect, clan, and family groups, based upon their provincial and regional origins in China, consolidated in Singapore through associations and social organisations, generally localised in territorially specific areas. Thus to create a society collectively mobilised for economic development was a formidable task which the government had to confront.[177]

Looking to their neighbours, the PAP government was suspicious of external interference. The PAP leadership was convinced that there was a serious possibility for Singapore to be taken over by a communist movement that could link up with the strong communist influence in Indonesia, in the shadow of the Chinese Communist Party, for whom many Singaporean

---

[175] Ibid., p. 34.

[176] Castells, Manuel (1988), *The Developmental City-State in An Open World Economy: The Singapore Experience*, University of California, Berkeley Working Paper, no. 31, p. 45.

[177] Ibid.

political militants had a nationalistic admiration.[178] With all this uncertainty, it was not surprising that economic growth during import-led was not as high as export-led industrialisation. It is important to point out these facts, as it puts in context the reasons why import-substitution policy was unsuccessful. Often, when an import-substitution industrialisation policy is being criticised or compared to export-led, it is usually done out of context. The criticism normally centres on the question of protectionism of local infant industries from international market forces. By implication, it is argued that domestic resources are utilised inefficiently thus leading to partial specialisation of a country's comparative advantage in international division of labour. However, the argument is that import-substitution or export-led industrialisation policy during uncertainty cannot attract foreign investors. Thus, it is not the policy, which is in question, but the events that led to the unsuccessful implementation of the policy.

Economically, entrepot trade was still declining in relative terms due to direct confrontation with Indonesia, which resulted in a negative growth rate of 4 per cent in 1964. As is shown in figure 3.2, the official unemployment rate during the 1960-65 period was the highest ever experienced. Although population growth rate was decreasing, it was still high enough to cause concern among economic planners as was confirmed in the 1961-64 Development Plan.[179]

The Plan drew attention to the critical nature of population growth and the consequent employment problems, stressing that there could be no significant reduction of dependence on entrepot trade within the Plan period even though industrialisation was to be pursued vigorously. As such, the main objectives of the 1960-65 industrial development strategy were to create 214,000 jobs by the end of the decade. This implied that the government would have to create a total of 10,000 to 20,000 job vacancies a year.

The vacancies would represent nearly 48 per cent of the total employment. Of the new jobs to be created, 98,000 would have to be found in manufacturing.[180]

---

[178] Ibid.

[179] Ministry of Finance (1969), *State of Singapore Development Plan, 1961-1964*.

[180] Chia, Siow Yue (1971), "Growth and Pattern of Industrialisation", in You, Poh Seng and Lim, Chong Yah (eds.), *The Singapore Economy*, Singapore: Eastern Universities Press, p. 193.

Table 3.3 Singapore: Growth Rates of GDP, Population and Unemployment, 1960-96

Year	GDP Annual Growth Rate	GDP Per Capita[1]	Population Annual Growth Rate	Unemployment Annual Growth Rate
IS Phase				
1960-65	4.7	2.3	2.8	13.4
1960	-	-	3.5	13.5
1961	8.6	5.1	3.3	15.0
1962	7.0	3.2	2.6	15.3
1963	10.5	9.9	2.5	14.0
1964	-4.3	8.6	2.5	13.8
1965	6.6	4.0	2.5	8.7
Export-Led Phase				
1966-73	12.7	10.7	1.8	6.4
1966	10.6	7.9	2.3	8.7
1967	13.0	10.6	2.0	8.1
1968	11.4	12.4	1.6	7.3
1969	13.4	11.7	1.5	6.7
1970	13.4	11.7	1.7	6.0
1971	12.5	10.6	1.8	4.8
1972	13.3	11.4	1.9	4.7
1973	11.2	9.4	1.9	4.5
Towards High-Tech Phase				
1974-78	6.9	5.3	1.4	3.2
1974	6.8	5.1	1.7	4.0
1975	4.0	2.5	1.5	4.5
1976	7.2	5.8	1.4	4.5
1977	7.7	6.4	1.4	3.9
1978	8.6	6.5	1.2	3.6
High-Wage Phase				
1979-84	8.7	7.4	1.5	2.9
1979	9.3	8.0	1.3	3.4
1980	10.2	18.9	1.3	3.0
1981	9.9	18.6	1.2	2.9
1982	6.3	5.1	1.2	2.6
1983	7.9	6.6	1.1	3.2
1984	8.3	7.1	1.1	2.7
Recession & Recovery Phase				
1985-96	7.76	-4.1	1.73	3.2`
1985	-1.8	-1.7	1.1	4.1
1986	1.8	7.1	1.0	6.5
1987	8.8	12.3	1.2	4.7
1988	11.0	10.8	1.5	3.3
1989	9.2	10.4	1.9	2.2
1990	8.3	6.2	2.2	2.0

Note:
1 At 1968 factor cost.

Sources: For unemployment estimates between 1960-64 period see Chalmers, W. E. (1967), *Crucial Issues in Industrial Relations in Singapore*, Singapore: Donald Moore Press, pp.180-82; Singapore, Department of Statistics; *Economic and Social Statistics 1960-82*; and *Yearbook of Statistics*, Singapore Department of Statistics, 1970-92.

Table 3.4 Singapore: Trade Unions Membership and Industrial Stoppages, 1960-96

	Employee Class		Industrial Stoppages		
Year	Unions	Total Membership	Number	Workers Involved	Total Man-days lost due to stoppages
IS Phase					
1960	130	144,770	45	5,939	152,005
1961	124	164,462	116	43,584	410,889
1962	122	189,032	88	6,647	165,124
1963	112	142,936	47	66,004	338,219
1964	106	157,050	39	2,535	35,908
1965	108	154,052	30	6,374	45,800
Export-Led Phase					
1966	108	141,925	14	1,288	44,765
1967	106	130,053	10	4,491	41,322
1968	110	125,518	4	175	11,447
1969	110	120,053	-	-	8,512
1970	102	112,488	5	1,749	2,514
1971	100	124,350	2	1,380	5,449
1972	97	166,988	10	3,162	18,233
1973	92	191,481	5	1,312	2,295
High-Tech Phase					
1974	90	203,561	10	1,901	5,380
1975	89	208,561	5	1,865	4,835
1976	91	221,936	10	1,576	3,193
1977	90	229,,056	1	406	1,011
1978	89	236,907	-	-	-
1979	85	249,710	-	-	-
High-Wage Phase					
1980-96	85	255,020	-	-	-
1986	83	200,613	1	-	-
1991	83	217,086	-	-	-
1992	81	228,686	-	-	-
1993	82	235,723	-	-	-
1994	82	232,927	-	-	-
1995	81	235,157	-	-	-
1996	83	255,000	-	-	-

Source: Department of Statistics, *Yearbook of Statistics*, 1980-96.

However, foreign manufacturing investment inflow between 1960-65, amounted to only $157 million. To improve FDI flow, the government established the Economic Development Board (EDB) in late 1961. Originally under the Ministry of Finance, and then the Ministry of Trade and Industry, the EDB was responsible for development planning of a general and sectoral nature. Its initial tasks, however, were to promote investment, develop infrastructure and facilities, and administer the Pioneer Industry Programme.

In addition, the EDB was also responsible for enquiries and arrangements from potential foreign investors. In 1968 the government decided to devolve many of the several functions of the EDB onto other new institutions. The Jurong Town Corporation (JTC) was then given the task of managing and developing industrial land, the Development Bank of Singapore was charged with the provision of long-term finance and the Singapore Institute for Standards and Industrial Research (SISIR) with ensuring product quality and promote industrial research.[181]

Using standard economic analysis, the import-substitution industrial phase was less successful as subsequent economic development periods. GDP grew at an annual rate of 6 per cent as shown in table 3.3. Entrepot trade continued to be the main contributor to GDP. However, in 1965, Singapore separated from Malaysia, and changed its industrial policy to that of export-led industrialisation.

Export-led Phase (1966-73)

By every traditional economic standards, the export-led industrial strategy was a success.[182] The period 1966-73, saw the highest rate of GDP growth of 12.7 per cent. Consequently, the unemployment rate fell from 8.7 per cent in 1965 to 4.5 per cent in 1973. Foreign investment flow also was at its peak. The first cumulative $1 billion hallmark was achieved in 1971. In short, the highest growth rate of foreign investment in the manufacturing sector was achieved in 1970 with 66 per cent of total direct investment, and 58 per cent in 1971.

---

[181] Chng, Meng Kng; Low, Linda and Toh, Mun Heng (1988), *Industrial Restructuring in Singapore: For ASEAN-Japan Investment and Trade Expansion*, Singapore: Chopmen, p. 13.

[182] Lim, Linda Y. C. (1983), "Singapore's Success: The Myth of the Free Market Economy", *Asian Survey*, 23 (6), pp. 753; Mirza, Hafiz (1986), *op. cit.*; Rodan, Garry (1989), *The Political Economy of Singapore's Industrialisation: National State and International Capital*, London: MacMillan; Lee, Yuan (1988), "The Government in Labour Market", in Krause, Lawrence B.; Koh, Ai Tee and Lee, Yuan (eds.), *The Singapore Economy Reconsidered*, Singapore: Institute of Southeast Asian Studies; Young, Alwyn (1992), *A Tale of Two Cities: Factor Accumulation and Technical Change in Hong Kong and Singapore*, Unpublished material for the National Bureau of Economic Research; Pang, E. F. and Komaran, R. V. (1985), "Singapore Multinationals", *Columbia Journal of World Business*, 20 (2), pp. 35-42; Aggarwal, Raj (1985), "Emerging Third World Multinationals: A Case Study of the Foreign Operations of Singapore Firms", *Journal of Contemporary Southeast Asia*, 7 (3), pp. 193-208; Lecraw, D. (1985), "Singapore", in Dunning, J. H. (ed.), *Multinational Enterprises, Economic Structure and International Competitiveness*, London: Wiley; Lim, M. H. and Teoh, K. F. (1986), "Singapore Corporations go Transnational", *Journal of Southeast Asian Studies*, 17 (2), pp. 336-365.

However, the tasks of implementing the export-led industrial policy were by no means an easy one. There were still a number of internal "hurdles" to jump. Most of these hurdles were already in existence during the import-substitution phase. Firstly, the local entrepreneurs during the import-substitution phase were inexperienced, too small in size, lacked the technology, overseas markets and industrial capital needed to make the new industrial strategy work.[183] But TNCs, with their enormous resources and international networks, were considered capable of offering jobs, production capacity, technology, know-how, and foreign markets in a single and continuous package, quickly and seemingly, without limit.[184] Secondly, the high unemployment level during the early 1960s industrial phase continued into the new industrial phase. Thirdly, wage rates were high compared to other countries in the region. Table 3.5 shows daily wage rates for the period 1964-68. Singapore's high wage rates were due mainly to fringe benefits, which were awarded as a result of the union's success in negotiating better conditions of services. The fourth hurdle was the announcement in April 1967 of the British government's intentions to withdraw from all military bases in Singapore. Originally the plan was to complete withdrawal by 1975, but later, in 1968, it was changed to 1971. British Military expenditure in Singapore contributed about one-sixth of total GDP and employed one-fifth of the labour force. The loss of jobs as a result of the withdrawal was estimated at around 100,000.[185]

Determined to succeed with export-led industrialisation, the government liberalised all investment policies and revised its incentives, removed all trade barriers that were introduced during IS period, introduced new legislation to limit various social institutions, and created an atmosphere that was suitable for investment to assure business community that Singapore was a viable place for industrial production.

In 1967 the government passed the Economic Expansion Incentives (Relief from Income Tax) Act which amended and consolidated the existing laws providing more incentives to potential investors. The Act introduced the following new incentives: first, tax relief in respect of exports profits for a period of at least fifteen years. Second, in approved cases, the tax on royalties, licenses, and technical assistance fees and on contributions to research and development costs, payable to overseas enterprises from Singapore plants, was

---

[183] Ibid.

[184] Rodan, Garry (1989), *op. cit.*, p. 18.

[185] Ibid., p. 99.

Table 3.5 Comparative Wage Rates in Selected Asian Countries, 1964-68 (US$ Per Day)

Year	South Korea	Taiwan	Hong Kong	Singapore
1964	0.5	1.1	1.6	2.5
1965	0.6	1.2	1.8	2.5
1966	0.7	1.3	1.9	2.4
1967	0.8	1.4	2.1	2.6
1968	1.0	1.6	2.2	2.5
Average 1964-1968	0.7	1.3	1.9	2.5

Note:
1 Prior to December 1971, the exchange rate was US$1.00 = S$3.03.

Source: Lee, S. Y., "Some Basic Problems of Industrialisation in Singapore," *Journal of Developing Areas* (7/2), January 1973, p. 204.

reduced to 20 per cent of total investment. Complete tax exemptions were granted over a three-year period and, in special cases, within the first year. Third, complete tax exemption was granted on interest received by overseas enterprises for individuals on approved loans to Singapore enterprises for the purchase of capital equipment. Tax on interest earned from deposits in Singapore banks by non-residents was reduced to 10 per cent. Modifications were introduced in 1970 for the Economic Expansion Incentives (Relief from Income Tax) (Amendment). The Amendment sought to encourage large scale investments in industries and to reduce prolonged tax relief periods for export enterprises. A firm needed a minimum of fixed capital expenditure of $1 million to qualify for pioneer status. This period of tax relief in respect of export of profits was reduced from fifteen years to eight years.[186]

With regard to industrial relations and the labour market, the government established a special relationship with the National Trade Union Congress (NTUC) which was formed in 1961.[187] Fundamentally, the aim was to maintain industrial stability and provide adequate economic policies for foreign

---

[186] Wong, K. P. (1980), *op. cit.* Also see Huang, S. H., "Measure to Promote Industrialisation", in You, Poh Seng and Lim, Chong Yah (eds.), *The Singapore Economy*, Singapore: Eastern Universities Press, 1971.

[187] Lee, Tsao Yuan (1988) 'The Government in the Labour Market', in Krause, Lawrence B.; Koh, Ai Tee and Lee, Tsao Yuan (eds.), *The Singapore Economy Reconsidered*, Singapore: Institute of Southeast Asian Studies, 1988, p. 176.

multinationals. In 1968, the Employment Act and Industrial Relations (Amendment) Act was passed. The Employment Act stripped workers of almost all their rights by standardising terms and conditions of employment to induce investment from abroad. The Act proposed a standard work week of 44 hours; a reduction in annual paid holidays from 16 to 11 days; a reduction of sick leave provision from 28 to 14 days; and strict control of overtime work. The Industrial Relations Act on the other hand, aimed at the provision of management prerogatives, which were not subject to union negotiation and defined the framework and procedures for negotiation and conflict resolution.

In 1972, the National Wage Council (NWC) was established with the aim of ensuring orderly wage awards.[188] The tripartite NWC was made up of representatives from the employers' federations, trade unions, and government. In principle the NWC wage guidelines are not mandatory. However, in practice, the NWC awards were endorsed by the Cabinet and were followed by the public and widely accepted by the private sectors.[189] The basis on which the NWC recommendations were made is not exactly known as these are not usually published. The awards were based upon criteria with regard to productivity growth, global and domestic inflation, changes in wage structure, company profitability, employment and unemployment situations, foreign investment, the world economic condition, and Singapore's international competitiveness.

The take-off of export-led manufacturing concentrated on the labour-intensive industries. Heavy industries were limited to the military reconverted base.[190] Between 1966 and 1973 manufacturing accounted for 30 per cent of the GDP.[191] All export-led industries experienced considerable growth. The petroleum industry in particular, accounted for 26 per cent of the total output of the manufacturing sector in 1973. The electronics and electrical industry contributed a total manufacturing output of $1,100 million and

---

[188] Lim, Chong Yah (1984), *Economic Restructuring in Singapore*, Singapore: Federal Publication. Also, see National Wage Council (1978) *Information Booklet*, Singapore: National Printers.

[189] Ibid., p. 179.

[190] Rodan, Garry (1989), *op. cit.*, p. 19.

[191] Chng, Meng Kng, Low, Linda and Toh, Mun Heng (1988), *op. cit*, p. 13.

employed over 45,000 persons in 1973. The basic metal, metal fabrication and engineering industries also expanded during this period. Its total output for 1973 was about $590 million, an increase of 34 per cent.[192] Shipbuilding and repairing industry increased output to over $500 million with a contribution of three-quarters from ship repair and one-quarter from new building activities. The total workforce in this industry increased to over 20,000 or 10 per cent of the manufacturing workforce. Traditional industry such as textiles and apparel also increased their output by 56 per cent to $604.3 million of which $483.5 million were directly exported to Europe. With the export-led industries firmly in place, Singapore's economy was now ready to embark on a new industrial phase.

Shift Towards High-Technology Phase (1973-78)

The rapid economic expansion experienced during the export-led phase was however, severely halted by the 1973/74 world oil crisis and subsequent recession of 1974/75. Singapore was more heavily hit than any other economy in the region. This was because of the fact that its manufacturing activities were heavily geared towards external markets, which meant that any external shock would have a more harmful impact on its domestic economy than most other economies.[193] GDP growth fell from an average rate of 12.7 per cent to 6.8 per cent in 1974 and 4 per cent in 1975. Total output and value added fell from 7.3 in 1974 to in 1975 3.7 per cent.[194]

The manufacturing sector in particular was seriously hit during this period. Total manufacturing sector contribution to GDP was only 2 per cent compared to an annual average rate of 16 per cent for the past six years. Value added in the sector declined to an average rate of 8.1 percent in 1973.[195] The construction sector, which declined by 9 per cent in real terms in 1973, was the only sector that recovered in 1974 with a real growth of 6 per cent. Value added at 1970 constant prices advanced by $23 million to reach $441 million 1974, stimulated by increased expenditure of both the government and statutory boards.

The most important consequence of the recession was the heavy loss of jobs, which mainly came from the manufacturing sector. A total of 16,900 workers were retrenched. About 66 per cent of those retrenched were working

---

[192] Ibid.

[193] Ibid.

[194] Ibid.

[195] Ibid.

in the electronic industries, while 4 per cent and 8 per cent were from textiles/garments and wood based industries respectively.[196] The effect of this retrenchment was cushioned by the return of foreign workers, mostly to nearby Malaysia.[197]

However, the economy recovered from the 1974/75 downturn due largely to the quick rebound of manufacturing investment spurred by a loosening of the Economic Expansion Incentives Act and the other EDB Schemes. These included the Capital Assistance Scheme and the Joint Venture Bureau, both established in 1975, the Small Industries Finance Scheme (SIFS) launched in 1976 and the Extended Small Industries Finance Scheme (ESIFS).[198] The manufacturing sector however, was the leading sector in the new industrial development. The sector grew by 12 per cent in 1978, representing its best performance since 1975, and increased its share of GDP to over 25 percent. The increase was largely due to favourable international demand. In 1978 industrial output rose by 11 per cent at current prices, while employment increased by 8 per cent to 236,700 workers.

Leading the manufacturing sector growth was metal and precision engineering whose output rose by 24 per cent to S$1,108 million. Stimulated both by expansion of the consumer product industries, and the marked revival of oil exploration activities worldwide, the output of the electrical and electronic industries increased by 11 per cent to S$2.9 billion.[199] This represented about 17 per cent of total manufacturing output. The industry was significantly boosted by the increased demand of radios, television sets, electronic calculators and electronic components especially semi-conductors.[200] Joining the growth-oriented industries was the transport equipment industry. Its output increased by 16 per cent in 1978. The reason was primarily because of the upsurge in rig building to meet demand for offshore exploration especially in the Gulf of Mexico and China. The shipbuilding and repairs sector on the other hand suffered considerably in 1978. The revenue of the industry dropped by 15 per cent in 1978 to S$1,045 million. Output of the garments industries reached S$663 million, the highest since embarking on export-led industrialisation. Over 80 per cent of this were as a result of export. The garment industry, being more adaptable to the fast changing pattern of world demand, contributed about two-thirds of the total output. Total employment increased to 36,000, that is, about 15 per cent of the total workforce in

---

[196] Rodan, Garry (1989), *op. cit.*, p. 115

[197] Ibid., p. 115.

[198] Chng, Meng Kng, Low, Linda and Toh, Mun Heng (1988), *op. cit.*, p. 15.

[199] EDB, Annual Reports, 1968-80.

[200] Ibid.

manufacturing.[201]

On achieving recovery from the turbulent world economic condition, the government became selective towards the types of multinationals encourage to invest in Singapore. The economy, between 1975-78, was now in full employment.[202] As such, the selective strategy was basically aimed at attracting multinationals that would adopt capital intensive methods of production, to relieve the dependence on immigrant workers from neighbouring countries and to supplement the local labour force which the government and its policy makers realised would not be the best solution for the long-run. Also, the government saw the continued importation of foreign workers as a source that would in the future dry up in that most of the neighbouring countries were also intensifying their development programme similar to that of Singapore.[203] Furthermore, guest workers were considered as increasing more racial tension among the existing Chinese, Malay, Indian and Cocatians.

According to the EDB, Singapore economic planners had already begun embarking on high technology industries as early as 1970. Table 3.4 below shows the distribution of employment and value added between 1960 to 1980. It indicates that before 1970, the Singapore economy relied heavily on labour-intensive methods of production. Since 1970 the manufacturing sector has been shifted from labour-intensive to capital-intensive industries.

High Wage Phase (1979-84)

While the economic expansion of the late-1970s continued into the new industrial phase, growth was still generated largely through labour force increases, mainly of foreign workers as there was already a domestic labour shortage.[204] In fact, the most serious constraint on further expansion between 1979-84 was a shortage of labour, and not a shortage of foreign investment as had been the case during the import-substitution phase of the early 1960s. By 1978, jobs in the Singapore's economy were being created at an average of about forty thousand per year while the workforce was expanding at an average of about thirty thousand per year, leaving a substantial shortfall (see table 3.7).

Industries most severely affected by the labour shortage in manufacturing

---

[201] Ibid.

[202] Rodan, Garry (1989), *op. cit.*, p. 115.

[203] Ibid.

[204] Chng, Meng Kng, Low, Linda and Toh, Mun Heng (1988), *op. cit.*, p. 15.

included electrical and electronics, textiles, garments, leather, wood and wood products, footwear and transport equipment as they depend on mostly unskilled labour force for production.[205] During the 1974-78 period, the government responded to labour shortages by liberalising the conditions of entry for foreign workers. In 1979, the government decided not to continue with the large importation of foreign workers and introduced the high-wage policy.

Table 3.6 Singapore: Distribution of Employment and Value Added in Manufacturing Industries, 1960-80 (Per cent of Total Manufacturing)

Year	Employment		Value Added	
	Low Value Added Industries[1]	High Value Added Industries[2]	Low Value Added Industries[1]	High Value Added Industries[2]
1960	68.6	31.4	68.2	31.8
1965	67.5	32.5	58.0	42.0
1970	57.9	42.1	38.5	61.5
1975	44.3	55.7	26.9	73.1
1976	42.7	57.3	28.7	71.3
1977	42.5	57.5	28.7	71.3
1978	42.7	57.3	28.8	71.2
1979	40.8	59.2	27.8	72.2
1980	38.4	61.6	24.2	75.8

Notes:
1 Low value added industries include broadly food and beverages, textile and garments, wood and paper products, leather and rubber products, non-metallic products, plastic products and miscellaneous.
2 High value added industries include broadly chemicals and chemical products, petroleum products, metals and metallic products, engineering, electrical and electronic products, transport equipment and precision equipment and photographic and optical goods.

Source: Economic Development Board (1982), *Annual Yearbook Report.*

---

[205] Tan, Augustine J. H., "Singapore's Economy: Growth and Structural Change", paper presented for a Conference on *Singapore and the United States into the 1990s*, November 6-8, 1985.

Table 3.7 Singapore: Percentage Growth Rate of Total Work Force, 1970-2000

Period	Average Growth Rate (%)	Contribution from	
		Indigenous Workers (%)	Foreign Workers (%)
Actual			
1970-1973	5.7	5.7	-
1974-1978	4.1	3.0	1.1
1979-1984	3.5	1.6	1.9
1985-1990	2.6	1.8	0.8
1990-1995	1.5	0.7	0.8
Forecast			
1996-2000	1.4	0.5	0.7

Source: *The Singapore Economy in the Nineties: The Leap to Maturity*, Singapore: Crosby Research, March 1997.

Wage-Productivity Increases (1972-92)

Though the high-wage period was to last for only three years (1979-81), the policy has been a major instrument for industrial transformation in Singapore even until the present day.[206] The main reason for the high-wage policy was that continued dependence on foreign labour would simply perpetuate a vicious cycle of low skilled, low productivity and labour intensive industries. These industries in turn could only afford to pay low wages, which in turn, caused them to depend on more imported labour to keep their wage cost down.[207] Thus, to end the vicious cycle, the government decided to redefine Singapore's comparative advantage by making the country less attractive to labour-intensive industries because of its relative high labour-capital requirements, and encourage more capital intensive industries as well as increasing manufacturing productivity. This was done largely through the NWC, which was responsible, for the country's wage awards. As indicated in tables 3.8 the

---

[206] Low, Linda and Toh, Mun Heng (1988), *op. cit.*, p. 15.
[207] Chng, Meng Kng, Low, Linda and Toh, Mun Heng (1988), *op. cit.*, p. 15, Ibid.

NWC recommendations in 1986 to 1996 made relatively high wage awards.[208] On average annual awards by the NWC increased by 16-33 per cent per year between 1979-84.[209] The high wage recommendations by the NWC were also reflected in real wage and labour cost[210] increases. Real wages between 1979-84 increased at an average rate of 7 per cent per annum, more that three-times the corresponding rate for 1973-78 period. Consequently, the rate of labour cost rose from an average rate of 1 per cent between 1973-78 to 10 per cent in 1979-84.

---

[208] Low, Linda and Toh, Mun Heng (1998), *op. cit.*, p.15.
[209] Chng, Meng Kng, Low, Linda and Toh, Mun Heng (1998), *op. cit.*, p.15, Ibid.
[210] Total labour costs includes CPF, SDF and payroll tax.

Table 3.8   Singapore: NWC Wage Increase Guidelines, 1986-96

Year	Guidelines
1986 and 1987	• Wage restraint.
1988 and 1989	• Total wage increase should be given in 2 parts – a moderate basic wage increase and a variable payment/bonus linked to company/individual performance or productivity; and total wage increase should lag behind productivity growth.
1990	• Built-in wage increase (annual increments plus wage adjustments) should lag behind productivity growth; and companies performing well should, however, reward employees with higher variable bonus.
1991	• Total wage increase should be lower than that of 1990, in line with the expected slower economic growth; and built-in wage increase should lag behind productivity growth. Companies performing well should, however, reward employees with higher variable bonus.
1992	• Total wage increase should be moderated in line with the expected slower economic growth; and built-in wage increase should lag behind productivity growth. Companies should pay as much of the wage increase as possible in the form of variable component.
1993	• Built-in basic wage increase should lag behind productivity growth. Total wage increase can, however, reflect the expected improved economic and business performance; and companies should pay as much of the total wage increase in the form of variable component. Those companies which had done exceptionally well should pay special bonus.
1994	• Built-in wage increase should lag behind productivity growth rates. Total wage increase should reflect the favourable performance of the economy; variable payment should reflect closely the performance of the company. For companies that have done exceptionally well, their variable bonus need not be rigidly capped at the existing agreed quantum. They should consider paying a one-off special bonus; and companies may wish to consider, in the payment of their wage increase, the inclusion of a dollar quantum instead of purely on a percentage basis.
1995 and 1996	• Total wage increase should reflect the performance of the economy; built-in wage increase should lag behind productivity growth rates; companies should pay as much as possible of their wage increase in the form of variable component; variable component should reflect the performance of the company; and companies should consider, in the payment of their wage increase, the inclusion of a dollar quantum instead of purely on a percentage basis.

Source: Ministry of Labour (1996), *Singapore Yearbook of Labour Statistics.*

Table 3.9 Singapore: Nominal, Real[1] Earnings and Productivity Growth Rates for All Industries and Manufacturing Sector, 1981-96

	1981	1982	1983	1984	1985	1986	1987	1988	1989	1990	1991	1992	1993	1994	1995	1996
Nominal Earnings																
All Industries	14.5	15.9	10.2	10.7	14.5	0.8	3.2	8.2	9.8	9.3	9.2	7.5	6.3	8.8	6.4	5.8
Manufacturing	17.2	10.7	11.7	9.0	17.2	1.2	3.4	10.6	11.4	12.2	11.3	8.6	7.8	9.7	8.1	7.6
Real Earnings																
All Industries	6.0	11.5	8.9	7.9	6.0	2.2	2.6	6.5	7.4	5.7	5.6	5.1	4.0	5.6	4.5	4.3
Manufacturing	8.4	6.6	10.4	6.3	8.4	2.6	2.9	8.8	8.9	8.5	7.5	6.2	5.5	6.5	6.2	6.1
Productivity																
All Industries	5.2	1.6	5.3	6.9	5.2	6.7	5.1	5.0	5.1	4.1	2.1	2.9	6.9	5.8	3.6	0.7
Manufacturing	9.2	-0.7	9.1	7.2	9.2	13.5	3.7	2.0	3.9	4.6	3.6	2.9	11.8	11.2	6.6	3.3
Productivity - Real Earnings Gap																
All Industries	-0.8	-9.9	-3.6	-1.0	-0.8	4.5	2.5	-1.5	-2.3	-1.6	-3.5	-2.2	2.9	0.2	-0.9	-3.6
Manufacturing	0.8	-7.3	-1.3	0.9	0.8	10.9	0.8	-6.8	-5.0	-3.9	-3.9	-3.3	6.3	4.7	0.4	-2.8

Notes:
1 Average monthly earnings are computed using data obtained from the CPF Board. It include bonuses, if any, but excludes employers' CPF contributions. From 1992, figures exclude all identifiable self-employed persons.
2 Deflated by the corresponding year's Consumer Price Index (October 1992 - September 1993 = 100).

Source: Earnings is from CPFB's Administrative Data. Productivity is from Department of Statistics.

Although the wage increases between 1979-84 were particularly aimed at restructuring Singapore's economy, they were not accompanied by productivity increases. Between 1973-78, productivity increased by an average of 3 per cent per annum and 5 per cent for the 1979-84 period. Although in the seventies, productivity growth (3 per cent) was lower, it was higher than in real wage (2 per cent) and total labour cost (1 per cent). In the eighties, though productivity (5 per cent) was higher than in the seventies, it was lower than real wages (7 per cent) and labour costs (10 per cent). By implication, the rapid increases in labour costs during the eighties led to drastic reductions of firms' profitability and undermined the country's competitiveness

69

vis-á-vis other NIEs.[211] The rate of return on capital in the private sector declined from 22 per cent in 1980 to 18 per cent in 1984. This decline was particularly severe in manufacturing from 33 per cent in 1980 to 17 per cent in 1984.

Most of the labour costs were in the form of the Central Provident Fund (CPF, meaning forced saving). For instance, contributions to CPF and other government funds accounted for 22 per cent of the increases in remunerations in 1980-84. CPF contributions were, on the one hand, accumulated, and on the other hand, used for housing purchases. This then implies that though wage cost increases were higher than other costs, the CPF contributed to labour cost increases which led to the significant loss of Singapore's competitiveness *vis-á-vis* the NIEs.

However, Singapore was not alone in the restructuring programme. The other East Asian NIEs were also transforming their respective economies but at a relatively slower rate taking into consideration their international competitiveness. Although among the East Asian NIEs, Singapore's productivity was the highest, its wage rate was higher than that of Korea, Taiwan and Hong Kong. As it is shown in tables 3.8 and 3.9, the productive-wage gap between Singapore and the East Asian NIEs has resulted in its loss of international competitiveness via the NIEs which is also reflected in the high cost of operating business in the country.

During the 1980-84 period, Singapore's unit labour cost (ULC)[212] for the manufacturing sector increased on an average of 38 per cent per annum and 43 per cent for the whole economy. The unit business cost[213] (UBC) increased by 16 per cent per annum in the same period. The increase in ULC and UBC was not at all surprising because of the high wage increases that were awarded by the NWC. The effect was the ultimate loss of the islands' international competitiveness, most especially in comparison with those of

---

[211] Castells, Manuel (1988), *op. cit.*, p. 60.
[212] The ULC is defined as the ratio of the average nominal wage of labour to real value added per worker. It depends on the industrial structure of the manufacturing sector. A manufacturing sector with more labour intensive industries, *ceteris paribus*, will have a higher ULC than a manufacturing sector with fewer labour intensive industries.
[213] Unit Business Cost here means total cost of doing business in Singapore.

Table 3.10 Productivity Performance among the East Asian NIEs, 1975-84

Country	1975 -79 Average Productivity Growth (%)	1980 - 84 Average Productivity Growth (%) [1]
Singapore	3.2	4.9
Hong Kong	8.4 [2]	3.7
Taiwan	6.6	4.1
Korea	6.1	4.3

Notes:
1 Real value added per worker.

2 1976 - 79.

Source: *The Singapore Economy: New Directions*, Report of the Economic Committee, Singapore: Ministry of Trade and Industry, February 1986.

Table 3.11 Hourly Wages of Production Workers in US Dollars, 1980-84

Country	1980	1984	% Increase
Singapore	1.47	2.37	61
Hong Kong	1.44	1.40	-3
Taiwan	1.27	1.90	50
Korea	1.08	1.32	22

Source: Tan, Augustine H. H., "Singapore's Economy: Growth and Structural Change", paper prepared for a Conference on *Singapore and the United States into the 1990s*, November 6-8, 1985.

Table 3.12 Singapore: Indices of Unit Labour Cost and Unit Business Cost (1983=100)

| | Unit Labour Cost | | Unit Business Cost |
	Overall Economy	Manufacturing	Manufacturing
1980	72.8	77.1	89.4
1981	80.7	83.4	97.9
1982	92.9	96.1	100.6
1983	100.0	100.0	100.0
1984	104.0	106.4	104.1
1985	105.0	113.6	104.0
1986	93.2	96.4	91.2
1987	89.3	91.3	88.0
1988	92.5	94.8	90.8
1989	98.2	103.1	96.6
1990	105.0	110.3	103.4
1991	123.2	126.3	118.6
1992	1277	134.2	118.6
1993	133.5	126.1	121.0
1994	133.5	126.1	120.2
1995	135.7	1242	122.7
1996	140	1279	125.5

Source: Lee, Tsao Yuan (ed.), *Singapore: The Year in Review 1991*, Singapore: The Institute of Policy Studies, 1992.

its neighbouring countries.[214]

In addition to the high wage there cost were increases in indirect taxes and other costs. These included: rental payments which, after steep increases in 1981-84, came down after the 1985 recession; interest costs which rose sharply since 1980 with the rise in interest rates; statutory board rates and fees, which have generally risen each year; indirect taxes, notably property taxes which have increased with the rise in property values; and taxes on transportation, where deliberate increases have been made to meet specific policy objectives and added to business costs thus further reducing profitability and international competitiveness.[215] Thus, when there was a world recession in 1985 Singapore was caught unawares.

During the recession practically all sectors of the economy registered declines in the first half of 1985. Key industries, such as oil-and marine-related industries, were adversely affected by the structural change in global demand and supply conditions. Quarterly GDP growth rates which stood at a high of 10.1 per cent in the first quarter of 1984 fell every subsequent quarter to register a negative 1.2 per cent growth for the second quarter of 1985, minus 3.5 per cent for the third quarter and minus 1.8 per cent for the whole of 1985. Singapore's GDP record in 1985 was the worst in the region, with Korea registering a growth rate of 5.4 per cent, 4.3 per cent for Taiwan and 3.5 per cent for Thailand. Actual real GDP for 1986 recovered to positive growth of 1.8 per cent, but was lower than that of Hong Kong (11.8 per cent), Korea (11.7 per cent) and Taiwan (10.6 per cent).

Apart from being severe in magnitude, the recession shocked the economy with its seeming suddenness. Tables 3.13 and 3.14 show annual and seasonal GDP growth rates between 1980-90 respectively. Looking at the annual rates of growth in real GDP from 1980 to 1984 one would hardly have anticipated such a severe drop in 1985.

But a careful examination of the growth pattern of the major industries indicates that their performance in the 1980s has been fluctuating or growing at decreasing rates. The same trend is not reflected in the overall rates for the economy because of the artificially high growth rates of the construction sector during these years. The dip in the overall economy could only be observed with seasonally adjusted data, which clearly shows that the 1985 recession started around the fourth quarter of 1984 and lasted till around the fourth quarter of 1985. Recovery began in the first quarter of 1986.[216]

The effects of the 1985 recession were widespread. Total employment fell

---

[214] Lee, Tsao Yuan (1992), *Singapore: The Year in Review 1991, Singapore*: The Institute of Policy Studies.

[215] Ibid.

[216] Lim, Chong Yah et al (1988), *op. cit.*, p. 24.

Table 3.13 Singapore: Percentage Change in the GDP of Major Economic Sectors (Annual Data), 1980-90

	1980	1981	1982	1983	1984	1985	1986	1987	1988	1989	1990
Total	10.2	9.9	6.3	7.9	8.2	-1.8	1.8	9.4	11.1	9.2	8.3
Manufacturing	11.8	9.7	-5.7	2.1	8.8	-7.3	8.4	17.3	18.0	9.8	9.5
Construction	10.9	17.5	36.3	29.3	15.5	-13.9	-22.4	-9.8	-4.4	1.5	7.2
Trade	7.2	5.7	5.9	4.4	5.8	-1.7	-0.5	11.1	16.6	8.3	7.8
Transport & Communications	13.9	13.8	12.0	8.0	9.8	3.3	8.1	8.5	10.6	9.4	8.8
Financial & Business Services	22.4	19.0	10.8	12.8	14.5	10.4	-1.1	20.4	10.1	15.1	14.9
Other Services	5.7	6.0	9.4	8.8	4.6	4.0	4.9	5.4	3.4	4.6	5.9

Sources: Lim, Chong Yah et al (1988), *Policy Options for the Singapore Economy*, p.25.; and *Ministry of Trade and Industry (1991), Economic Survey of Singapore*.

Table 3.14 Singapore: Seasonally Adjusted* Percentage Change in Major Economic Sectors (Quarterly Data, 1985 Market Prices), 1983-86

	Total	Manufacturing	Construction	Trade	Transport & Comm	Financial & Bus.	Others
1983 I	10.8	21.0	24.3	5.1	10.6	7.9	3.6
II	9.8	5.7	38.1	5.8	10.0	7.8	4.1
III	8.2	17.0	16.8	5.2	7.4	2.8	9.1
IV	10.1	17.3	34.3	5.6	9.1	2.2	5.4
1984 I	13.4	4.7	21.5	6.6	13.5	36.1	8.6
II	4.9	6.9	1.0	1.1	18.0	1.3	7.0
III	3.9	-2.4	6.6	8.5	-4.1	15.2	3.3
IV	2.0	-1.6	-10.6	12.2	6.5	12.1	-7.8
1985 I	-0.5	-12.8	1.2	-4.7	-4.4	17.4	26.4
II	-9.2	-13.3	52.2	-4.5	4.3	15.3	-4.4
III	-5.0	-6.3	-2.7	-18.4	0.2	8.4	2.1
IV	-4.0	-7.9	-28.9	-3.3	10.2	6.4	3.2
1986 I	4.3	6.2	-16.4	7.7	14.8	-0.3	6.1
II	10.7	43.9	-6.9	9.5	3.6	5.8	0.3
III	5.5	21.4	-41.1	-6.3	15.6	11.8	11.4
IV	3.3	6.9	-21.9	4.6	1.6	9.2	7.7

Note:
1 * Annualized percentage changes over preceding quarter.

Source: Lim, Chong Yah et al (1988), *Policy Options for the Singapore Economy*, p. 28.

by about 96,000 in 1985 for the first time in more than two decades.

The bulk (83 per cent) of the job losses occurred in the construction and manufacturing sectors. Two-thirds of those affected were foreign workers. Despite this, unemployment amongst Singaporeans was high, about 5 per cent by the end of 1985.[217] Productivity growth fell from 6.4 per cent in 1984 to 3 per cent in 1985. Productivity growth in fact would have been much lower than minus 1.4 per cent if the construction sector were excluded. Productivity in the manufacturing sector actually declined by 2 per cent. New foreign investment commitments fell by 32 per cent to $900 million. The manufacturing sector's output fell by 7 per cent when after expanding strongly in 1984. The decline was particularly pronounced in the export-led industries.[218] The electronics industry suffered a decline of 6 per cent because of excess global production. Production of personal computers and computer peripherals fell. This adversely affected the demand for electronic components. Output of the petroleum refineries declined by 9 per cent as traditional suppliers began refining their own oil. Demand for oil in the world market was also depressed. The surplus capacity in world shipping led to a 17 per cent drop in output of its shipyards. The printing and publishing, chemical products and industrial chemicals were the only industries that experienced positive growth.[219]

Most importantly, high labour costs, coupled with an appreciating Singapore dollar, as measured by the export weighted effective exchange rate index led to increasing loss of Singapore's comparative advantage. Between 1974 and 1980, Singapore's dollar had appreciated by 7 per cent and 28 per cent in 1980-85 alone.[220] Unlike other Asian NIEs, high wage costs were accompanied by depreciation of local currency. Also, the high savings policy via CPF and public sector surpluses had some effect on the economy during the recession.[221] The CPF rate as at 1985 was about 50 per cent, and was blamed mostly for the weak domestic demand. Moreover, the surplus funds were used in the construction sector, which during the recession was in a slump, rather than in productive investments in the manufacturing sector.

---

[217] Chng, Meng Kng, Low, Linda and Toh, Mun Heng (1988), *op. cit.*, p. 16.
[218] Ibid.
[219] Ministry of Trade and Industry (1985), *Economic Survey of Singapore*, p. 9.
[220] Krause, Lawrence B., Koh, Ai Tee and Lee, Tsao Yuan (1988), *op. cit.*
[221] Ibid.

Externally, the slowdown in world trade (from 8.6 per cent in 1984 in real terms to 3.2 per cent in 1985) and regional economic activities, mainly with the ASEAN countries, the stark reduction in United States growth (from 6.4 per cent in 1984 to 2.7 per cent in 1985), and increasing protectionism as a result of regional market groupings were identified as the main causes. The slowdown in global demand increases, which was largely due to the depressed economic conditions of the industrialised countries, had a severe impact on Singapore exports. In 1985, Singapore's exports in volume terms dropped by 0.9 per cent. In value terms, exports fell by 2.3 per cent to S$50 billion, compared with a growth of 11 per cent in 1984.[222]

The severity of the recession as compared to other Southeast Asian NIEs led to the forming of an Economic Committee in April 1985, to review Singapore's development over the coming decade. The Committee formed eight Sub-Committees to look at key sectors of the economy, involving a wide spectrum of senior public and private managers. The final report was produced in February 1986. In the report the Committee recommended both short and long-term measures to stimulate recovery. Among the various recommendations made by the Committee were a reduction in the employers' contribution to the CPF from 25 per cent to 10 per cent, which would immediately reduce wage costs by 12 per cent.[223] In addition, a two-year wages freeze was recommended. To increase the investment rate it proposed an immediate reduction in the corporation tax rate from 40 per cent to 30 per cent from the start of the 1987 fiscal year, and a new investment allowance on investment in machinery and equipment. In the long run, the report suggested that Singapore should expand its trade in services, such as banking, insurance, tourism, consultancy and professional services. At the same time, the state's direct participation in the industrial sector should be reduced, and the private sector given greater freedom.[224]

In the same year, the government implemented the recommendations and gradually recovery was sustained through 1987 and the year end with real GDP growth of 9.5 per cent, much higher than the predicted figure of 6 per cent. In 1988 GDP growth further increased to 11 per cent and declined steadily to 9 per cent in 1989 and 8 per cent in 1990. The recovery itself was made possible through cuts in employer and employee taxes and wage restraint as

---

[222] Ministry of Trade and Industry (1985), *Economic Survey of Singapore*.

[223] Ministry of Trade and Industry (1986), *The Singapore Economy: New Directions*, Singapore: National Printers.

[224] Kirkpatrick, Colin (1986), 'Singapore at the Crossroads: The Economic Challenges Ahead', *National Westminster Bank Quarterly Review*, May, p. 49.

suggested by the Economic Committee. Although labour costs declined in real terms, they were still high enough to make Singapore comparatively disadvantaged for labour-intensive industries. With regards to long term sustainable growth, the government revised the wage bargaining process by allowing greater flexibility and productivity related awards to be introduced. Personal and corporate taxes were reduced and a value-added tax introduced. The aim of these measures was to increase firms' rate of return on capital in Singapore. As a proportion of GDP, profitability in Singapore had been steadily declining during the high wage policy. In fact, profitability as a share of GDP was at it lowest during the recession.

Manufacturing Investment Inflow (1960-92)

In general, Singapore's industrial strategy has always been synonymous with its foreign investment policy. The special relationship is evident whenever the state advocates or unveils a new industrial plan. Typically, a long list of incentives for foreign multinationals is announced immediately.[225] Such a symbiotic relation has earned Singapore the most favourable investment site in the whole of Southeast Asia.

Often each policy has been designed to make Singapore more attractive to foreign investors. As is evident in table 3.10, when the high wage policy was introduced in 1979, the government provided a list of incentives ranging from 100 per cent status to tax exemption on profits. The aim of the incentives was to compensate foreign investors for the high domestic wage costs and attract more capital intensive industries. The result has always been positive. As shown in table 1.2, even during the recession period, foreign inward manufacturing investment in Singapore was higher than the corresponding inflow for Taiwan, Hong Kong and Korea. In particular, between 1979-84 inward-manufacturing investment increased on average by 16 per cent a year.

---

[225] Chia, Siow Yue (1971), "Growth and Pattern of Industrialisation" in You, Poh Send and Lim, Chong Yah (eds.), *The Singapore Economy*, Singapore: Eastern Universities Press; Chia, Siow Yue (1986), "Direct Foreign Investment and the Industrialisation Process in Singapore, in Lim, Chong Yah and Lloyd, Peter J. (eds.), *Singapore: Resources and Growth*, Oxford: Oxford University Press; Lim, Linda Y. C. (1983), "Singapore Success: The Myth of the Free Market Economy", *Asian Survey*, 23 (6), p. 753; Krause, Lawrence B.; Koh, Ai Tee and Lee, Yuan (1988), *op. cit.*; Young, Alwyn (1992), *A Tale of Two Cities: Factor Accumulation and Technical Change in Hong Kong and Singapore*, Unpublished material for the National Bureau of Economic Research.

Table 3.15 Singapore: List of Tax Incentives

- Pioneer status for approved manufacturing and service activities - exemption of tax on profits; tax relief period of 5-10 years.

- Expansion incentive for approved manufacturing and service activities - exemption of tax on profits in excess of pre-expansion level; tax relief period of up to 5 years.

- Approved foreign loan scheme for manufacturing and service activities - exemption of withholding tax on interest.

- Approved royalties for approved manufacturing and service activities - half or full exemption of withholding tax on royalties.

- Export incentive for approved export activities - 90 per cent tax concession on approved export profits.

- Double tax deduction for expenses on export promotion and development.

- Double tax deduction for expenses on research and development.

- Accelerated depreciation allowance.

- Investment allowance for approved manufacturing and service activities, approved research and development activities, approved construction operations, and approved projects for reducing consumption of potable water.

- Post pioneer incentive for approved companies enjoying pioneer status or export incentive as follow up to pioneer incentive - corporate rate of not less than 10 per cent for up to 5 years upon expiry of pioneer or export incentive.

- Ten per cent concessionary tax on income of Asian Currency Units, offshore income of insurance companies and income from offshore gold transactions.

- Tax exemption on income from approved syndicated loans and syndicated credit facilities.

- Tax exemption on income of Singapore-registered ships.

Table 3.15 Singapore: List of Tax Incentives (cont'd)

- Fifty per cent tax concession on export income of approved warehousing, technical or engineering services.

- Fifty per cent tax concession on export income of approved consultancy services.

- Fifty per cent tax concession on export income of approved international trading companies.

- Concessionary 10 per cent on income from approved headquarters operations.

- Venture capital incentive for investment by eligible companies and individuals in approved new technology projects - losses incurred from the sale of shares, up to 100 per cent of equity invested, can be set off against the investors other taxable income.

Source: Lim, Chong Yah (1988), *Policy Option for the Singapore Economy*, London: McGraw-Hill, table 9.7, p. 258; adapted from Singapore's Economic Development Board handbook.

As noted in figure 3.7, in particular, cumulative inflow of FDI between 1979-84 was two-times the corresponding amount for the 1973-78, more than three-times of 1965-73, and forty-six-times 1960-65 periods. The low level of foreign manufacturing investment between 1960 and 1965 reflected the difficulties of attracting foreign investors under an import-substitution strategy, and the unfavourable domestic political and labour conditions. However, the achievement of political as well as labour market stability between 1966-78, and the increased promotional incentives for export-led industrialisation, led to the accelerated foreign manufacturing investment.

The sharp decline between 1973-77 period, was due to external factors; namely, the international monetary and oil crisis and recession, and political uncertainties in Southeast Asia following the fall of South Vietnam to the communists.[226]

---

[226] Chia, Siow Yue (1986), *op. cit.*, p. 88.

Table 3.16 Singapore: Foreign Investment Commitments in the Manufacturing Sector (in Gross Fixed Assets), 1960-96

Year	Annual Amount ($M)	Cumulative Amount ($M)	Annual Growth Rate
IS Phase			
1960-65	.	517	.
Export-Led Phase			
1966-73	..	2,502	43.3
1966	82	239	52.2
1967	64	303	26.8
1968	151	454	49.8
1969	146	600	32.2
1970	395	995	65.8
1971	580	1,575	58.3
1972	708	2,283	45.0
1973	376	2,659	16.5
Towards High-Tech Phase			
1974-78	..	2,589	14.7
1974	395	3,054	14.9
1975	326	3,380	10.7
1976	359	3,739	10.6
1977	406	4,145	10.9
1978	1,097	5,242	26.5
High-Wage Phase			
1979-84	..	7,282	15.7
1979	1,107	6,349	21.1
1980	1,189	7,538	18.7
1981	1,221	8,759	16.2
1982	1,162	9,921	13.3
1983	1,269	11,190	12.8
1984	1,334	12,524	11.9
Recession & Recovery Phase			
1985-96	..	..	11.8
1985	888	13,412	7.1
1986	1,190	14,602	8.9
1987	1,448	16,050	9.9
1988	2,657	18,707	16.6
1989	1,625	20,332	8.7
1990	2,217	22,549	10.9
1991	2,461	25,010	10.9
1992	2,733	27,743	11.0
1993	3,177	30,920	16.0
1994	4,327	35,247	36.0
1995	4,852	40,099	12.0
1996	5,716	45,815	17.0

Sources: For 1960-79, Chia, Siow-Yue, Direct Foreign Investment and the Industrialisation Process in Singapore, in *Singapore: Resources and Growth* (eds), Lim, Chong-yah and Lloyd, Peter J., Oxford: Oxford University Press, Table 4.1. Economic Development Board, *Annual Reports and Yearbook*, 1970-92.

As is shown in table 3.17, Europe and in particular, UK was the main source of FDI in the early 1950s and 1960s. UK's position since the mid-1970s, as the single most important investor in the city-state declined dramatically as American and Japanese investors began to dominate manufacturing investment. In 1981-84, US investment accounted for half the total manufacturing investment commitments (excluding petrochemicals). Japanese investments, on the other hand, showed some relative decline (from about 15 per cent of the total in 1981 to 12 per cent in 1984) as Japanese firms invested in more industrialised western countries to counter protectionist pressures, and were deterred from investing in Singapore because of persistent labour shortages and the government's determination to phase out labour intensive activities. Japanese firms have led the resurgence of foreign investment inflows since 1986, responding to a rising yen, new government incentives, local cost cutting measures and the regional economic boom.[227]

Table 3.17 Singapore: Investment Commitments in Manufacturing by Country of Origin, 1980-96

Country	1980	1981	1982	1983	1984	1985	1986	1987	1988	1989	1990	1991
United States	505.7	674.4	533.3	571.7	805.9	427.3	443.4	543.5	586.6	520.2	1,054.8	969.2
Japan	135.3	212.1	73.7	166.6	166.6	244.1	493.8	601.1	691.3	541.2	708.2	713.2
Europe	360.4	228.7	421.9	394.1	325.1	201.0	218.8	285.8	358.1	544.2	435.3	684.2
European Community (EC)	269.9	166.3	386.9	338.8	318.9	180.9	204.8	241.0	345.1	525.4	395.5	615.9
United Kingdom	129.5	83.1	283.1	207.5	186.6	69.4	93.4	42.4	56.6	174.6	89.9	186.5
Netherlands	1.0	1.2	62.8	99.2	70.3	75.2	57.1	70.9	82.9	174.0	72.6	216.2
Germany	69.2	11.5	31.4	12.8	14.3	20.1	16.7	90.3	46.7	26.4	165.7	60.2
France	18.8	1.7	1.3	6.8	0.0	15.1	27.8	15.2	86.0	106.0	60.4	75.2
Italy	45.4	62.5	2.4	5.1	44.8	-	5.1	22.0	68.0	32.8	-	70.1
Other EC	6.0	6.3	5.9	7.4	2.9	1.1	4.7	0.2	4.9	11.6	6.9	7.7
Switzerland	35.8	17.0	22.0	15.4	2.7	4.7	7.7	27.8	10.1	0.9	32.7	12.6
Sweden	53.6	38.3	11.1	12.5	0.3	14.9	5.4	8.7	-	-	7.1	1.2
Other European Countries	1.1	7.2	1.8	27.4	3.3	0.5	0.9	8.3	2.9	18.0	-	54.5
Others	187.7	106.2	133.9	137.4	37.1	15.6	34.6	17.6	21.7	19.8	19.2	94.5
Total Foreign	1,189.1	1,221.4	1,162.5	1,269.8	1,334.7	888.0	1,190.6	1,448.0	1,657.8	1,625.4	2,217.5	2,461.1
Total Local	224.4	641.6	542.0	506.0	493.7	232.4	259.4	295.0	349.6	333.3	266.8	472.9
Total (Foreign & Local)	1,413.5	1,862.9	1,704.5	1,775.8	1,828.4	1,120.4	1,450.0	1,743.0	20,007.3	1,958.7	2484.3	2934

[227] Lim, Linda Y. C. and Pang, Eng Fong (1991), *op. cit.*, p. 55.

Table 3.17 Singapore: Investment Commitments in Manufacturing by Country of Origin, 1980-96 (Cont'd)

Country	1992	1993	1994	1995	1996
United States	1,201.4	1,452.2	2,451.7	2,075.8	2,262.0
Japan	858.0	779.4	913.8	1,152.5	1,960.4
Europe	618.7	881.9	907.0	1,526.3	1,389.1
European Community (EC)	555.7	806.2	893.0	1,510.8	1,320.5
United Kingdom	305.5	357.8	525.8	771.6	397.6
Netherlands	43.1	7.7	175.6	391.4	517.8
Germany	106.4	204.6	91.8	183.9	246.4
France	34.1	124.9	54.0	140.5	59.1
Italy	26.7	43.3	38.9	12.8	53.9
Other EC	20.6	62.9	7.6	10.6	45.7
Switzerland	63.1	66.3	11.4	13.2	60.1
Sweden	19.3	5.0	-	-	-
Other European Countries	20.6	62.9	7.6	10.6	45.7
Others	55.0	63.5	54.9	97.8	104.8
Total Foreign	2,733.0	3,177.1	4,327.4	4,852.4	5,716.2
Total Local	748.0	745.5	1,437.2	1,956.7	2,368.9
Total (Foreign & Local)	3,481.0	3,922.6	5,764.6	6,809.1	8,085.1

Notes:
1 S$800 million investment commitments in the petrochemical complex.
2 S$790 million investments in the petrochemical complex.

Source: Economic Development Board, (1991), *Annual Reports and Yearbook*.

     This dominant role of foreign capital in the manufacturing sector is in large measure due to the fact that the Singapore government is independent of local capital, and often does not even represent its interests, at least not *vis-á-vis* competition with foreign products or foreign corporations. Rather, the state's policy of free trade and competition in effect favours large, established TNCs over small local firms.[228] The government on the other hand, argues that the Republic's dependence on TNCs is not a disadvantage, as the TNCs foster an economic environment in which local enterprise has blossomed, providing capital, technology, management expertise and ready markets. However, the increasing presence of the TNCs makes the country's economic

---

[228] Ibid., p. 53.

structure depend on foreign investors and the state.

The increase of foreign investment in Singapore's manufacturing sector can also be measured through the contribution of foreign firms in the domestic output. Table 3.11 shows the distribution of important manufacturing activities by group of investors and by gross output, value added, employment and direct exports. It shows that as at 1970, wholly foreign owned subsidiaries in Singapore contributed 43 per cent to manufacturing gross output; the proportion increased to 56 per cent by 1975, 59 per cent by 1980 and declined to 55 per cent by 1985.

These figures are much higher when majority foreign-owned firms are added to wholly foreign subsidiaries in Singapore. For instance, employment by foreign companies instead of 32 per cent in 1975 would now be 53 per cent. Likewise, direct export contribution for all foreign owned companies would be 84 per cent in 1975, 85 per cent in 1980, and 82 per cent in 1985. Again, this confirms the fact that most of the foreign multinationals established in Singapore are export-orientated.

Local contribution to the manufacturing sector has been minimal. Contribution to gross output for instance, declined from 18 per cent in 1975 to 15 per cent in 1980, with a slight increased in 1985. The decline in 1980 indicates the effect of the high wage policy introduced in 1979 right through 1984. A rate of decline is also noted in the local contributions to value added, employment and direct exports. Even the combined totals of local and majority local owned contributions are enough to offset the serious imbalance between in the manufacturing sector.

Table 3.18 Singapore: Distribution of Major Manufacturing Activities by Investors, 1975-85

	Gross Output	Value Added	Employment	Direct Exports
1975 Per Cent Share Of:				
Wholly Foreign Owned	56.2	47.4	31.5	66.1
Majority Foreign Owned	15.1	15.3	20.5	18
Wholly Local Owned	18.0	24.3	32.8	8.9
Majority Local Owned	10.7	13.0	15.1	7
1980 Per Cent Share Of:				
Wholly Foreign Owned	58.7	54.1	39.9	71.5
Majority Foreign Owned	15	13.3	18.5	13.2
Wholly Local Owned	15.6	19.1	28.1	7.1
Majority Local Owned	10.7	13.5	13.5	8.2
1985 Per Cent Share Of:				
Wholly Foreign Owned	54.5	54.9	41.6	65.7
Majority Foreign Owned	15.9	9.9	11.8	16.5
Wholly Local Owned	20.3	23.4	33.5	11.4
Majority Local Owned	9.3	11.8	13.1	6.4

Source: Department of Statistics, *Report on the Census of Industrial Production*, Singapore,1975-86.

Table 3.19 shows an even worse picture of the imbalance between foreign and local owned companies in the manufacturing sector. Even though total and foreign net investment commitments in the manufacturing sector have been on the increase since the 1970s, local participation in the sector has been increasing but at a decreasing rate. For instance, the local share for 1977 was 4 per cent and then increased to 21 per cent in 1985 and declined considerably to 9 per cent in 1990.[229]

Most of the decline in the 1980s was due to increased wage costs and labour shortages. Since a good number of Singaporean owned firms are in labour intensive manufacturing, many had to relocate in other countries to be competitive. The other factor, which also drastically reduced the local participation during the 1980s, was the industrial policy to restructure the Singapore economy in general and manufacturing in particular. The aim, according to the government, was to shift production from labour intensive to capital intensive methods. While this industrial restructuring programme was aggressively pursued by the state to restructure the manufacturing sector towards capital-intensive activities, it nonetheless neglected the helpless local entrepreneurs. This was also a conclusion that was reached by the commission set up to examine the cause of the 1985 recession.[230]

---

[229] Chia, Siow-Yue (1986), "Direct Foreign Investment and the Industrialisation Process in Singapore", in Lim, Chong Yah and Lloyd, Peter J. (eds.), *Singapore: Resources and Growth*, Oxford: Oxford University Press, p. 87.
[230] Ibid.

Table 3.19 Singapore: Net Investment Commitments in Manufacturing, 1973-95

Year	Total	Foreign ($M)	% Share	Local ($M)	% Share
1973	447	376	84.1	71	15.9
1974	518	395	76.3	123	23.7
1975	385	326	84.7	59	15.3
1976	401	359	89.5	42	10.5
1977	439	406	92.5	33	7.5
1978	1,143	1,097	96.0	46	4.0
1979	1,227	1,107	90.2	120	9.8
1980	1,413	1,189	84.1	224	15.9
1981	1,862	1,221	65.6	641	34.4
1982	1,704	1,162	68.2	542	31.8
1983	1,775	1,269	71.5	506	28.5
1984	1,827	1,334	73.0	493	27.0
1985	1,120	888	79.3	232	20.7
1986	1,449	1,190	82.1	259	17.9
1987	1,743	1,448	83.1	295	16.9
1988	3,007	2,657	88.4	349	11.6
1989	1,958	1,625	83.0	333	17.0
1990	2,443	2,217	90.7	226	9.3
1991	2,934	2,461	83.87	473	16.12
1992	3,481	2,733	78.51	748	21.48
1993	3,923	3,177	80.98	746	19.01
1994	5,765	4,328	75.0	1,437	24.92
1995	6,809	4,852	71.25	1,957	28.74

Source: Department of Statistics, *Economic & Social Statistics, 1960-82*. Economic Development Board, Annual Report and Yearbook, 1970-92.

The Role of the State

The literature on the role of the state in Southeast Asia is well documented.[231] Singapore is not an exception to where the state has been the main determining force of its industrialisation and comparative advantage in the international division of labour. However, what is different with Singapore as compared to other Southeast Asian countries is the fact that the popularity of the government is closely linked to the success of TNCs in the country. In other words, the ability of the PAP government to continue as the wining party in Singapore depends on the success of TNCs and the continues flow of inward manufacturing investment. However, like every other government, the Singapore government uses intervention policies involving widespread state participation in economic activity financed, in the main, by extensive taxation of income.[232]

Government revenue has been increasing at a steady rate even during the recession years. Although all governments differ in how they derive their revenues from various sources, Singapore is peculiar in two respects.[233] First, a high proportion of its revenue is derived from taxes on income, which is usually in the form of forced savings — namely through the CPF. Established in the 1955 as a social security programme with individual accounts, the initial contribution rate to the Provident Fund was set at 5 per cent of the employees salary, with a matching 5 per cent contribution from the employer. But as industrial transformation began to take place the government need for more and more revenues led to rates being raised to 15 per cent during the 1970s. By

---

[231] Amsden, A H. (1985), "The State and Taiwan's Economic Development" in Evans, P., Rueschemeyer, D. and Skocpol, T. (eds.), *Bringing The State In*, London: Cambridge University Press, pp. 78-106; Amsden, A. H. (1989), *Asia's Next Giant: South Korea and Late Industrialisation*, Oxford: Oxford University Press; Appelbaum, R. P. and Henderson, J. (1992), *States and Development in the Asian-Pacific Rim*, Newbury Park: Sage Publications; Deyo, F. C. (1989), *Beneath the Miracle: Labour Subordination in the New Asia Industrialism*, Berkeley: University of California Press; Wade, R. (1990), *Governing the Market: Economic Theory and the Role of Government in East Asian Industrialisation*, Princeton: Princeton University Press; White, G. (1988), *Developmental States in East Asia*, London: Macmillan.

[232] Young, Alwyn (1992), *op. cit.*, p. 10.

[233] Mirza, Hafiz (1986), *op. cit.*, p. 14.

1984, the rate had increased to 25 per cent apiece and currently 18 per cent/22 per cent, after being found as one the major causes of the 1985 recession. Participants may have used their fund balances to purchase housing (usually built by the Housing Development Board) or government shares, but, otherwise has a limited ability to withdraw their balances, even upon retirement. As of 1980, fully 95.1 per cent of the fund was invested in government securities. At peak, in 1985, CPF contributions amounted to a staggering 14.9 per cent of GNP, or 36 per cent of the GNS.[234]

Secondly, the yield from property taxes has been very high because the state takes advantage of the country's land shortage — a shortage which has actually resulted in the reclamation of land from the sea, especially in Singapore city. Thirdly, there is a great deal of property income which mainly derives from (i) commercial and user-charge profits of state owed enterprises; and (ii) the dividends, profits and other returns from the government's large holdings of overseas portfolio and direct investments.[235] However, government taxes on TNCs have been very minimal thus providing the incentives for more FDI and free repatriation of profits. Above all, the state has been involved in huge infrastructure development programmes, industrial estates, free trade ports, industrial training, incentive schemes and a whole range of other activities, with the basic objective of satisfying foreign rather than local investors.[236]

The incorporation of some 450 (excluding statutory boards) state enterprises which have influence in almost every aspect of the Singapore's economy is more than just free market economy. Generally, the role of the state enterprises do not get in the way of the foreign producers, but compete extensively with the local private entrepreneurs.[237] Therefore, the "crowding out" of local capital not only pertains to foreign companies but also to state-owned firms. The state often argues that if it had not set up some of the companies in major areas of business, such as Singapore Airlines and Neptune Orient Lines in transportation, or Keppel and Sembawang in ship repairing, the opportunities would simply have passed the country. No local entrepreneurs would have sprung up to take the place of the state owned corpora-

---

[234] Young, Alwyn (1992), *op. cit.*, p. 14.

[235] Ibid.

[236] Ibid.

[237] Lim, Linda Y. C. and Pang, Eng Fong (1991), *op. cit.*, p. 53.

tions, as they would not have had the financial resources to take up such a huge task. Furthermore, it makes no difference economically to Singapore whether a company is owned by private Singaporean shareholders or by the Minister for Finance on behalf of the Government, as its contribution to the GDP is the same.[238]

The real question is whether the company is operating efficiently, and competing fairly against other companies. If a company wins business because it can offer a better product or service, or submits lower bids for projects because its costs are lower rather than just because it is a government company, then it should be allowed and encouraged to get the business. For the fiercer the competition, the greater the incentive for all firms to operate as efficiently as possible, or be squeezed out.[239]

Other state activities include the expansion of investment incentives administered by the EDB under the Economic Expansion Incentives Act, which was first introduced in 1959 and has been substantially amended since then.[240] Since the 1985 recession, the government has enacted policies to encourage Singapore firms to invest overseas in order to grow, to gain access to foreign markets and to acquire new technology. In 1988, the EDB established an International Direct Investments (IDI) programme to help local firms expand overseas and eventually become TNCs themselves. Some of the financial incentives offered include: (a) Overseas Tax Incentive, allowing companies to reduce their losses through tax write offs; (b) tax exemption for foreign income repatriated to Singapore; and (c) feasibility grants for the hiring of consultants needed to evaluate overseas investment opportunities. The government now also provides free consultancy services to local firms venturing abroad, and is willing to participate jointly with any local companies in overseas investments.[241]

---

[238] *Singapore Business*, January 1992, p. 5.
[239] Ibid.
[240] Lim, Linda Y. C. and Pang, Eng Fong (1991), *op. cit.*, p. 53.
[241] Ibid.

Conclusion

Singapore's experience of economic development is undoubtedly a unique one because of its small size and strategic location as an entrepot for Southeast Asia. However, the development process has two major economic implications. Firstly, the fundamental importance of the state as the main architect of the country's economic success since 1957. The state has been responsible for laying the ground for economic growth and actually guiding the overall process. By implication, this means that Singapore development was not as a result of a *laissez-faire* state. For though the economy is open to TNCs, it does not mean that the state is performing a passive role in the economy. Rather, it is the dynamic combination of the nation-based state and an internationally oriented market economy, which sets the centre stage for achieving development. It is such a state, intervening in the international economy on behalf of the "national interest", that is called the developmental state in economic development literature.[242]

Secondly, Singapore's economic transformation indicates the importance of FDI inflow for a country's development. As noted, contrary to the simplistic assumptions of radical views, TNCs are largely responsible for the development of Singapore, not only through their investment and exports, but also through their multiplier effects on the economy as a whole.

On the other hand, excessive dependence on TNCs could result in slower pace of the country's economic development. For instance, if the state wants to up-grade the economy to a higher stage of technological development and economy autonomy at a faster pace, it could encounter difficulties.[243] Unless there is an autonomous, government-led effort in education and R&D, the TNCs will improve the quality of their productive lines only to a limited extent and according to the pace required by their parent company, not necessarily coincident with the host economy.

However, the continuous FDI inflow has resulted in the successful transformation of Singapore's economy from that of entrepot trades to manufacturing-service activities. Success has also resulted in its loss of comparative advantage in labour intensive industries. The latter has been one of the prime motivators for labour intensive manufacturing investment abroad. This is what I turn to next.

---

[242] Castells, Manuel (1988), *op. cit.*, p. 74.
[243] Ibid.

4 Extent of Singapore's Overseas Investments

ABSTRACT

Traditionally, Singapore is known to be a safe haven for FDI by TNCs. In recent years, Singapore has emerged as a capital-exporting nation. This chapter argues that outward direct investment from Singapore is due to the changes in the price of factor inputs which influences firms' ability to maximise profit. It is assumed that if the present growth rate of Singapore's investments abroad is maintained until the year 2000, cumulative FDI outflow will be about four to six times the size of inflow. This could have a devastating impact on Singapore's economy considering the fact that it relies heavily on FDI in sustaining future growth. Finally, it is argued that the relative strengths of Singapore's investment abroad is reflected in its ability within the Asia region and its weakness is shown in its inability to venture into unfamiliar markets.

Introduction

As noted in the last chapter, between 1965 to 1979 Singapore's economy has depended on its ability to gain access to foreign markets because of its limited domestic market. Traditionally, this was achieved via high quality and competitively priced exports. But as the country began to achieve full employment, it was evident that future development was impossible with the present factors of production, except if production methods were changed and factor prices increased to discourage the use of labour for low value-added activities. Given such constraints, the government formally launched an economic restructuring strategy programme in 1979. The restructuring programme was essentially a response to then prevailing and anticipated changes in Singapore's comparative advantage.[244] Thus domestic labour costs were increased primarily to reflect real wage growth and this resulted in keen competition from other low wage economies and Singapore's comparative advantage, which it initially enjoyed as a low cost, labour-intensive export country was eroded.[245]

Apart from the loss of comparative advantage, the economic restructuring policy relatively weakened an already vulnerable group of indigenous entrepreneurs. Traditionally, local entrepreneurs had a long trading legacy (from the entrepot trade) which hindered the emergence of a sizeable group of local industrial firms. The few local firms who had attempted to invest in the industrial sector did so in the labour-intensive industries. However, unlike Malaysia where indigenous firms as infant industries enjoyed the privilege of being protected by the state, until 1985 when industrial policy was changed in favour of export-led growth, Singapore local firms were not given the same nurture which is vital for indigenous entrepreneurship. Even during the 1960s and 1970s, the government generally refused to shoulder training costs, provide managerial training, or give technical, financial, and market development assistance. Instead, foreign and government enterprises have competed with domestic private entrepreneurs for the small Singapore market.[246] However, the lack of technical and managerial expertise amongst the local entrepreneurs made it very difficult for these firms to adjust to the government up-grading programme. Economic restructuring requires a major investment in education, manpower training, and R&D, which these firms could not afford. Moreover, the few well-educated and capable persons who could have been employed by the local firms for the government upgrading were

---

[244] Lim, Chong Yah (1988), *op. cit.*, p. 268.

[245] Ibid.

[246] Ibid.

already absorbed into high remunerative employment in the public sector and TNCs.[247] Thus, the relocation of local entrepreneurship abroad was due to the specialisation of these firms in labour-intensive activities, which the government was phasing out because of the constraint on existing factors of production.

The effect of the government industrial strategy was also reflected in the total overseas investment, which included direct and portfolio investment, capital transactions with overseas subsidiaries and associates, and other foreign assets which have increased fourteen-fold between 1979 and 1990.

Over 55 per cent of the total direct investment abroad are by local entrepreneurs: indicating the relative effect of the high-wage policy on the local firms. However, before I fully examine to what extent Singapore based firms have invested abroad, I would like to first distinguish between local, foreign and government owned firms in Singapore.

Types of Overseas Investors in Singapore

The idea that Singaporean firms are investing abroad is a relatively new phenomenon. Usually, when Singaporeans referred to "foreign investment", they meant industrial capital put into Singapore factories by foreign TNCs with the active environment of the EDB. In recent years, outward investment by Singaporean firms has gained strong recognition from the government who recently published its first data, through the Department of Statistics, on the subject.[248]

The published data however should be treated with caution. The figures are not actual investment flows, but FDI stock-based data from the Department's survey of companies registered in Singapore. The data may not even include the earlier exodus of local firms whom, through the discriminative government wage policy in 1979, may have relocated their entire businesses out of Singapore. This is because of the fact that the Singaporean authorities may never trace these firms. Even more worrying is the fact that local firms in Singapore investing abroad do not need to inform the Department of Statistics of their overseas projects. Therefore, current official data may even underestimate the real extent of Singapore's overseas activities. It is also possible that many of the companies surveyed may even

---

[247] Ibid.

[248] Department of Statistics (1991), *Singapore's Investment Abroad 1976-1989*, Singapore: National Printers.

decide to underestimate the real value of their overseas investments because of taxation. Moreover, since Singaporean firms are allowed to invest overseas freely without any official records, they may do so without registering the subsidiaries as Singapore owned. The real extent of Singapore overseas investments may then be difficult to estimate.

Moreover, the predominant role of TNC subsidiaries in Singapore's economy has made the classification of the nature, origin and ownership of overseas investment by firms based in Singapore very difficult. According to the Department of Statistics' own classification, overseas investors based in Singapore are classified as follows.

(i) Wholly local owned companies with 100 per cent of ordinary paid up shares owned locally and with total control over overseas investment decisions.

(ii) Majority local owned companies with at least 50 per cent of ordinary paid-up shares owned locally, also with a considerable influence over the decisions to carry out overseas investments.

(iii) Wholly foreign-owned companies with 100 per cent of ordinary paid-up shares owned by foreign investors, mostly TNCs.

(iv) Majority foreign-owned companies with more than 50 per cent but less than 100 per cent of ordinary shared owned by foreign investors.

The fundamental problem with the above official classification is that it fails to make the distinction between state-owned, state-linked corporations and local private firms. Although it is understandable that the state may not want its citizens to know "where" and "what" state funds have been used for, because of the political and/or economic consequences that may arise, the failure to make the simple distinction has rendered critical analysis on state TNCs and small local private firms impossible.

Internationally, the Government of Singapore Investments Corporation (GIC) invest a sizeable share of government surpluses in a diversity of stocks in several sectors and in many countries.[249] Although specific information on those investments is not public, they are believed to be very large and strategically targeted around two basic criteria: access to privileged knowledge and contacts in international financial networks; and safe investments with satisfactory levels of return. Although the arguments on this matter are a bit speculative, it is significant to notice that, the criteria for investment are apparently more strategic than strictly profit-making, although

---

[249] Castells, Manuel (1988), *op. cit.*, p. 32.

money-losing operations are not allowed. The main reason for these investments abroad is the government's feeling about the vulnerability of the Singapore's economy.[250] Only by diversifying its assets and further interpenetrating Singapore in the core financial and industrial networks of the advanced economies can the government expect to overcome the catastrophic consequences of a dramatic shrinkage of world trade and internationalised production that could damage Singapore's nodal role in an open economy.[251]

The government's investment is nominally managed by the GIC, but this seems to be mainly a coordinating and administrative body. In terms of overall investment policy, however, it is the top-level government that decides. In terms of individual GLCs or government-link firms, such as Singapore Telecom, Singapore Airways and Sheng-Li Holdings, decisions are left to the management of each firm, so that they are not reserved, in general, if they fail to make profits.[252] Thus, the state is a net overseas investor and as such, it needs to be distinguished from local (including majority local) firms and multi-national subsidiaries (that is, wholly foreign and majority owned foreign companies). Although none of the current official data supports this unique classification, it is nevertheless important to have the distinction in mind as it enables us to focus analytically on the extent of local, as opposed to state-owned overseas investment. According to the Department of Statistics, the present data excludes government-owned firms. Therefore, the data is a reflection of private-owned firms based in Singapore.

Nevertheless, overseas direct investment by local and majority local private owned firms can be traced as far back to when Singapore and Malaysia were in a federation. It began with family businesses, mostly Chinese-owned, who because of the geographical proximity, invested in Malaysia to tap into the large domestic market, cheaper labour and raw material.[253] In recent years, both the motives and push factors have changed. The main push factor is the labour shortage of unskilled workers, constant appreciation of the Singapore dollar, and discriminative government policies such as the high wage policy which was introduced in 1979. Although the main aim was to up grade Singapore's economy, and in particularly, its industrial base, the policy nonetheless led to the premature exit of many of the local private firms to neighbouring countries who at the time were in labour-intensive industries

---

[250] Ibid.

[251] Ibid.

[252] Ibid.

[253] Lim, Linda Y. C. and Pang, Eng Fong (1991), *Foreign Direct Investment and Industrialisation: in Malaysia, Singapore, Taiwan and Thailand*, Development Centre: Organisation for Economic Co-operation and Development, p. 60.

such as plastics, food and beverages, wood products and furniture, textiles and garments.[254] The displacement of the local firms would not have been as bad as it was if the government had at least provided some kind of "safety net" for the "poor" private firms who could not compete with GLCs and TNC subsidiaries. This is, in fact, the most likely explanation why FDI investment by local firms has been in the lead until recently. In total, the local firms between 1981-90 accounted for over 55 per cent of Singapore overseas direct investment (figure 4.2). Secondly, the introduction of incentives and regulations, which favoured TNC subsidiaries instead of local private firms, led to unfair competition between the two and consequent relocation of the latter. This has in effect led to crowding out of the local firms during the 1979-85 period, and the possible explanation for the huge flow of investment by this group of investors.

Most of the local private firms which survived through this government high-wage period did so with no official help or special cooperation with fellow firms to form some sort of competitive force, as is the case in Japan (Kereitsu) or Korea (Chaebol).[255] However, the significance here is that overseas direct investment by local firms is mainly from small-sized firms, with no specific advantages such as financial resources and manpower, technology, and experience.

Apart from the state and local private direct investment, the other major group of investors in Singapore consist of multinational subsidiaries. These firms invested in Singapore during export-led industrialisation and are now investing overseas because of the loss of Singapore's comparative advantage, either with the NIEs or with the neighbouring countries.[256] Most of these foreign firms are now beginning to realise that Singapore is no longer a cheap location for industrial production. Like the local private firms, these foreign subsidiaries relocate some production facilities to resource-rich neighbouring countries as a result of severe labour shortage, high wage costs, appreciating Singapore dollar, and limited industrial space for expansion. However, Singapore remains the headquarters for most of their operations in the region because of its excellent infrastructure, highly skilled labour force, R & D centres and superb telecommunication facilities.

The decision of these foreign subsidiaries to relocate overseas questions Singapore's international competitiveness via the NIEs. It also points to two fundamental conclusions with regards to FDI: Firstly, that Singapore is no longer a low cost production site. Secondly, that in order to compete in the world market, firms will have to search for cheaper location sites. Whether

---

[254] Ibid.

[255] Ibid.

[256] Ibid.

Singapore succeeds in future to attract more capital intensive industries than its competitors in the region depends on its ability to continue to up-grade its present infrastructure, communication facilities, R & D centres, and maintain the country as the region's financial centre.

Trend and Extent of Overseas Direct Investment

Nature

The nature of Singapore's direct investment over the last fifteen years has changed dramatically. According to the Department of Statistics, most of Singapore's direct investment abroad between 1976 and 1982 was from the manufacturing sector.[257] Due to the lack of data, it has not been possible to examine the characteristics of Singapore overseas investment before 1990. Table 4.1a. shows the nature of direct investment activities by matching the industrial activities of the firms set up overseas with that of the local investor firms based in Singapore. As at the end of 1990, the bulk of Singapore's direct investment abroad was from the financial sector (51 per cent) which covers mainly investment holding firms, followed by manufacturing sector (19 per cent) with firms mostly in the labour-intensive industries including textiles and garments, electrical and electronics, plastic, food and beverages. The decline in manufacturing investment in the late-1980s is due to the government's emphasis an positioning Singapore as the financial headquarters of Southeast Asia.

This pattern is also reflected in the number of subsidiaries established abroad by Singapore-based firms (see tables 4.1a - 4.2b). Most of the established branches are from the financial, commerce and manufacturing sectors which together accounts for 80 per cent of the total overseas subsidiaries set up abroad.

---

[257] This is a fact that is confirmed in the Department of Statistics owned publication entitled Singapore's Investment Abroad 1976-89, pp. 2-6.

Table 4.1a Singapore: Nature of Direct Investment by Activity of Investors in Singapore and Activity Abroad, 1990 (in Percentage)

Activity Abroad	Manufacturing	Construction	Commerce	Transport	Financial	Real Estate	Business Services	Others	Total
Activity of Investors									
Total	100.0	100.0	100.0	100.0	100.0	100.0	100.0	100.0	100.0
Manufacturing	40.1	0.5	5.0	3.4	18.6	0.9	5.1	7.6	19.1
Construction	0.2	55.1	0.3	0.3	0.4	18.6	0.0	0.0	2.0
Commerce	8.8	0.0	29.2	0.2	1.1	4.4	1.7	14.0	5.9
Transport	0.6	0.0	0.1	67.2	2.2	4.2	4.7	0.0	3.4
Financial	39.5	34.7	59.3	21.3	55.6	47.7	25.1	60.7	50.5
Real Estate	0.2	3.4	4.9	0.1	6.6	20.7	44.7	6.0	7.1
Business Services	10.7	6.3	1.2	7.5	15.5	3.5	18.7	0.6	11.8
Others	0.0	0.0	0.0	0.0	0.0	0.0	0.0	11.0	0.1

Source: Department of Statistics, *Singapore's Investment Abroad 1976-1990*, Singapore: National Printers, 1993.

Table 4.1b Singapore: Nature of Direct Investment by Activity of Investors in Singapore and Activity Abroad, 1995 (in Percentage)

Activity Abroad	Manufacturing	Construction	Commerce	Transport	Financial	Real Estate	Business Services	Others	Total
Activity of Investors									
Total	100.0	100.0	100.0	100.0	100.0	100.0	100.0	100.0	100.0
Manufacturing	58.7	36.0	10.2	1.20	32.5	1.0	6.1	7.0	32.5
Construction	0.3	37.2	0.3	-	0.3	18.4	0.6	0.2	2.0
Commerce	8.0	0.3	40.3	3.5	5.1	6.7	2.0	6.1	9.2
Transport	0.5	0.1	0.6	73.5	4.3	1.3	0.2	-	4.6
Financial	26.7	21.8	38.9	11.7	47.5	53.2	22.5	67.7	40.1
Real Estate	0.2	3.2	1.7	-	7.6	16.3	12.9	4.2	5.7
Business Services	5.6	1.5	8.1	10.1	2.6	3.1	55.5	5.7	5.7
Others	0.0	0.0	0.0	0.1	0.0	0.1	0.2	9.1	0.2

Source: Department of Statistics, *Singapore's Investment Abroad 1976-1990*, Singapore: National Printers, 1994-95.

Table 4.2a Singapore: Nature of Established Firms Abroad by Activity of Investors and Activity Abroad, 1990 (in Percentage)

Activity Abroad / Activity of Investors	Manufacturing	Construction	Commerce	Transport	Financial	Real Estate	Business Services	Others	Total
Total	100.0	100.0	100.0	100.0	100.0	100.0	100.0	100.0	100.0
Manufacturing	51.9	1.3	11.0	3.5	5.0	4.0	17.4	6.0	18.0
Construction	1.0	69.2	0.6	1.2	1.4	3.4	0.0	2.0	3.3
Commerce	15.1	0.0	59.0	2.9	4.1	7.4	11.0	22.0	24.5
Transport	0.6	0.0	0.7	69.4	3.8	4.0	3.2	1.0	6.8
Financial	25.4	26.9	23.4	19.7	74.3	47.7	21.3	49.0	35.6
Real Estate	0.8	1.3	1.6	0.6	6.0	28.9	1.3	3.0	4.0
Business Services	5.3	1.3	3.6	2.9	4.8	4.7	45.8	2.0	7.0
Others	0.0	0.0	0.1	0.0	0.5	0.0	0.0	15.0	0.8

Source: Department of Statistics, *Singapore's Investment Abroad 1976-1990*, Singapore: National Printers, 1993.

Table 4.2b Singapore: Nature of Established Firms Abroad by Activity of Investors and Activity Abroad, 1995 (in Percentage)

Activity Abroad / Activity of Investors	Manufacturing	Construction	Commerce	Transport	Financial	Real Estate	Business Services	Others	Total
Total	100.0	100.0	100.0	100.0	100.0	100.0	100.0	100.0	100.0
Manufacturing	52.8	27.6	15.0	2.5	7.4	6.3	13.5	5.8	22.4
Construction	0.8	44.7	2.8	-	0.9	2.5	2.2	2.2	2.3
Commerce	17.7	2.0	55.2	4.9	6.9	10.0	4.2	17.3	22.5
Transport	1.2	1.3	0.9	75.0	3.6	3.8	2.2	1.4	6.5
Financial	23.3	18.4	22.3	15.7	71.4	52.9	27.1	38.8	34.6
Real Estate	0.8	3.9	1.3	-	6.9	22.1	0.5	4.3	3.9
Business Services	3.4	2.0	4.7	1.5	2.6	1.8	49.5	2.9	6.9
Others	-	-	0.1	0.3	0.2	0.8	0.7	27.3	0.9

Source: Department of Statistics, *Singapore's Investment Abroad 1976-1990*, Singapore: National Printers, 1994-95.

In terms of diversification, the financial sector was the most diversified. Sixty-two per cent of such firms set up abroad in a wide spectrum of activities like commerce, manufacturing and real estate (see tables 4.3a - 4.3b). The business services, real estate and manufacturing sectors were moderately diversified with 55, 52 and 35 per cent respectively. Overall, about 70 per cent of the firms set up abroad remained in the same activities as their parent firms in Singapore. However, the main reason for diversification was to spread their political, economic and business risks. For adverse developments are unlikely to take place simultaneously in many different countries and thus, while business in one country (say, Singapore) may be bad it may be much better in another country so that the overall performance of the firm is protected from the swings in any one country's political, economic and business environment.[258]

Table 4.3a Singapore: Diversification in Terms of Types of Companies Set Up Abroad, 1990

Activity of Investor in Singapore	No. of Companies Set Up Abroad in a Different Activity	Same Activity	Total
Agriculture	2	6	8
Mining	0	2	2
Manufacturing	140	265	405
Construction	22	54	76
Commerce	150	411	561
Transport	36	120	156
Financial	505	310	815
Real Estate	47	43	90
Business Services	87	71	158

Source: Department of Statistics, *Singapore's Investment Abroad 1976-1990*, Singapore: National Printers, 1993.

---

[258] Aggarwal, Raj (1985), *op. cit.*

100

Table 4.3b Singapore: Diversification in Terms of the Amount of Direct Investment Abroad, 1995

Activity of Investor in Singapore	Amount ($ Million)	Per Cent of D3 in a Different Activity (%)
Manufacturing	15,040.5	56
Construction	929.2	80
Commerce	4,257.8	57
Transport & Communication	2,131.0	53
Financial	18,559.2	41
Real Estate	2,627.3	79
Business Services	2,623.8	72

Source: Department of Statistics, *Singapore's Investment Abroad 1994-95*, Singapore: National Printers, 1995.

Trends

According to the Department of Statistics data, outward direct investment by Singapore-based firms dates back to the mid-1970s. As is illustrated in table 4.4, Singapore's international direct investment between 1976-90 grew at an average rate of 16 per cent per annum. The bulk of the overseas direct investment occurred during the period of 1979-85. In fact, outward direct investment between 1979-85 period was higher than total overseas direct investment between 1981-90 period in Korea and Taiwan. Such a magnitude of overseas direct investment during the 1979-85 period shows the effect of the government's high-wage policy which eroded Singapore's international competitiveness via the NIEs and neighbouring countries such as Malaysia, Indonesia and Thailand, who were gaining comparative advantage in labour-intensive industries.[259]

---

[259] Chaponniere, Jean-Rapheal (1992), *op. cit.*, p. 1.

Table 4.4 Singapore: Extent of Overseas Investments, 1976-90

Year	Total	Growth Rate	Share	DI	Growth Rate	Share	PI	Growth Rate	Share	TO	Growth Rate	Share	Other	Growth Rate	Share
High-Tech Phase															
1976-78	8304.8	16.2	..	3426.1	8.5	..	1771.9	23.2	..	1317.0	3.6	..	1789.8	42.6	..
1976	2200.4	-	100.0	1015.1	-	46.1	446.9	-	20.3	412.5	-	18.7	325.9	-	27.4
1977	2706.6	23.0	100.0	1120.0	10.3	41.4	525.6	17.6	19.4	457.5	10.9	16.9	603.5	85.2	31.8
1978	3397.8	25.5	100.0	1291.0	15.3	38.0	799.4	52.1	23.5	447.0	0.0	13.2	860.4	42.6	38.6
High Wage Phase															
1979-84	42691.4	20.4	..	11519.7	11.1	..	9288.3	17.4	..	5554.9	22.7	..	16328.5	32.5	..
1979	4372.6	28.7	100.0	1506.8	16.7	34.5	1046.8	30.9	23.9	508.6	13.8	11.6	1310.4	52.3	37.8
1980	4989.3	14.1	100.0	1615.9	7.2	32.4	1196.8	14.3	24.0	523.7	3.0	10.5	1652.9	26.1	56.7
1981	6723.0	34.7	100.0	1677.7	3.8	25.0	1484.2	24.0	22.1	733.2	40.0	10.9	2827.9	71.1	44.2
1982	7654.3	13.9	100.0	2086.9	24.4	27.3	1605.6	8.2	21.0	988.7	34.8	12.9	2973.1	5.1	43.0
1983	8751.6	14.3	100.0	2233.1	7.0	25.5	1888.9	17.6	21.6	1339.2	35.5	15.3	3290.4	10.7	48.8
1984	10200.6	16.6	100.0	2399.3	7.4	23.5	2066.0	9.4	20.3	1461.5	9.1	14.3	4273.8	29.9	54.5
Recession & Recovery Phase															
1985-90	101159.0	21.9	..	23.572.7	24.7	..	26151.0	26.1	..	16352.5	31.5	..	35082.9	20.7	..
1985	12702.3	24.5	100.0	2257.2	0.0	17.8	2982.9	44.4	23.5	1906.3	30.4	15.0	5555.9	30.0	44.5
1986	12899.5	1.6	100.0	2597.6	15.1	20.1	2922.7	0.0	22.7	1724.5	0.0	13.4	5654.7	1.8	32.0
1987	12040.6	0.0	100.0	2961.5	14.0	24.6	3333.3	14.0	27.7	1617.9	0.0	13.4	4127.9	0.0	35.8
1988	12968.3	7.7	100.0	2993.9	1.1	23.1	3736.9	12.1	28.8	1921.7	18.8	14.8	4315.8	4.6	62.4
1989	22714.0	75.2	100.0	5288.7	76.6	23.3	5535.9	48.1	24.4	3790.9	97.3	16.7	8098.5	87.6	32.3
1990	27834.3	22.5	100.0	7473.8	41.3	26.9	7639.3	38.0	27.4	5391.2	42.2	19.4	7330.1	0.0	0.0

Notes:
1 DI   Direct Investment.
2 PI   Portfolio Investment.
3 TO   Transactions with Overseas.
4 Other   Other Foreign Assets.

Source: Department of Statistics, *Singapore's Investment Abroad 1976-90*, Singapore: National Printers.

The magnitude of the investment abroad however shows the effect of the loss of comparative advantage particularly by the local investors. Over 55 per cent of the total outward direct investment between 1981-90 was from local entrepreneurs (see table 4.5). The bulk of these local firms were from the labour-intensive industries such as textiles and garments, footwear and leather, food and beverages and packaging. The local share of outward direct investment in 1990 alone was nearly three times the total manufacturing investment inflow in Singapore. Such a gap between the local investor's FDI inflow and outflow confirms the impact of Singapore's loss of international competitiveness. This is also evident with existing TNC subsidiaries based in Singapore. The average rate of foreign TNCs investment outside Singapore is more than two-fold the inflow of manufacturing investment.

Most of the foreign firms that have relocated are characterised by assembly-line production, such as electrical, electronics and plastic industries. Although the motivation by this group is similar to that of the local investor, the order of importance is slightly different. The similarity and differences of the causes, push and pull factors for outward direct investment, will be examined empirically in the next chapter. However, I now turn briefly to what these push and pull factors are with regard to Singapore's direct investment abroad.

Extent of Overseas Involvement[260]

Table 4.5 shows FDI inflow and outflow in Singapore since 1981 as published by the Department of Statistics, and a number of characteristics stand out. Firstly, cumulative FDI outflow from Singapore (as measured in Singapore dollars) between 1981-90 is almost twice the corresponding inflow of FDI by TNCs.

---

[260] Because there are differences in the way each government raises its data, caution should be used in interpreting individual country figures. In the case of Singapore, the inward direct investment represent manufacturing investment commitments as at year end. This is often documented by the Department of Statistics which then publishes its annual figure. However, the data on outward direct investment is not as reliable as the inward investment. This is because there are no official statistics of the same nature for FDI outflow as there are for inward direct investment. The data used here was based on a survey carried out by the Singapore government between 1981-90. As is discussed in chapter 4, the figures do not include the earlier mass exodus of local firms who, through the discriminative government wage policy in 1979 (see Chapter 3), have relocated their entire business operation out of Singapore. In the case of Korea, it is claimed that the FDI data represent actual investment as at year end. Taiwan's figures represent total stock of FDI as at the end of the year. There is no data for Hong Kong because the government does not keep track of FDI outflow.

Table 4.5 Singapore: Inward and Outward Direct Investment, 1981-93[1]

	Inward Investment						Outward Investment					
Year	Total	%[2]	Foreign	%	Local	%	Total	%	Foreign	%	Local	%
1981	1862	-	1221	-	641	-	1678	-	800	-	878	-
1982	1704	-8.5	1162	-4.8	542	-15.4	2087	24.4	988	23.5	1099	25.2
1983	1775	4.2	1269	9.2	506	-6.6	2233	7.0	1007	1.9	1226	11.6
1984	1827	2.9	1334	5.1	493	-2.6	2399	7.4	1004	-0.3	1396	13.9
1985	1120	-38.7	888	-33.4	232	-52.9	2257	-5.9	585	41.7	1762	26.2
1986	1449	29.3	1190	34.0	259	11.6	2598	15.1	745	27.4	1853	5.2
1987	1743	20.3	1448	21.7	295	13.9	2962	14.0	1125	51.0	1836	-0.9
1988	3007	72.5	2657	83.5	349	18.3	2994	1.1	1095	-2.7	1899	3.4
1989	1958	-34.9	1625	-38.8	333	-4.6	5289	76.7	3047	178.3	2242	18.1
1990	2443	24.8	2217	36.4	226	-32.1	7474	41.3	4051	33.0	3423	52.7
1991	2934	18.0	2217	11.0	473	75.2	18608	149.0	8937	120.6	9671	82.5
1992	3481	18.6	2733	11.1	748	58.1	22442	20.6	10818	21.0	11624	20.1
1993	3923	12.7	3177	16.2	746	-0.3	28159	25.5	14178	31.1	13981	20.2
Cum. total	29,270	-	23,382	-	5,887	-	101,180	-	48,380	-	52,890	-
Average	-	10.1	-	12.6		5.2	-	31.3	-	43.9	-	31.5

Notes:
1 Figures in Singapore dollar (million).
2 Percentage growth rate.

Source: Department of Statistics, *Singapore's Investment Abroad 1976-93*, Singapore: National Printers.

Though inward direct investment into Singapore's economy over the last ten years has been increasing, firms based in Singapore have generally preferred to invest abroad. However, the difference between the amount invested in Singapore's economy and abroad becomes even more interesting when it is compared on a yearly basis. For instance, in 1990 alone, the FDI outflow was three times higher than manufacturing investment inflow into Singapore's economy. In fact, it is assumed that if the present growth rate is maintained until the year 2000, cumulative FDI outflow will be about four to six times the size of inflow. This could have a devastating impact on Singapore's economy considering the fact that it heavily relies on FDI in sustaining future growth. Secondly, the local share of FDI outflow has increased more than four times local investment in Singapore's economy. In fact, the compound growth rate for the local investment inflow in Singapore's manufacturing sector is negative. Furthermore, local direct investment abroad accounts for over 55 per cent of total overseas direct investment from Singapore. The dramatic increase of the local direct investment calls into question Singapore's industrial policy, which is almost totally dependent on FDI. Above all, the imbalance between foreign and local confirms the relative weakness and decline of local entrepreneurship in Singapore.

Thirdly, the outflow of FDI by foreign subsidiaries is almost the same as the total investment inflow in Singapore's economy.

Table 4.6 Inward and Outward Direct Investment Among the East Asian NIEs,[1] 1981-90[2]

	Singapore				Korea				Taiwan			
Year	Inward	%[3]	Outward	%	Inward	%	Outward	%	Inward	%	Outward	%
1981	909	-	819	-	145	-	28	-	466		11	-
1982	808	-11.1	990	20.9	189	30.3	101	260.7	396	-15.0	12	9.1
1983	835	3.3	1,050	6.1	269	42.3	109	7.9	380	-4.0	11	-8.3
1984	839	0.5	1,101	4.9	422	56.9	50	-54.1	404	6.3	39	254.5
1985	532	-36.6	1,072	-2.6	532	26.1	113	126.0	558	38.1	41	5.1
1986	669	25.8	1,199	11.8	354	-33.5	181	60.2	702	25.8	57	39.0
1987	875	30.8	1,487	24.0	1,060	199.4	410	126.5	1,419	102.1	103	80.7
1988	1,545	76.6	1,539	3.5	1,284	21.1	216	-47.3	1,183	-16.6	219	112.6
1989	1,031	-33.3	2,784	80.9	1,090	-15.1	570	163.9	2,418	104.4	931	325.1
1990	1,408	36.6	4,307	54.7	803	-26.3	955	67.5	2,302	-4.8	1,552	66.7
Cum. total	9,451	-	19,348	-	6,148	-	2,733	-	10,228	-	2,976	-
Average	-	9.3	-	20.4	-	30.1	-	71.1	-	23.6	-	88.4

Notes:
1   Hong Kong is not included because of the lack of official data.
2   Figures in U.S. dollar (million).
3   Percentage Growth Rate.

Sources: Department of Statistics. *Singapore Investment Abroad 1976-90*. Investment Commission and Ministry of Economic Affairs, *Statistics on Overseas Investment*, Republic of China, 1993. *Outward direct investment from Korea*, London: Korean Embassy, 1993.

The average rate of growth by foreign investors is more than twice the rate at which they invest in Singapore's manufacturing sector. The surge of outward direct investment by the foreign TNCs based in Singapore raises the question of Singapore international competitiveness.

Fourthly, as is shown in table 4.6 above, outward and inward direct investment in Singapore, as compared to the East Asian Newly Industrialising Economies (NIEs), has been unusually high. Between 1981-90, cumulative outward direct investment from Singapore was seven-times the amount Korean firms invested abroad and six-times that of Taiwan.[261] In total, Singapore accounts for over 77 per cent of the NIE's direct investment abroad and is now the largest investor in the region after Japan. Such magnitude of FDI outflow for an industrialising economy questions its international competitiveness *vis-á-vis* the NIEs. Moreover, the surge in outward direct investment from Singapore and the simultaneous economic slow down in recent years raises the fears of a country's dependence on FDI for development.

Finally, as is evident in table 4.7, outward direct investment from Singapore as a proportion of GDP and exports is the highest of any of the NIEs. On average, outward direct investment as a proportion of gross domestic product (GDP) increased by 9 per cent between 1981-90 in Singapore. In contrast, the corresponding compound growth rate for Korea was 2 per cent and 5 per cent in Taiwan.

Table 4.7 Outward Direct Investment as a Percentage of GDP and Export Among the East Asian NIEs, 1981-90

Year	Singapore		Korea		Taiwan	
	Investment/GDP	Investment/Export	Investment/GDP	Investment/Export	Investment/GDP	Investment/Export
1981	5.7	3.9	0.4	0.1	0.9	0.1
1982	6.4	4.8	1.4	0.5	0.9	0.1
1983	6.1	4.8	1.4	0.4	0.7	0.1
1984	6.0	4.6	0.5	0.2	2.1	0.2
1985	5.8	4.7	1.3	0.4	1.7	0.2
1986	6.7	5.3	1.7	0.5	2.1	0.2
1987	7.0	5.2	3.0	0.9	2.6	0.3
1988	6.0	3.9	1.2	0.4	4.4	0.5
1989	9.3	6.2	2.7	0.9	15.2	1.8
1990	11.8	8.2	4.0	1.6	23.8	2.2
Average	8.7	5.2	1.8	0.6	5.4	0.6

Sources: Direction of Trade Statistics Yearbook, 1991. IMF, *Financial Statistics*, 1993.

---

[261] The figure excludes Hong Kong.

The average proportion of outward investment in terms of exports for the same period in Singapore was 5 per cent and the corresponding rate for Korea and Taiwan was less than 1 per cent. This shows the magnitude of outward direct investment from Singapore, and also, the widening-gap between Singapore's comparative advantage and the NIEs. Thus, Singapore's future attractiveness as an investment site is seriously questioned.

However, the above cursory review of some of the unique features in the Singapore economy and the doubts about its future development still does not change the minds of many economists who believe that FDI and international trade are the keys to economic growth. Such conviction is founded on Singapore's economic success in achieving the following two criteria for economic development. Firstly, that as a country's per capita income and stock of human capital rises, it shifts from being a net importer of investment, technology and skills to being a net exporter. Secondly, that as a country moves from labour-intensive to capital-intensive production techniques, it loses its comparative advantage as a low cost production investment site to lower income countries. The present outflow, it is argued, is another phase of economic development in which Singapore needs to pass through.

Before I examine the prevailing view in Singapore's investment abroad, I need to distinguish between FDI and portfolio investment. The purpose for the distinction is twofold. Firstly, to provide adequate meaning to the term FDI, as before 1960s, the term was used to mean one form of international capital movement, responding to just differences in rates of return on capital. Thus, the distinction will enable us to distinguish between the old and modern use of the term. Secondly, the distinction will provide a framework, which will be used throughout the book. Since I will concentrate on inward manufacturing rather than portfolio investment into Singapore's economy. However, the data for outward direct investment does not distinguish between the various forms of direct investment. I shall then use the term FDI in a relative sense, which will cover all forms of industrial production abroad. Finally, the distinction is to provide the basis for understanding the theoretical causes of FDI.

Geographical Distribution

Asia-Pacific

The data on the geographical distribution of Singapore's international direct investment is only available from 1981 onwards. However, the current distributional pattern, by region and country shows, the relative importance of comparative advantage of the different destination countries.[262] It also reflects the fact that Singapore investors, particularly the Chinese firms, preferred a business environment in which they have close personal, cultural and language ties.[263] Although in recent years, Singapore's direct investment in the region has declined by more than 25 per cent due to the increasing diversification of investment to advanced countries, the region remains an important investment site for Singapore's investors.

Tables 4.8 and 4.9 shows the distribution of Singapore's direct investment abroad and established firms by top recipient countries and activity of the investors respectively.

Table 4.8 Singapore: Distribution of Direct Investment by Country and Activity, 1990

Host Country	% Share of Total DFI	Manufacturing %	Financial %	Commerce %	Real Estate %
Malaysia	22	38	24	22	7
Hong Kong	12	26	37	9	22
New Zealand	11	0	95	4	0
Netherlands	8	1	99	0	0
Australia	7	4	64	5	25
USA	4	20	25	3	8
Taiwan	3	16	13	63	0
Thailand	3	57	14	18	5

Source: Department of Statistics, *Singapore's Investment Abroad 1976-90*, Singapore: National Printers.

---

[262] Department of Statistics, *Destination, Activity, and Returns of Singapore's Direct Investments Abroad*, Singapore: National Printers, 1992, p. 2.

[263] Hill, Hal and Pang, Eng Fong (1991), *op. cit.*, p. 561.

Among the top recipient countries are Malaysia and Hong Kong. Together, they account for over 30 per cent Singapore's total investment in Asia indicating the importance of these countries to Singapore firms as a destination of its FDI. Also, the two countries also account for the bulk of the established branches in the region.

Table 4.9 Singapore: Distribution of Established Companies Abroad in the Top Five Host Countries, 1990

Activity Abroad	Malaysia		Hong Kong		Thailand		Australia		United States	
	No	%	No	%	No	%	No	%	No	%
Total	1,007	100	365	100	144	100	88	100	86	100
Manufacturing	270	27	34	9	44	31	8	9	11	13
Commerce	387	38	103	8	41	28	22	25	17	20
Financial	93	0	129	35	15	10	23	26	24	28
Others	257	26	99	27	44	31	35	40	34	40

Source: Department of Singapore, *Singapore's Investment Abroad 1976-90*, Singapore:National Printers.

In Malaysia, about 1,007 (44 per cent) subsidiaries were set up, followed by Hong Kong 365, (16 per cent) and Thailand 144, (6 per cent). One of the possible determinants of Singapore's investment in Malaysia is the proximity of the country to Singapore and the relatively cheap labour costs. In Hong Kong, 35 per cent of the firms set up were in the financial sector, most of which were investment holding companies and nearly 28 per cent in commerce. In Thailand, 31 per cent of the companies set up were manufacturing companies and 28 per cent were in the commercial sector (see appendix). China's share has increased quite dramatically in recent years. Between 1986-90, Singapore subsidiaries in China were 193 worth S$461.6 million.[264] But by January 1992, Singapore firms invested in almost 500 projects worth more than S$1.3 billion, thus becoming the fourth biggest foreign investor in the Republic. Of the total, manufacturing direct investment accounts for over

---

[264] Singapore Business, *Global Opportunities*, September 1989, p. 48.

60 per cent, mainly in the form of joint ventures with either the local entrepreneurs or state enterprises. Nearly 90 per cent of the established subsidiaries are in labour-intensive industries such as textiles and garments, food processing and beverage, computer assembly, furniture and metal. The main attractions were the Republic's open-door policy, political and social stability (though the Tian-An-Men Square event slow down the investment activities for sometime). Also, the availability of infrastructure and service facilities, especially in the costal cities, change of foreign ownership laws and reform of approvals of investment projects, change of investment attitudes towards foreign investors, availability of cheap and abundant labour, huge domestic market (over one billion), shared dialects, strong family ties, and a vibrant local economy.[265]

In India, the main determinant of Singapore's direct investment was the huge population - which includes a prosperous middle class that numbers some 100 million - and a growing economy.[266] However, when compared to China, Singapore's FDI in India was very low. As at the end of 1991, only about 11 projects were signed by Singapore firms involving construction, ship repairing and manufacturing. According to the Singapore Business, the general lack of interests in India is due to the endless red tape, bureaucratic and administrative drawbacks and inconsistent foreign investment policy.[267] Similarly, in Sri Lanka, Singapore firms have been adopting a more cautious approach. In general, the continual internal political struggle and unclear FDI policies have put off Singapore investors. So far there are more than 55 Singapore approved projects in the island nation. The largest are Prima flour's S$120 million flourmill, Singapore's Sapphire Company, and Tien Wah Press.

In Vietnam and Cambodia, the current trend shows that Singapore direct investment is likely to increase in the future, as the two countries are now experiencing political stability.[268] Recently, the Singapore government signed a treaty with the Vietnamese authorities to guarantee all Singapore investments, including American subsidiaries in Singapore. As at mid-1992, total Singapore investment in Vietnam was about US$48.46 million, mostly in the garment, cigarette making, food processing and, drinks industries, and hotel construction. Prominent among these industries were Asia-Pacific Breweries Ltd, which has invested about US$25.5 million to brew beer, and Representations International Pte Ltd, which has committed US$5 million to produce soft drinks.

---

[265] Ibid.
[266] Ibid.
[267] Ibid.
[268] Ibid.

Singapore's overseas investment in the NIEs, particularly in Korea and Taiwan, is relatively low. With the exception of Hong Kong, which is the second largest recipient of its investment in Asia after Malaysia, Singapore investment in Taiwan and Korea is minimal. In Taiwan, Singapore firms have a small foothold of 58 subsidiaries worth S$222.7 million in 1990. Over 17 per cent of these firms are in the manufacturing industries and the rest in the financial and business services. There was no Singapore direct investment in South Korea until 1988, when a small fraction of the total investment, mostly in the financial and business sectors, was registered. However, the high coefficient as noted in table 4.5, resulted because of the recent liberalisation policy in the country, which has influenced Singapore firms to invest due to the high profit potential. At the end of 1981, there were only 118 Singapore established firms in Hong Kong, worth S$181.8 million. Nine years later, Singapore direct investment had increased to S$908.5 million in 360 established projects, mostly joint ventures in the manufacturing industries such as textiles and garments, and food processing. The current slowdown in Singapore direct investment in Hong Kong was due to the government's confrontation with Beijing's authorities towards British plans to increase democracy in the colony before 1997. In Australia, Singapore's investment ranked fifth, as the largest source of the country's foreign investment. Most of the investments were in the financial services (64 per cent), real estate (25 per cent), commerce (5 per cent) and manufacturing (4 per cent).

ASEAN

As noted in table 4.5, the coefficient of the Asean countries as a whole was similar to that of the Asia-Pacific region. This indicates that the major determinant of Singapore's direct investment in the Asean region is due to the relative high rate of return. In addition, the region has a large internal market - a combined population which exceeds 290 million - plus its abundant natural resources and cheap labour force. Between 1981 and 1990, there were over 9,645 Singapore subsidiaries worth S$12.8 billion (ie over 61 per cent of the total direct investment for the period). Again, Malaysia is the most important recipient of Singapore's direct investment in the Asean region. In 1981, Malaysia accounted for over 60 per cent of Singapore's overseas direct investment. In recent years, Malaysia's share has declined considerably to 22 per cent, but the country is still regarded by many Singapore investors as the most favourite site. The decline has been because of the increasing labour cost and ownership policy. However, the main attractions of Singapore investment in Malaysia are the geographical proximity, political stability, vibrant domestic economy, and change of economic orientation (from import-substitution to export-led). The evidence for this can be seen in the dramatic increase of FDI in the country since the change of industrial policy in 1985. Between 1985 to 1990, Singapore's direct investment in the country has increased by over 71 per cent. Of total Singapore FDI in 1990, 38 per cent was in manufacturing activities, and 24 per cent in financial investments; 38 per cent of the Singapore subsidiaries investment in Malaysia was in commerce and 27 per cent in manufacturing activities.

In Indonesia, Singapore is the biggest source for foreign investment. Between 1981-85, Singapore's direct investment was very low due to the country's import-substitution policy, which created artificial barriers to the movement of factors of production between national boundaries. Since then, Singapore's direct investment in the country has more than quadrupled, most of which has been made after 1987 because of the growth triangle initiative as discussed below.

The Growth Triangle

Whereas much has been written about the concept,[269] problems,[270] and the complementarity[271] of the Johor-Singapore-Raiu growth triangle, little is known about the detailed concentration of Singapore's direct investment in the growth triangle.

Coined by the then Singapore First Deputy Prime Minister Goh Chok Tong in December 1989, the term "Growth Triangle" describes the process of

---

[269] Kumar, Sree and Lee, Tsao Yuan (1991), "Growth Triangles, Belts and Circles", *Trends*, 28 April, Singapore: Institute of Southeast Asian Studies; Kumar, Sree and Lee, Tsao Yuan (1991), "A Singapore Perspective", in *Growth Triangle: The Johor-Singapore-Riau Experience*, in Lee, Tsao Yuan (ed.), Singapore: Institute of Southeast Asian Studies.

[270] Ng, Chee Yuen and Wong, Poh Kam (1991), *op. cit*, pp. 123-152; Lee, Tsao Yuan (1992), "Global Regionalism and Regional Economic Zones in the Asia-pacific: The Promise and Challenge of the 90s", *Business Times*, 15 April 1992; Perry, Martin (1991), *op. cit.*, Vatikiotis, M. (1991), "Search For a Hinterland: Singapore Appeals to Neighbours' Enlightened Self-interest", *Far Eastern Economic Review*, 3rd January.

[271] Lee, Tsao Yuan (1992), "Regional Economic Zones in the Asia-pacific: A Conceptual Overview", paper presented at the conference on *Regional Cooperation and Growth Triangles in ASEAN*, jointly organised by Centre for Business Research and Development, Faculty of Business Administration and the Centre for Advanced Studies, Faculty of Arts & Social Sciences, National University of Singapore, 23-24 April; Lau, Geok Theng, et al (1991), *Marketing the Growth Triangle: The Batam Case*, Faculty of Business Administration, National University of Singapore, mimeo.

economic integration between Singapore, Indonesia's Batam Island and the Malaysia state of Johor. The main objective was to encourage the governments of the three countries involved to work together to expedite this process, exploiting the complementary endowments of the three regions to attract foreign investment. However, the growth triangle initiative has since then become a centrepiece of Singapore's regional diplomacy and its economic development strategy, especially since Goh took over as Prime Minister at the end of 1990.

The integration process to which Goh referred to was nothing new, but an official declaration or acknowledgment of the process that began since the early 1980s. Singapore has sought to overcome its domestic land and labour constraints by encouraging firms to invest in adjacent areas of Malaysia and Indonesia. Singapore concluded a bilateral agreement with Indonesia to jointly develop Batam, 20 kilometres Southeast of Singapore, as an export-processing zone. A number of Singapore-based firms have since established manufacturing operations on Batam, primarily in the electronics industry. Many others have set up operations across the causeway in Johor, although there is no such bilateral agreement in effect.[272]

Informal economic ties with Johor are already substantial, and businessmen and state-level officials in Johor have received Goh's initiative enthusiastically. But there has been long-standing concern among federal authorities in Kuala Lumpur, and some Johoreans, that the initiative might not be consistent with Malaysia's national development strategy. Albeit, a number of joint projects have been proposed, including a high-technology park. As yet, there are no special arrangements for direct investments between Singapore and Johor.[273]

While at the political level, there are still some problems for final agreement, at the economic level substantial progress has been made with regards to the relocation of Singapore's labour-intensive firms.[274] In Batam island, for instance, Singapore is the largest investor, accounting for over 44 per cent of the total foreign investment, followed by the United States 19 per

---

[272] The Embassy of the United States of America, Singapore Office (1992), *The Growth Triangle: Singapore-Johor-Riau*, Report prepared as a guide to U.S. investors, May.

[273] Ibid., p. 1.

[274] Perry, Martin (1991), "The Singapore Growth Triangle: State, Capital and Labour at a New Frontier in the World Economy", *Singapore Journal of Tropical Geography*, 12 (2), pp. 138-151.

cent, and Japan 7 per cent. In Malaysia as a whole, Singapore has been among the top five investors over the last decade. Since the late-1980s, Singapore firms have accounted for over 20 per cent of FDI in Johor state of Malaysia.[275] The main determinants include geographical proximity, cheap labour force, and above all, the change of economic orientation from import substitution to export-led industrialisation. For over three decades, Malaysia and Indonesia pursued a strategy of import-substitution where economic nationalism was foremost in the minds of its leaders. The driving force for such an inward looking strategy, was realised through tariff and non-tariff barriers, has been through economic nationalism that goes beyond modern day economic rationality.[276] The feeling of economic nationalism in resource rich countries are sometime explained by the fear of begin exploited by those which are less endowed.[277] What is generally over-looked is that barriers erected to keep competitors out, although comfortable to domestic producers, destroy motivations and incentives to innovate, to strive for greater efficiency, to upgrade, above all, to allow the free movement of mobile factors of production such as industrial capital.

Apart from this, the attitudes of both countries towards foreign investment before the change of industrial policy in the mid-1980 was very biased.[278] Malaysia for instance, before 1986, required local participation in all investment projects. However, the Investment Act in 1986, relaxed the equity guidelines to allow for 100 per cent equity in cases where no local partners could be found. Pioneer statues, which grants a company a five-year tax relief period, was also granted to deserving companies. In Batam island, 100 per cent foreign ownership for the first five years was also allowed, after which there should be a 5 per cent divestment. If the company exported 100 per cent of its products, then no further divestment was required.[279] This special preference in Batam island is however, because of the growth triangle. This is in contrast to the rest of Indonesia, where domestic ownership must reach 51 per cent for at least 15 years.[280] It then shows that economic liberalisation, after all, can change a country's locational advantage.

However, the region's comparative advantage shows that Singapore firms will continue to invest in the growth triangle to increase exports, even though

---

[275] Ng, Chee Yuen and Wong, Poh Kam (1991), *op. cit.*, p. 134.
[276] Ibid.
[277] Ibid.
[278] Ibid.
[279] Lee, Tsao Yuan (1992), *op. cit.*, p. 11.
[280] Ibid.

Singapore based firms are increasingly diversifying their investment to advanced countries such as Europe and the U.S.

Europe

The coefficient of Singapore's direct investment in Europe has been insignificant due to the relative low level of FDI and rate of return. Again, this shows that Singapore firms do not possess ownership specific advantages, but also lack financial resources, market intelligence, manpower to manage and control long distance projects, and experience. In 1981, of the total 2,290 Singapore companies established abroad only 30 (3 per cent of overall total) were located in Europe: with the United Kingdom having 20 per cent (2 per cent of overall total, due mainly to historical colonial ties, familiarities in language, culture, and business environment), 7 per cent (0.7 per cent of overall total) in Netherlands, 3 (0.3 per cent of overall total) in other European countries mainly in France and Germany. By the end of 1990, the number increased to 113 (5 per cent of overall total): of the total, 63 (3 per cent) were located in the United Kingdom, 12 (0.5 per cent of overall total) in Germany, 20 (0.9 per cent) in the Netherlands, and 18 (0.7 per cent of overall total) in other countries in Europe.

In general, the main attraction of Singapore's FDI in Europe was as a result of the fear that post-1992 EC, would mean a "Fortress Europe", in which exports would no longer act as the best alternative to direct investment.[281] With a population of 325 million people, compared with 246 million in the US and 123 million in Japan, the EC post-1992 was seen to be a large, wealthy marketplace offering considerable growth potential as the internal frontiers in which the free movement of goods, persons, services and capital is ensured. In other words, the sheer size and scope of the European Market and the fear of ultimate protectionism, have been the prime motives for Singapore firms with aspirations towards globalisation to invest in Europe.

However, there is little information on Singapore firms in Europe. Among the few firms that have managed to invest in Europe, include the Singapore Food Technologies (SFI), which bought a 20 per cent stake in a British food

---

[281] This fear of the Single Market has been explained by Development Bank of Singapore (1989), *An Integrated European Market in 1992: Implications for Singapore*, Singapore: DBS Bank; Lee,Tsao Yuan (1990), "EC-1992: The Perspective of the Asian NIEs", Paper prepared for a conference on *The EC After 1992: Perspective from the Outside*, by University of Basel; Probert, Jocelyn (1991), *op. cit.*; Lall, S. *op. cit.*; Tan, Loong-Hoe (1992), "Single European Market in 1992: Implications and Responses from Singapore", paper presented at *Colloquium on ASEAN and Europe 1992*, Kuala Lumpur; Chaponniere, Rean-Raphael (1992), *op. cit.*

company in a deal which also gives it the options to full ownership the firm by the end of 1994. Under the deal, SFI - a member of the Singapore Technologies Industrial Corporation - and another local company, Novo Technology Development (NTD), have together combined resources to enable them to be competitive in Europe and at the same time increase their market share and gain access to market intelligence.

North America

A major attraction of Singapore's direct investment in the U.S. in particular, was the relative high rate of return. In addition, Singapore firms invested in the country because of the fear of the North American Free Trade (NAFTA). As at 1981, there were 46 (2.8 per cent) established Singapore companies in the US, worth S$31.8 million (1.9 per cent). By the end of 1990, the number of established companies had increased to 86 (3.8 per cent), worth S$331 million (4.4 per cent). With the exception of 1989, where an extraordinary investment was made in real estate, including a sizeable one in California by the government, the late-1980s generally experienced low FDI from Singapore investors.[282] This was due to the sluggish U.S. economy and the general downtrend of the world economic conditions. However, by the end of 1989, one-fifth of Singapore direct investment in the U.S. has been in the manufacturing and over 20 per cent in 1990, mostly in the primary and fabricated metals and machinery, chemicals, food processing and electronics.

Among the many projects that are in operation is that of Yeo Hiap Seng's US$52 million joint purchase (with Temasek Holdings) of American Canned Oriented food maker, Chun King.[283] Tee Yih Jia bought a U.S. oriental food company in May 1988 and made its way into the American market via a ready-made distribution network. In May 1991, Leo Sakata electronics, a local electronics firm set up a joint venture plant with Earnway Industries (Canada), worth S$4.5 million in Canada. Based at Thunder Bay, Ontario, the plant is expected to serve the U.S. market, which is already, the firm's biggest export

---

[282] Singapore Business, *Global Opportunities*, September 1989, p. 48.
[283] Ibid.

market.[284]

Although Singapore's global investment is not evenly distributed, its existing pattern reflects the sorts of investment that are being carried out and the motivation for them. As is been earlier discussed, the bulk of the investment in Asia shows the intensity of labour-demanding activities that have been relocated from Singapore. The investment in Europe and America indicates the market elements of Singapore investment in the last 5 years.

Conclusion

Having examined, in general, the extent and motivations of Singapore's direct investment overseas, it now appears that foreign investment by firms based in Singapore will continue to grow into the year 2000. However, as compared to the East Asian NIEs, Singapore firms will continue to increase their overseas investment but not as much as Korean, Taiwanese or even Hong Kong firms. The major reason for this is that Singapore depends heavily on FDI by TNCs themselves and as such may want to continue to up-grade its local infrastructure and other facilities, which may lead to a slow down in overseas investment. Also, the local firms are not as strong as Korean or Taiwanese firms who because of the government backing will continue to venture abroad into the foreseeable future.

As for the East Asian NIEs as a whole, FDI outflow will continue to grow in the 1990s. This assertion is based on the facts that the factors that caused the NIEs's FDI to rise dramatically in the past decade are still present and, if anything, growing stronger.[285] However, Korea is expected to lead the "new FDI" in the region because of its concentrated and advanced industrial structure, with the "chaebol" able to muster vast resources and deploy a range of sophisticated technologies. The main attraction of this new FDI in the Asian region in particular, will not be so much cheap labour *per se*, but rather promising domestic markets and availability of natural resources. Much of Taiwanese FDI on the other hand, will depend on the ability of domestic enterprises to up-grade and the effectiveness of support provided by the government. Most of the investment will be in China even though there is no official approval from the Taiwanese government for such investment.

However, it is evident from this chapter that as the Singapore government changes the country's comparative advantage, firms that are unable to adjust to the new policy will relocate to countries whose comparative

---

[284] Ibid.
[285] Lall, Sanjaya (1992), *op. cit.*, pp. 23-24.

117

advantage are in line with their production technique. It then follows that Singapore's investment abroad is not due to ownership advantages but loss of comparative advantage. The loss of comparative advantage in Singapore can also be empirically tested through the desire of firms to invest in countries other than Singapore. This is what I turn to next.

5 Empirical Findings: Testing for FDI Motivations

ABSTRACT

This chapter is based on four main propositions. Firstly, there is a correlation between FDI and profitability. Empirically, the analysis of this hypothesis is based on the simple Ordinary Least Square's (OLS) regression of FDI on profitability. Secondly, the motivations of Singapore-based firms for FDI is determined by certain "push" and "pull" factors. The results from the Student t-tests and stepwise regressions are used to examine the determinant push and pull factors between foreign and local firms. Thirdly, investing abroad entails a large initial cost of search and investigation and as such, overseas direct investment will be carried out by mainly large or firms with monopolistic advantage. A Cross-Tabulation is used to show the difference between foreign TNCs in Singapore that are claimed to possess monopolistic advantages and local firms that are small in size and as such, respond only to macroeconomic determinants of FDI. Fourthly, the strengths of Singapore's firms lie in their ability to engage in joint ventures and minority stake projects. The results from Spearman's Rank Correlation Coefficient tests are used to examine the relative difference between foreign and local investment decisions. The results of the Chi-Square (X^2) is used to show the mean distribution of each group of investors.

Introduction

The primary objective of the fieldwork in Singapore was to examine what influences a firm's initial decision to engage in outward direct investment from Singapore. More specifically, the fieldwork was undertaken to determine factors that motivate firms to invest abroad and whether foreign and local firms behaved in similar manners. Thus, the fieldwork survey was to examine subjective or behaviourial variables, which influence firm's decisions to carry out FDI.[286]

As noted in chapter 2, the neoclassical investment theory ignores subjective variable determinants of FDI. The theory claims that a firm's foreign investment can only be explained through objective conditions of relative profitability for capital as determined by market forces and economic theories. The rejection of subjective aspects of firms' decisions by neoclassical theory not only damages theories which purport to explain realistic investment, but also empirical evidence which seeks to explain firms Behaviour, as human beings, to be equally affected in their decision-making by subjective preferences.[287] As pointed out by Richardson, the importance of these subjective variables is at an apex of a structure of a series of discrete (non-incremental) investment decisions such as that to go abroad, where the structure of a firm's operations is changed noticeably in a very short period of time.[288] However, as it is argued later, subjective factors for FDI are as equally important as objective conditions for capital.

Fieldwork Survey

Background: Survey Methodology

Questionnaire Design The methodology used in collecting the primary data involved an initial questionnaire, followed by telephone calls, fax, and face-to-face interviews. The survey questions were designed after an initial study of the country and discussion with some academic staff at the National University of Singapore (NUS), Nanyang Technological University (NTU), and Singapore Manufacturers Association (SMA). The fieldwork itself was conducted mainly in Singapore, but supplemented by several visits to Johor

---

[286] Richardson, J. D. (1971), *op. cit.*

[287] Ibid.

[288] Ibid.

state in Malaysia, and Indonesia's Batam island because of the growth triangle initiative.

Characteristics of Firms/Ownership The firms surveyed were selected on a random basis using three important Singapore directories: the Tradelink 1991/2, published by the SMA; Singapore Manufacturers and Products Directory 1990, published by Department of Statistics; and the Directory of Singapore Exporters 1990, compiled and published by MSA Trade Services Company. Questionnaire was sent to 100 firms out of 250 firms in the above-mentioned directories. Out of 30 industrial classifications, the survey focused on 8 manufacturing industries (textiles and garments, footwear and leather, food and beverages, tobacco, fabricated metal and machine tools, electronics products and components, chemicals, and wood and furniture). These were particularly chosen because of their sensitivity to labour supply, costs and government industrial policies. However, companies surveyed were asked to rank their response to each factor between 1 and 10, where the rank ordering was in a decreasing order of importance.

A total of 64 companies responded.[289] Of this total, 4 firms were in the process of completing an agreement and/or signed for an overseas project. However, in summarising the result, I have included the 4 companies, as their pattern of response was in line with those firms that were already investing overseas.

All state corporations and state-linked companies declined interview and refused to participate in the survey. As shown in table 5.1 above, which

---

[289] The response was very good (considering the difficulties in convincing most of the company directors that the survey was only for an academic exercise).

Table 5.1 Singapore: Total Respondents by Manufacturing Industries

Type of Industry	Industrial Code*	Foreign[1]	Local[2]	Total
I Food & Beverages	311/3	2	4	6
II Textiles & Garments	321	-	18	18
III Footwear & Leather	323/4	1	6	7
IV Tobacco	314	3	2	5
V Fabricated Metal & Machine Tools	381	7	2	9
VI Electrical and Electronics	384	9	1	10
VII Wood & Furniture	331/2	1	4	5
VIII Chemicals	351/2	4	-	4
Total		27	37	64

Notes:
1   Include majority foreign owned companies.
2   Include majority local owned companies.
*   Industrial classification according to Singapore Industrial Classification 1990.

Source: Fieldwork Survey conducted in Singapore, 1993.

presents a breakdown of responding firms by manufacturing sector, 37 of the total respondents (64) were local firms and 27 were foreign subsidiaries in Singapore.

Size of Firms Over 50 per cent of the companies surveyed were established before 1975, 35 per cent between 1975-85, and 15 per cent after 1985. Of the 37 local owned companies who responded, 80 per cent were established before 1982. Table 5.2. below shows the size of firms by industry. About 42 per cent of the respondents had a total number of employees between 1-100. More than 32 per cent of the companies had a labour force between 101-200 and only 3 per cent had workforce of 301 and over.

The Size of Investment Flow Table 5.3 shows that 53 per cent of the firms surveyed have an investment less than S$20 million. Less than 13 per cent had an investment between $21 - $40m and less than 20 per cent had invested more than $41m. Table 5.4 shows the strategy in which Singapore firms investment overseas. Over 48 per cent of the companies surveyed indicated that they have joint venture projects overseas.

122

Table 5.2 Singapore: Size of Firms Surveyed

Number of Employees	I[1]	II	III	IV	V	VI	VII	VIII	Total
1 - 100	4	10	7	3	1		2		27
101 - 200	2	6		2	4	3	3	1	21
201 - 300		2			4	5		2	13
301 - 400						2		1	3
401 and over									0
Total	6	18	7	5	9	10	5	4	64

Note:
1   See table 5.1 for corresponding classification.

Source: Fieldwork Survey conducted in Singapore, 1993.

Table 5.3 Singapore: Size of Respondents Overseas Engagements by Industry

Investment Flow (S$M)	I	II	III	IV	V	VI	VII	VIII	Total
1 - 20	6	14	4	2	1	2	5		34
21 -40		2	3	1	1	1			8
41 - 60		2		2	2	4		2	12
61 - 80					5	2		1	8
81 - 100								1	2
101 and over									0
Total	6	18	7	5	9	10	5	4	64

Note:
1   See table 5.1 for corresponding classification.

Source: Fieldwork Survey conducted in Singapore, 1993.

Table 5.4 Singapore: International Direct Investment Strategy

Mode of Involvement	I	II	III	IV	V	VI	VII	VIII	Total
Joint Venture	6	6	1	1	5	6	5	2	31
Minority Stake		10	6	4	3	3			26
100% Equity		2	1		1	1		2	7
Others									0
Total	6	18	8	5	9	10	5	4	64

Note:
1 See table 5.1 for corresponding classification.

Source: Fieldwork Survey conducted in Singapore, 1993.

Analysis of Findings The analysis of the fieldwork data begins with the displays of the normal frequency distribution and the ranking of variables as shown in tables 5.5 and 5.6. The purpose for the distribution was to see the normal disparity of the mean scores and standard deviation of all the factors for foreign and local firms. The variations between foreign and local mean scores for each variable shows the relative importance of each of the factors to an investor. For instance, the push factor GSP has a mean score for local firms twice that of foreign firms, thus indicating the relative importance of this factor to local firms rating. Two factors account for the relative importance of the GSP factor to the local firms. Firstly, the GSP factor was the main channel for encouraging exports by local firms to the USA and other industrialised countries. Secondly, the GSP factor was a means to overcome competition from the other Southeast Asian countries who are producing the same kind of products. Likewise, the mean score for the locational-induced factor SLCR for local firms is three times the corresponding rating by foreign firms. The other reason for the descriptive presentation of the mean distribution was to enable the proper use of the computed data to examine the various propositions as is set out below.

Table 5.5 Distribution of Push Factors for FDI by Group of Investors

All n=64, Foreign n=27, Local n=37.

	All Firms		Foreign Firms			Local Firms		
	Mean	Stdv	Mean	Stdv	Rank	Mean	Stdv	Rank
GSP	2.297	2.454	1.480	0.640	10	2.890	3.060	9
ASD	4.672	1.968	5.300	2.150	5	4.220	1.720	7
GS	1.703	0.728	1.850	0.600	9	1.590	0.800	10
HOC	5.078	1.954	4.560	1.970	7	5.460	1.880	6
DPR	3.219	1.750	2.560	1.530	8	3.700	1.760	8
HLRC	8.047	1.527	8.000	1.240	3	8.080	1.720	3
HLC	8.578	1.366	8.670	1.360	1	8.510	1.390	2
LDM	6.141	2.468	5.040	2.410	6	6.950	2.210	4
GIRS	6.406	1.561	6.590	1.530	4	6.270	1.590	5
LS	8.828	1.254	8.410	1.450	2	9.140	1.000	1

Notes:
1 GSP   Loss of General System of Preference status.
2 ASD   Appreciating Singapore Dollar.
3 GS   Government Support.
4 HOC   High Operating Costs.
5 DPR   Diversification of Products/Risks.
6 HLRC   High Land/Rent Costs.
7 HLC   High Labour Costs.
8 LDM   Limited Domestic Market.
9 GIRS   Government Industrial Restructuring Strategy.
10 LS   Labour Shortage.

Source: Fieldwork Survey conducted in Singapore, 1993.

Table 5.6 Distribution of Pull Factors for FDI by Group of Investors

All n=64, Foreign n=27, Local n=37.

	All Firms		Foreign Firms			Local Firms		
	Mean	Stdv	Mean	Stdv	Rank	Mean	Stdv	Rank
TAX	3.813	2.513	2.930	2.300	8	4.000	2.740	8
FIC	4.547	2.329	4.000	2.420	7	4.950	2.210	7
TB	3.469	2.456	2.740	1.810	10	4.000	2.740	9
PTS	5.203	1.945	4.560	2.010	6	5.680	1.780	5
GI	4.625	2.800	6.220	2.100	5	3.460	1.850	10
SLCR	5.609	3.053	2.850	1.830	9	7.620	2.000	3
ACL	8.047	1.527	8.560	1.220	1	7.680	1.630	2
CLR	6.922	1.986	7.370	1.860	2	6.590	2.030	4
LM	6.156	2.191	6.960	2.520	4	5.570	1.720	6
PS	7.516	2.024	7.110	2.150	3	7.810	1.900	1

Notes:
1 TAX   Tax Incentives.
2 FIC   Favourable Investment Climate.
3 TB   Trade Barriers/ Market Protection.
4 PTS   Proximity to Singapore.
5 GI   Good Infrastructure.
6 SLCR   Shared Language, Cultural & Religion.
7 ACL   Availability of Cheap Labour.
8 CLR   Cheap Land & Raw Materials.
9 LM   Large Market.
10 PS   Political Stability.

Source: Fieldwork Survey conducted in Singapore, 1993.

Proposition 1: There is a Correlation between FDI and Profitability

Table 5.7 shows the results of an Ordinary Least Square's (OLS) regression of FDI on profitability. The data is taken from the Singapore Department of Statistics for the period 1981-90. Of the twenty-three cases used in the estimates only seven had a slope coefficient that is insignificant.

Among the Asian countries, where results were expected to be highly significant were Malaysia, Hong Kong and China. Surprisingly, Korea showed a highly significant coefficient and a high R^2 (adjusted), indicating that 90 per cent of Singapore's direct investment in Korea is profit motivated. The other 10 per cent can be explained by the subjective desires of individual firms as is examined empirically in the next section. However, Philippines and Japan have both produced coefficients that are just significant which is reflected in the low R^2. Although Indonesia has a high coefficient of 6.6, it is not significant because of the uneven distribution of Singapore's investment in the country as confirmed by the low R^2. This is not surprising as the bulk of Singapore's investment in the country occurred during the growth triangle (1988 onwards) period. Also, the recent surge in FDI in Indonesia has been due to of the government policies of foreign investment and economic strategies towards export-led and strict implementation of structural adjustment policies. The result also reflects the fact that most of Singapore's investment in Indonesia can be explained by factors other than the rate of return. In the case of the EC, the coefficient is not significant because of the low t-ratio. Surprisingly, Germany emerged as the only European country with a significant coefficient and a high R^2. This indicates that there is a good positive correlation between Singapore's investment and the rate of return from Germany. In the U.S., Singapore's direct investment is highly correlated with profitability, which is reflected through the high R^2 and high t-ratio.

The OLS regression results are in line with the neo-classical capital arbitrage theory, which claims that capital moves from a country with relatively low rate of return to a country with higher rate of return. However, the results do not support the neo-classical conclusion that FDI is only responsive to objective profitability for capital.

Table 5.7 An OLS Regression of FDI and Profitability from Abroad (Annual Data) 1981-90

Country / Region	R^2	Slop Coef. (β) / (t-ratio)	Stdev of (β)	p-value
Total	63.9	10.058 (4.11)**	2.445	0.003
Asian Countries	64.3	3.6327 (4.15)**	0.8759	0.003
ASEAN	51.6	3.828 (3.26)**	1.176	0.012
Malaysia	55.0	3.3449 (3.47)**	0.9647	0.008
Philippines	29.8	1.1838 (2.20)*	0.5390	0.059
Hong Kong	78.4	2.5995 (5.80)**	0.4483	0.000
Japan	41.2	9.384 (2.70)*	3.474	0.027
China	57.1	9.821 (3.60)**	2.729	0.007
Korea	89.5	11.118 (8.81)**	1.262	0.000
Taiwan	29.2	0.9804 (2.17)*	0.4514	0.062
Others	27.9	9.046 (2.12)*	4.274	0.067
Germany	61.5	4.491 (3.92)**	1.145	0.004
Australia	71.1	1.9509 (4.81)**	0.4053	0.000
US	91.2	2.2030 (9.73)**	0.2265	0.000
Other	78.5	14.306 (5.83)**	2.455	0.000

Notes:
1 *Significant at 95 per cent confidence level.
2 **Significant at 99 per cent confidence level.
3 # Referred to appendix for detailed table

Source: Singapore's Department of Statistics, *Singapore's Investment Abroad 1976-90*, Singapore: National Printers.

127

Proposition 2: The Motivation of Singapore-based Firms for FDI is determined by Certain "Push" and "Pull" factors

The second test investigates the significant push and pull variables for local and foreign companies. The results in table 5.8 shows that push variables GSP, LS, DPR, and LDM were highly significant for local firms than foreign subsidiaries. By implication, the results suggest that most local firms have relocated because of the loss of Singapore's eligibility for United States General System Preferences (GSP) status, which was withdrawn in January 1989. Most of these firms relocated to countries such as Malaysia to continue the eligibility for the U.S. GSP. This is because the variable GSP was a U.S. eligibility to import goods such as textiles and garments to the U.S. market. The loss of the status in 1989 by Singapore resulted in the loss of special privilege of the local firms right to import goods into U.S. markets and led to the relocation of local firms to countries who were still eligible for the U.S. import quota.

Similarly, the significance of LS variable indicates severe shortage of unskilled and semi-skilled labour, which emerged in the early 1970s because of Singapore's achievement of full employment led to the mass exodus of labour-intensive industries. In the past, the government has been importing foreign workers to relieve labour shortages and any tension brought about by rising labour costs. In 1989, for example, the number of immigrant workers was 161,000 and this does not include the number eligible for permanent residence or citizenship.

Table 5.8 Student t-test of Investment, Push and Pull Factors by Ownership

	Investment	GSP	ASD	GS	HOC	DPR	HLRC	HLC	LDM	GIRS	LS
Foreign	27	27	27	27	27	27	27	27	27	27	27
Local	37	37	37	37	37	37	37	37	37	37	37
t-ratio/Pooled Variance	0.949 (.06)	0.022 (2.35)*	0.029 (2.24)*	0.164 (1.41)	0.067 (1.86)	0.009 (2.72)**	0.836 (.21)	0.661 (.44)	0.002 (3.28)**	0.419 (.81)	0.021 (2.38)*
t-ratio/Separate Variance	0.951 (.06)	0.010 (2.72)*	0.036 (2.16)*	0.146 (1.47)	0.070 (1.85)	0.007 (2.78)**	0.827 (.22)	0.661 (.44)	0.002 (3.24)**	0.416 (.82)	0.030 (2.25)*

	TAX	FIC	TB	PTS	GI	SLCR	ACL	CLR	LM	PS
Foreign	27	27	27	27	27	27	27	27	27	27
Local	37	37	37	37	37	37	37	37	37	37
t-ratio/Pooled Variance	0.015 (2.51)*	0.109 (1.63)	0.042 (2.08)*	0.022 (2.36)*	0.000 (5.57)**	0.000 (9.74)**	0.022 (2.36)*	0.124 (1.56)	0.011 (2.63)**	0.174 (1.38)
t-ratio/Separate Variance	0.014 (2.54)*	0.115 (1.60)	0.031 (2.21)*	0.025 (2.31)*	0.000 (5.46)**	0.000 (9.88)**	0.061 (2.47)*	0.119 (1.58)	0.017 (2.48)**	0.183 (1.35)

Notes:
1 Push Factors: Loss of General System of Preference status (GSP).
2 Appreciating Singapore Dollar (ASD); Government Support (GS).
3 High Operating Costs (HOC).
4 Diversification of Products/Risks (DPR).
5 High Land/Rent Costs (HLRC).
6 High Labour Costs (HLC).
7 Limited Domestic Market (LDM).
8 Government Industrial Restructuring Strategy (GIRS).
9 Labour Shortage (LS).
10 Pull Factors: Tax Incentives (TAX).
11 Favourable Investment Climate (FIC).
12 Trade Barriers/ Market Protection (TB).
13 Proximity to Singapore (PTS).
14 Good Infrastructure (GI).
15 Shared Language, Cultural & Religion (SLCR).
16 Availability of Cheap Labour (ACL).
17 Cheap Land & Raw Materials (CLR).
18 Large Market (LM).
19 Political Stability (PS).
20 * Significant at 95 per cent confidence level.
21 ** Significant at 99 per cent confidence level.

Source: Fieldwork Survey conducted in Singapore, 1993.

The major problem with market size theory is that the method for measuring a country's market size rests solely on GDP or GNP per capita. The use of GDP or GNP per capita estimates to measure a country's market size could be misleading in the sense that a small country such as Singapore with a high GNP per capita of over US$12,000 may be more attractive than the neighbouring Malaysia where GNP per capita is just US$2,320: much lower but spread over a population of over 18 million compared to Singapore with 3 million. Though Singapore has a much higher GNP per capita as in 1990, its total GNP which should also reflect the total market size, if the above hypothesis is to be followed strictly, is lower than that of Malaysia with lower GNP per capita for the same year.

The factors such as TAX, TB and SLCR were highly significant for local firms. The importance of TAX to the local firms is due mainly to the fact that it replaces the disadvantage that firms have to face in Singapore. In other words, the variable TAX gives the local firms the edge of being able to produce in the host country market. However, the significance of the TB variable contradicts Kojima's model, which claims that large firms invest abroad because of the fear of protectionism. Here, the result indicates that local as well as foreign firms were investing abroad because of the fear of trade barriers.

It may be noted that the increasing land and rent prices in Singapore were not significant in the empirical test. In the past, land use for public facilities, residential and industrial estates, and infrastructure came mainly from the release of British military land, the contraction of agricultural land and forestry, and the expansion of the sea front.[290] However, the reclamation programme increased Singapore total landmark from 581.5 kilometre to 639.2 kilometre between 1966 to 1992, but further reliance on this method is by no means limited given the small geographical size of the country. Given this limitation in recent years, land prices have consistently increased on an average of 30 - 40 per cent per year between 1986 and 1990. This in effect, has made Singapore one of the most expensive locations in the world in terms of industrial, office, and commercial sales and rental costs. A survey by property consultants Richard Ellis at the end of 1989 found Singapore ranking the costliest in office rental among major cities in the world (after Tokyo, London, Hong Kong, and Paris).[291] A year after, another survey found Singapore's price of shopping rental space third in the world (after Tokyo and New York).[292] With such phenomenal rises in land and rental prices, it is not surprising that many local and foreign enterprises have decided to relocate their industrial activities where they can compete more favourably in world markets.

---

[290] Ng, Chee Yuen and Wong, Poh Kam (1991), *op. cit.*; Lee, Tsao Yuan (1992), *op. cit.*
[291] Ibid.,p. 130.
[292] Ibid.

The next test is based on stepwise multiple regression of investment, as the dependent variables and the push and pull factors for FDI as the independent variables (see tables 5.9-5.11). Because it is a stepwise regression, variables, which are not significant, are not included in the results.

The purpose of this test was to examine which of the variables were the most important for both foreign and local firms' decision to invest abroad. Values of the adjusted R^2 in the regression are relatively low. However, the result shows the coefficients of CLR, ACL, GSP, LDM and PTS variables to be significant for both foreign and local firms. However, when the data were tested for individual groups of investors, three coefficients were significant for foreign firms and five for local firms. Foreign subsidiaries particularly, considered LM, LS and ACL as the most significant variables for their FDI.

In the case of local firms, HLRC, LS, SLCR, HLC and ACL emerged as the most important factors for investment decision abroad. The significance of LS, HLRC, HLC and ACL between foreign TNCs and local firms shows the sensitivity of Singapore based firms to factor costs. Most especially,

Table 5.9 Stepwise Multiple Regression for Foreign and Local Firms

All: n= 64; Foreign: n= 27; Local: n= 37.

	R^2	CLR	ACL	GSP	LDM	PTS	p-value
step 1	11.8	5.227830 (3.072)**					.0032**
step 2	17.6	5.67420 (3.427)**	4.990998 (2.316)*				.0239*
step 3	21.5	6.019776 (3.703)**	4.524603 (2.138)*	2.636774 (2.002)*			.0498*
step 4	26.1	6.765089 (4.191)**	5.364511 (2.567)**	2.803708 (2.190)*	2.830906 (2.174)*		.0337*
step 5	33.7	7.209089 (4.688)**	4.689030 (2.351)*	2.921883 (2.408)*	4.388477 (3.239)**	4.691490 (2.782)**	.0073**

Notes:
1 Dependent Variable: Investment.
2 Independent Variables: Push and Pull factors.
3 *Significant at 95 per cent confidence level.
4 **Significant at 99 per cent confidence level.

Source: Fieldwork Survey conducted in Singapore, 1993.

Table 5.10 Stepwise Multiple Regression for Foreign Firms

n=27

	R^2	LDM	LS	ACL	p-value
step 1	25.6	7.158489 (3.157)**			.0041**
step 2	34.4	8.237062 (3.759)**	7.605993 (2.086)*		.0478*
step 3	44.3	8.600762 (4.246)**	9.183792 (2.678)*	5.139418 (2.293)*	.0313*

Notes:
1 * Significant at 95 per cent confidence level.
2 ** Significant at 99 per cent confidence level.

Source: Fieldwork Survey conducted in Singapore, 1993.

Table 5.11 Stepwise Multiple Regression for Local Firms

n=37

	R^2	HLRC	LS	SLCR	ASD	ACL	p-value
step 1	26.3	8.031392 (3.722)**					.0007**
step 2	36.4	7.584888 (3.769)**	8.818469 (2.556)*				.0152*
step 3	49.5	13.520066 (5.188)**	10.911258 (3.469)**	7.155176 (3.138)**			.0036**
step 4	54.8	13.217712 (5.350)**	10.484869 (3.515)**	7.286976 (2.198)*	3.761773 (2.198)*		.0353*
step 5	58.8	12.766078 (5.393)**	10.077183 (3.532)**	7.452817 (3.616)**	3.902466 (2.389)*	3.5402570 (2.389)*	.0499*

Notes:
1 * Significant at 95 per cent confidence level.
2 ** Significant at 99 per cent confidence level.

Source: Fieldwork Survey conducted in Singapore, 1993.

the factors LS, HLRC and HLC have been the main push for FDI by firms based in Singapore. Thus, it is reasonable to conclude that the relocation of industrial capital abroad by firms based in Singapore is due to Singapore's loss of comparative advantage in factor prices.

Proposition 3: The Strengths of Singapore's Firms Lie in Their Ability to Engage in Joint Ventures and Minority Stake Projects

Proposition 4: Investing Abroad Entails a Large Initial Cost of Search and Investigation and as such, Overseas Direct Investment Will Be Carried Out by Mainly Large or Firms with Monopolistic Advantage

The main purpose of these propositions was to empirically examine two major claims in FDI literature. Firstly, the claim that investing abroad entails a large initial cost of search and investigation and as such, overseas direct investment will be carried by large and/or oligopolistic firms. Secondly, the claim that small firms normally will seek to invest in joint or minority ventures rather than 100 per cent ownership as is the case with large firms. In both tests, I have substituted Kojima's methodology of "large" for foreign subsidiaries and "small" for local firms.

Tables 5.12 displays the percentage distribution and actual values of the proportion of firms size in each category. To determine whether or not there is a relative difference between foreign TNC subsidiaries and indigenous firms, one compares the actual and/or the percentage (figures in parenthesis) mean values of one group against the other. For instance, the expected and observed mean values of all firms with workers less than 100 shows that local firms have relatively the highest mean scores of 23 and 62. In fact, the percentage mean value for local firms is four-times the corresponding mean value for foreign TNCs in Singapore. On the other hand, the number of foreign TNCs employing more than 100 workers is twice that of local firms.

Table 5.13 shows the difference between foreign and local firms investment strategy abroad. In joint venture projects abroad, foreign firms (63) has the highest proportion of activities as compared to local firms (38). Local firms (54) adopts more minority strategy than foreign corporations (22).

The X^2 value shows that the mean distribution of each group of investor is significantly different from each other at 99 per cent confidence level. Thus, it is reasonable to conclude that foreign TNCs and local firms are significantly different in size. In other words, the result supports the first claim that local firms are relatively smaller in size than foreign TNCs in Singapore. As noted in chapter 2, two major factors accounted for the relatively small size

Table 5.12 Firm Size (Foreign and Local) Cross-tabulation of Expected and Actual Values of the Proportion of Firms in each Category

Size (Employment)	Foreign	Local	Total
1 - 100	4 (14.8)	23 (62.2)	27 (42.2)
101 - 200	14 (51.9)	7 (18.9)	21 (32.8)
201 - 300	7 (25.9)	6 (16.2)	13 (20.3)
301 - 400	2 (7.4)	1 (2.7)	3 (4.7)
Total	27 (42.2)	37 (57.8)	64 (100)
Chi-Square (X^2)	Value 14.91561	df 3	p-value 0.00189**

Note:
1 **Significant at 99 per cent confidence level.

Source: Fieldwork Survey conducted in Singapore, 1993.

Table 5.13 Strategy (Foreign and Local)

Strategy	Foreign	Local	Total
Joint Venture	17 (63)	14 (37.8)	31 (48.4
Minority Stake	6 (22.2)	20 (54.1)	26 (40.6)
100% Ownership	4 (14.8)	3 (8.1)	7 (10.9)
Total	27 (42.2)	37 (57.8)	64 (100)
Chi-Square (X^2)	Value 6.56953	df 2	p-value 0.03745*

Note:
1 *Significant at 95 per cent confidence level.

Source: Fieldwork Survey conducted in Singapore, 1993.

of local firms in Singapore.[293] Firstly, the Singapore government has been employing a deliberate strategy of relying on development based entirely on foreign direct investment by TNCs to lead the economy into advanced technology, without providing specific promotion for local entrepreneurs to develop advanced technology. Secondly, local entrepreneurs have traditionally been seen by the state as inexperienced and mostly in low value-added activities and as such may not been able to sustain future growth. According to Lall, it is the combined effect of these two factors which relatively weakens and steadily declines the role of local entrepreneurship as reflected in their size.[294]

Theoretically, the result of the first claim produces a mixed result. On the one hand, the result supports Cave's claim that investing abroad requires an initial large cost of search and investigation which is mostly appropriate for large firms.[295] As noted in the theoretical chapter, this line of argument has been the premise of existing literature on FDI, which claims that investing firms must possess intangible capital to invest overseas. As pointed out by Lall, the possession of intangible capital for FDI was not only peculiar to TNCs from the DCs, but also TNCs from LDCs.[296] According to Lall, there are five ways LDC firms can possess ownership advantages for FDI. Firstly, TNCs from LDCs have specific advantage in technical knowledge which is localised around a completely different set of production techniques from that of the DCs, and more relevant to factor price and quality conditions in other LDCs.[297] Secondly, the product may be specific to Third World conditions, or adapted in such a way that many of the "frills" (or high-performance, luxury characteristics) are dropped while retaining its essential functions. Thirdly, Third World firms may possess technological advantages not merely because their processes and products are better adapted to local factors prices, factor quality, and demand conditions. Fourthly, Third World firms may develop differentiated consumer products which compete with branded products of DC TNCs. Finally, all these advantages may be strengthened by the ability to function better in the environment of other LDCs.[298] Although the argument was not whether firms from LDCs possess intangible assets or not, the

---

[293] Lall, Sanjaya (1991), *op. cit.*, p. 21.
[294] Ibid.
[295] Caves, R. E. (1971), *op. cit.*, pp. 1-27.
[296] Lall, Sanjaya (1983), *op. cit.*, p. 6.
[297] Ibid.
[298] Ibid.

question was whether the size of a firm has a significant influence towards its decision to invest abroad. As has been argued by Chung, the possession of intangible assets can lead to the mistaken belief that only large firms carry out FDI.[299]

On the other hand, the result supports Kojima's claim of clear distinction of local and foreign firms size. That is, local firms are relatively smaller in size than foreign firms. However, the result does not support Kojima's claim that FDI by local firms are macroeconomic while FDI by large firms are microeconomic. The second cross-tabulation results shows than the mean scores of strategy adopted by foreign and local firms are significantly different at 95 per cent confidence level. By implication, the result supports the claim that small firms, because of their relative size and inexperience in overseas projects will be in minority ventures rather than foreign firms. The results do not support Kojima's claim that large firms normally invest only in 100 per cent ventures because of their size. Instead, the result shows that foreign firms would prefer joint ventures than minority projects overseas. One possible explanation why the cross-tabulation results did not support Kojima's claim is that Kojima's original work was on the distinction between American TNCs and Japanese firms. In this case, I have substituted American TNCs for foreign subsidiaries and Japanese firms for local investors. Usually, foreign subsidiaries would not have the autonomous power to decide on whether to invest in joint or 100 per cent ventures. Depending on the nature and the size of the commitment and the internal policies of the firm, the final official decision-making body is either the officers of the division in which the subsidiary is located or the board of directors of the entire corporation.[300] However, since the distinction in the thesis was on foreign subsidiaries and local firms it is possible that the decision to invest abroad did not come from the Head Office. Thus, Kojima's distinction of large and small firms could not be directly measured and the second claim cannot hold. However, it is argued that small firms will undertake minority stake venture abroad because of the financial, management and technical resource constraints which confront them.

The question then is; are there differences between foreign and local subjective motivations for FDI? To examine this question, I have computed various push and pull factors using Spearman's rank correlation coefficient to show the differences in investment decisions between the two groups of investors.

In order to assess and test the relationship between foreign and local push factors for FDI an important non-parametric technique called the

---

[299] Lee, H. Chung (1984), *op. cit.*, pp. 713-23.

[300] Goodman, Louis W. (1987), *Small Nations, Giant Firms*, London: Holmes & Meier, Chapter 4.

Spearman's rank Correlation has been used. From tables 5.14 and 5.15, I find that Spearman's r for push factors by foreign an local firms is estimated at 0.915 and for pull factors by foreign and local firms is calculated at 0.539. A positive value of Spearman's r suggests that there is a strong direct correlation between foreign and local push factors for FDI and a relatively weak correlation the choice for the locational decisions. The relatively weak correlation of the pull variables indicates the significant difference between the way foreign and local firms choose their investment decisions. In general, the statistical test criterion indicates that if the rank correlation coefficient is +1, there is a perfect correlation between the rankings of two factors under consideration. If the rank correlation is -1, there is a perfect inverse relationship between the two factors. However, the detailed individual significant testing of the factors are shown in the appendices.

Table 5.14 Spearman's Rank Correlation Coefficient for Push Factors by Foreign and Local Firms

Factors	Foreign Rank	Local Rank	d	d²
GSP	10	9	1	1
ASD	5	7	2	4
GS	9	10	1	1
HOC	7	6	1	1
DPR	8	8	0	0
HLRC	3	3	0	0
HLC	1	2	1	1
LDM	6	4	2	4
GIRS	4	5	1	1
LS	2	1	1	1

Notes:
1 Spearman's $r = 1 - \frac{6\ Sd2}{n\ (n^2 - 1)} = \mathbf{0.915}$.

2 The significance of the Spearman's test is determined when r is near 1 or equals 1.

Source: Fieldwork Survey conducted in Singapore, 1993.

Table 5.15 Spearman's Rank Correlation Coefficient for Pull Factors by Foreign and Local Firms

Factors	Foreign Rank	Local Rank	d	d²
TAX	8	8	0	0
FIC	7	7	0	0
TB	10	9	1	1
PTS	6	5	1	1
GI	5	10	5	25
SLCR	9	3	6	36
ACL	1	2	1	1
CLR	2	4	2	4
LM	4	6	2	4
PS	3	1	2	4

Note:
1   Spearman's $r = 0.539$.

Source: Fieldwork Survey conducted in Singapore, 1993.

Case Study

Mido Textiles Limited[301]

Mido Textiles Limited is a family company registered in Singapore as wholly local-owned. Like most of the local-owned firms in the textile industry, Mido Ltd began its operation over 30 years ago with two brothers in a small shophouse in Singapore. Today, the company is still wholly family local-owned by three Ng brothers: Lawrence, Michael and Freddy. The industry is a highly competitive one. Most of the competition is from Hong Kong and China which has a long tradition in the production of textile garments followed by Sri Lanka, Malaysia, Indonesia, Thailand, Bangladesh and recently Vietnam and Cambodia. The industry is highly dependent on labour for production. Thus availability of cheap factor prices will enable a firm in the industry to compete vigorously in the export markets. If located in a relatively higher factor prices country, FDI will be seen as the most obvious strategy for international competition. This is what the Mido strategy has been in

---

[301] The interview was conducted with Mr. L. Ng, the Managing Director, Mido Textiles office in Singapore, 4th of January, 1993.

138

the last ten years. As at 1992, the company employed about 100 staff in Singapore and has an annual turnover of S$19 million and group net assets in excess of S$10 million. Encouraged by its success, the company now have a niche in the local fashion market as the sole agent for China made woollen and mixed suiting. The firm is also one of the leading importers-exporters and wholesales of silk, cotton and synthetic fabrics.

Its first silk shop outlet was established in 1976, known as the China Silk House, and presently the company has over eight chain outlets. The company decided to invest overseas in 1980 because of the government introduction of the high wage policy in 1979. In 1985, the company initiated a joint venture, Smart Garments Ltd, in Beijing, China, and in which it presently holds 50 per cent of the equity.

In 1987, the company, though in another venture, diversified into the travel industry. Singa China Travel Service Pte Ltd was set up in Singapore together with Hong Kong's China Travel Service (one of the largest travel agents in the world) to cater to the rapidly growing China tourism market. Mido Textiles owns 40 per cent of Singa China Travel Service which handles international and inbound tours as well as other travel related services. Furthermore, Mido Textiles through its wholly owned subsidiary, Peing Hoe Pte Ltd, owns commercial, industrial and residential properties in Singapore. It is also among the top 10 shareholders of the Industrial and Commercial Bank of Singapore. While its lists of success goes on and on, the question here is what activated its overseas direct investment in China, and, what were the main reasons for recent diversifications.

Reasons for Investing Abroad According to Mr. Lawrence Ng, managing director Mido Textiles in Singapore office, the main push for "our overseas direct investment in the 1980s and 90s includes high wage cost in Singapore, severe shortage of unskilled labour force due to the government clampdown on importation of foreign workers, the loss of GSP status, rising Singapore dollar which makes exports of textile materials to be expensive as compared to other Asian countries, deliberate government policies to phase out labour intensive industries, the introduction of quota system which have led to dramatic loss of revenue, and the loss of Singapore's competitiveness *vis-à-vis* the East Asian NIEs and semi industrialising countries in Asia".[302]

In a separate interview, Mr. Patrick Lee, managing director of Sing Lun Pte Ltd, another well known wholly local family textile company, agreed with

---

[302] 4th January, 1993.

Mr. Lawrence Ng that "one of the greatest pushes for his company's overseas direct investment has been high costs of doing business in Singapore".[303] He added, "that it is not only wage cost that is high, but other costs which makes company operation in Singapore expensive". The government, he explained instead of addressing the problem directly, keeps talking of the industry needing to increase productivity. Accordingly, "in the textile and garment industry, productivity can only be increased to a limit, as the industry's production process is ever-changing due to the changing world of fashion. By investing a huge sum of industrial capital in a particular machine, in less than no time the machine will become obsolete as the machine can no longer handle the new fashion. Thus, the industry requires much labour force to handle some of the changing fashion techniques".[304]

However, Mr Ng argued that if Singapore's labour cost was not as high as it is today and if Singapore had not lost its GSP status to Malaysia his company and many of the firms in the industry would not have been investing overseas. The loss of the GSP status has been one of the most significant setbacks for the industry. The GSP was a scheme, which allowed Singapore textiles firms to export all its output to America. In its place was introduced the quota system. The new quota system allocates 75 per cent of the year's available quotas on past performance, the remaining 25 per cent is rationed through an open bidding system. Because of the decision to auction the additional quotas, profit margins of most of the industry manufacturers have been eroded.[305]

Reasons for Diversification Finally, Mr. Ng gave three reasons for his company's investment diversification. Firstly, Mr. Ng pointed out that it was because of uncertainties. "Though I have relocated most of our production to China due to the fact that it is cheaper to produce in China as compared to Singapore, but there are still uncertainties which makes us to go into properties, travel agents and other non related businesses".[306]

Secondly, "I still want to have good solid ground in Singapore, so I have taken the step by diversifying our resources to other businesses".

Thirdly, "as a company I aim to make as much profit as I can. Thus, if I know of areas of business that will generate profits to our company I cannot say because it is not related to our business so lets hands off".

---

[303] 5th January, 1993.

[304] Ibid.

[305] 4th January, 1993.

[306] Ibid.

Investment Strategy The investment strategy used by the Mido Textiles involves a minority stake and franchising in Malaysia, and a joint venture in China. As a family business, cash flow is very limited and thus large projects would have to be in conjunction with a second or third party. Sing Lun limited on the other hand, prefers wholly owned projects rather than joint venture because of its experience in Bangladesh with a corrupt partner in which the company lost millions of dollars. Mr. Lee argued that "though he is not against any joint venture but it's got to be in an area you know very well". However, Mr. Lee's case also shows how vulnerable some local firms can be overseas. Most Singaporean firms prefer especially to go into joint ventures most especially, in markets they do not know so well. The main reason for the minority stake is because of lack of financial resources, experience in foreign investment and ownership advantages. The lack of ownership advantages is something, which contradicts the result of Lall and others who have studied FDI by Third World TNCs.[307] However, unlike the TNCs from Hong Kong, Brazil and India as quoted by Lall who possess ownership advantages, firms from Singapore do not possess advantages because of the relative weakness of these firms in the local economy. In Hong Kong local and foreign firms are given an equal chance to compete for both local and foreign markets. Moreover, Hong Kong entrepreneurs have a longer history than Singapore. In Singapore, foreign firms dominate the local production and markets.

Conclusion

The empirical analysis shows that profitability, limited domestic market, product diversification and risks, labour shortage, trade barriers, shared language, culture and religion, tax incentives and General System of Preference Status are some of the main determinants of outward direct investment in Singapore. Furthermore, the empirical tests confirm the hypothesis that Singapore's direct investment abroad is determined by two

---

[307] Lall, Sanjaya (1983), *op. cit.*, Chapter 1.

sets of phenomena. Firstly, the objective conditions of profitability for capital as largely determined by factor prices. That is, labour-intensive firms in Singapore, which are losing comparative advantage, will relocate to countries, which are gaining comparative advantage in the same industry. Secondly, the subjective motivations of Singapore-based firms for FDI as influenced by state policies and firms desire to invest in places other than Singapore.

6 Conclusion

ABSTRACT

The primary focus of this book has been to examine the main determinants of FDI inflow and outflow in Singapore's economy. The empirical findings presented in chapter 5 have shown that Singapore's overseas investments are determined by two sets of phenomena. Firstly, that Singapore's firms respond to rate of return differentials between the "home" and the "foreign" locations. Secondly, that subjective factors such as limited domestic market, product diversification and risks, labour shortage, trade barriers, shared language, culture and religion, tax incentives and General System of Preference Status are some of the main push and pull motivations for investment abroad. However, it is concluded that Singapore's experience could be very relevant for other countries considering a liberalisation of policies toward FDI for development in at least three aspects. Firstly, it shows the role of the state in laying the ground for economic growth and actually creating the country's comparative advantage. Secondly, it shows the importance of FDI by TNCs for development purposes. Thirdly, it shows the fact that a country's comparative advantage is never static, but evolves with capital accumulation and technological change where, as labour becomes more expensive in Singapore and capital is cheaper, firms in Singapore use less labour and more capital by substituting capital for labour.

Summary

Singapore's economic performance during the thirty-two years after its independence (1965-97) is nothing short of extraordinary.[308] Using traditional economic measures, Singapore's economic growth rate of 8-10 per cent during 1965-92 period was the highest in the world. Although there was some variation between sub-periods, the high growth was achieved with relatively low inflation rate (CPI of 2.5 per cent between 1965-96), and with very little borrowing from external financial sources[309] (see tables 6.1 and 6.2). Unemployment, which was at its highest levels in the early 1950s and 1960s (averaging 14 per cent), declined to 3-4 per cent in the 1970s, and 2.4 in the 1990s. Furthermore, entrepot trade which accounted for over 70 per cent of GDP in the late 1950s, declined in real terms to less than 20 per cent, leaving the manufacturing, construction, and financial sectors as the main pillars for sustainable growth in the 1980s.

The generally broader base of the economy to a degree insulated Singapore from the 1979-82 world recession. Even at the time the world was experiencing recession, the Singapore government was still determined to continue with its industrial restructuring from labour-intensive to capital-intensive production. Overall, the high economic growth and transformation achieved in the last two and the half decades have filtered down to the great majority of the population. This is reflected in the size of home ownership. For instance, over 85 per cent of the population are housed in government flats, 70 per cent of them in home-ownership status. Primary education is mandatory, universal and free, while secondary education is also generally provided by the state.[310] In general, the educational system in Singapore is closely tied to the needs of domestic and, most especially, foreign manufacturing concerns. For instance, four main areas have been extensively developed in recent years: higher education, where the emphasis has been on the production of engineering graduates; vocational training, aimed primarily at school leavers; the Skills Development Fund which reimburses employers for sponsoring training and the updating of skills; and the training centres and units funded jointly by the EDB and various TNCs.[311]

---

[308] Castells, Manuel (1988), *op. cit.*, p. 1.
[309] Ibid.
[310] Castells, Manuel (1988), *op. cit.*, p. 2.
[311] Dixon, Chris (1991), *op. cit.*, pp. 162-236.

Table 6.1a Singapore: Key Indicators of Economics Balance, 1994-2000

Indicator		1994	1995	1996	1997(F)	1998(F)	1999(F)	2000(F)
Inflation	(%)	3.1	1.7	1.4	2.3	2.2	1.9	1.7
Unemployment	(%)	2.6	2.4	2.4	2.5	2.6	2.4	2.5
Current Account	(S$bn)	18.5	20.4	19.9	18.8	20.6	22.6	26.3
as % GDP	(%)	17.1	16.9	15	12.9	13.1	13.2	14
Government Budget	(S$bn)	9.2	9.3	8.9	7.5	6.8	6.1	7
as % GDP	(%)	8.4	7.7	6.7	5.2	4.3	3.6	3.7
Monetary Growth, M2	(%)	14.4	8.5	9.8	10.1	11.3	9.9	10.21
Prime Rate	(%)	6.5	6.3	6.3	6.7	6.3	6.3	6.3
3-Month Inter-bank Rate	(%)	4.3	3	3.3	5.5	3	2.9	3.1

Note:
1 (F) Forecast.

Source: Gross-Gen, Quarterly Economic Review, 1997.

Table 6.1b Singapore: Forecasts by Sectors and Demand Aggregates, 1994-2000

Percentage change	GDP	1994	1995	1996	1997(F)	1998(F)	1999(F)	2000(F)
1990 Constant Prices	Share							
Overall GDP	100	10.5	8.8	7	7.5	5.5	7.3	7.6
GDP by Sectors								
Manufacturing	28	12.7	10	3.4	3.8	5.5	7.9	7
Contruction	7.4	16.2	8.5	18.4	11.5	12	8.6	5
Commerce	18.3	9.1	9	6	6	3	5.9	6.5
Tpt/Communication	13.1	10.7	10.8	8.1	9.4	7.4	6.8	9.6
Financial/Business Services	26.7	9.7	7.6	8.2	10.5	4.2	8.9	9.1
GDP by Demand Aggregates								
Private Consumption		5.4	5.3	8	7.4	3.4	5.8	6.4
Public Consumption		0.1	9.6	18.9	5.2	4.3	6.7	9.4
Investment		8.1	9	16.1	10.1	8.6	7.7	5.7
External Demand		93.9	15.3	-14	-8.3	12	12.5	13.7

Notes:
1 Sectoral weights do not sum to 100 due to the exclusion of some minor sectors.
2 (F) Forecast.

Source: Gross-Gen, Quarterly Economic Review, 1997.

Table 6.2 Singapore: Long Term Indicators, 1989-2000

Long Term Indicators	1989	1990	1991	1992	1993	1994	1995	1996
NATIONAL ACCOUNTS								
(At 1990 Prices)								
Private Consumption (S$m)	28,595.0	30,762.0	32,560.0	34,717.0	38,473.0	40,774.0	42,924.0	46,376.0
(Real % chg.)	8.5	7.6	5.8	6.6	10.8	6	5.3	8
Public Consumption (S$m)	6,106.00	6,780.00	7,304.00	7,540.00	8,381.00	8,392.00	9,200.00	10,935.00
(Real % chg.)	5.6	11	7.7	3.2	11.2	0.1	9.6	18.9
Total Investment (S$m)	19,569.00	21,578.00	24,465.00	27,552.00	30,804.00	33,368.00	36,371.00	42,230.00
(Real % chg.)	15.8	10.3	13.4	12.6	11.8	8.3	9	16.1
Increase in Stocks	1,071.00	2,771.00	605.00	208.00	1,483.00	-899	-182.00	-1,865.00
(Real % chg.)	-21.1	158.8	-78.2	-65.7	614.5	-160.60	-79.8	925.1
Net Exports of G&S (S$m)	6,648.00	5,988.00	7,932.00	7,668.00	7,021.00	13735	15,836.00	13,625.00
(Real % chg.)	10.1	-9.9	32.5	-3.3	-8.4	95.60	15.3	-14
Statistical Discrepancy	300.00	42.00	-56.00	-330.00	-769.00	-977	-1,497.00	-1,515.00
(Real % chg.)	-23.9	-85.9	-232.1	490	132.7	27.1	53.2	1.2
GDP (S$m)	62289	67921	72811	77353	85393	94393	102652	109787
(Real % chg.)	9.6	9	7.2	6.2	10.4	10.5	8.8	7
PRICES AND LABOUR								
CPI (YoY % chg.)	2.4	3.4	3.4	2.3	2.4	3.1	1.7	1.4
Unemployment (%)	2.2	1.7	1.9	2.7	2.7	2.6	2.4	2.4
BALANCE OF PAYMENTS								
Merchandise Trade Balance (S$m)	-3,707	-6,704	-4,382	-6,367	-7,981	-1,600	1,855	-746
as % Nominal GDP	-6.2	-9.9	-5.8	-7.9	-8.5	-1.5	-1.5	-0.6
Current Account Balance (S$m)	5,739	5,613	8,437	9,146	6,795	18,546	20,448	19,944
as % Nominal GDP	9.7	8.3	11.2	11.3	7.2	17.1	16.9	15
Average Exchange Rate (S$/US$)	1.950	1.813	1.728	1.629	1.616	1.527	1.417	1.410
Year End Exchange Rate (S$/US$)	1.894	1.745	1.631	1.645	1.608	1.461	1.414	1.400
FISCAL POSITION								
Government Budget Balance (S$m)	2497	1820	3522	4937	6973	9162	9278	8864
as % GDP	4.2	2.7	4.7	6.1	7.4	8.4	7.7	6.7
MONEY AND INTEREST RATES								
Money Supply M2 (S$m)	51,546	61,845	69,542	75,729	82,130	93,981	101,967	111,951
(% Chg.)	22.5	20.0	12.4	8.9	8.5	14.4	8.5	9.8
3-Month Inter-bank Rate (%)	5.6	4.9	3.0	2.2	3.3	4.3	3.0	3.3
Prime Rate (%)	6.3	7.7	7.1	5.6	5.3	6.5	6.3	6.3

Source: Gross-Gen, Quarterly Economic Review, 1997.

Sources of Economic Success

As noted in chapter 3, three major factors have contributed to the dramatic economic performance in Singapore since 1965. The first main factor is the labour force. In the 1960s when, unemployment averaged 9-14 per cent a year, and population grew at 3.3 per cent, labour force participation was 42 per

Table 6.2 Singapore: Long Term Indicators, 1989-2000 (cont'd)

Long Term Indicators	1997(F)	1998(F)	1999(F)	2000(F)
NATIONAL ACCOUNTS				
(At 1990 Prices)				
Private Consumption (S$m)	49,800.0	51,500.0	54,500.0	58,000.0
(Real % chg.)	7.4	3.4	5.8	6.4
Public Consumption (S$m)	11,500.00	12,000.00	12,800.00	14,000.00
(Real % chg.)	5.2	4.3	6.7	9.4
Total Investment (S$m)	46,500.00	50,500.00	0.54	57,500.00
(Real % chg.)	10.1	8.6	7.7	5.7
Increase in Stocks	-300.00	-1,500.00	-1,800.00	-1,600.00
(Real % chg.)	-83.9	400	20	11.1
Net Exports of G&S (S$m)	15,315.00	17,015.00	18,938.00	20,888.00
(Real % chg.)	12.4	11.1	11.3	10.3
Statistical Discrepancy	-2,000.00	-2,000.00	-2,000.00	-2,000.00
(Real % chg.)	32	0	0	0
GDP (S$m)	118000	124500	133650	143800
(Real % chg.)	7.5	5.5	7.3	7.6
PRICES AND LABOUR				
CPI (YoY % chg.)	2.3	2.2	1.9	1.7
Unemployment (%)	2.5	2.6	2.4	2.5
BALANCE OF PAYMENTS				
Merchandise Trade Balance (S$m)	-5,636	-2,680	-2,912	-1,255
as % Nominal GDP	-3.9	-1.7	-1.7	-0.7
Current Account Balance (S$m)	18,830	20,622	22,645	26,271
as % Nominal GDP	12.9	13.1	13.2	14
Average Exchange Rate (S$/US$)	1.525	1.590	1.490	1.425
Year End Exchange Rate (S$/US$)	1.650	1.530	1.450	1.400
FISCAL POSITION				
Government Budget Balance (S$m)	7500	6800	6100	7000
as % GDP	5.2	4.3	3.6	3.7
MONEY AND INTEREST RATES				
Money Supply M2 (S$m)	123,258	137,186	150,767	166,146
(% Chg.)	10.1	11.3	9.9	10.2
3-Month Inter-bank Rate (%)	5.5	3.0	2.9	3.1
Prime Rate (%)	6.7	6.3	6.3	6.3

Note:
1 (F) Forecast.

Source: Gross-Gen, Quarterly Economic Review, 1997.

cent. However, as political stability and the institutional apparatus of export-led manufacturing activities were in place, unemployment during the late 1970s and 1980s, fell to an average rate of 3.2 per cent (mainly structural), and the rate of labour force participation increased to 64 per cent (largely as a result of women joining the labour market). As pointed out by Dixon, job creation during the late 1970s was more than the supply of labour.[312] About 40,000 vacancies a year were created while there were only 32,000-33,000 new entries to the labour market. The gap was increasingly met by the influx of foreign labour, particularly from Malaysia. Foreign workers in the early 1980s, accounted for about 10 per cent of the labour force. There were two clear choices open to the government: either increase reliance on foreign workers or move towards more capital-intensive production. The government opted for the second strategy and in 1979 initiated the high-wage policy otherwise known as the second industrial revolution to encourage the development of higher value added production and financial services. Thus, a significant share of the economic growth achieved was the result of the rapid incorporation of labour into the production system.

The second source of growth was the massive, efficient, capital investment between 1965 and 1990. In fact, Singapore's economy during this period became the showcase for standard economic theory, in which investment is the fundamental engine of growth. This investment had three major sources: gross national savings mainly the CPF, FDI, and private local investment.

Set up in 1955, as an employment insurance fund, the CPF became a major source of saving. In the 1950s, employer and employees each contributed 5 per cent of labour costs, to provide pensions, welfare payments and, later, the means of purchasing housing. By the 1980s, the contributions had been successively increased to 50 per cent (later reduced to 40 per cent in 1986 after the 1985 recession). At its peak in 1984, the rate of saving was the equivalent of 42 per cent of GDP, the highest in the world. The equivalent figure for Japan was 31 per cent. This extraordinary level of forced savings meant that the CPF had ceased to be primarily an insurance fund, but had become a major instrument of public finance. With the addition of the Post Office Saving Bank, the government has been in a position to direct the investment into public infrastructure (particulary public housing and transportation), and in private corporations in which the government participates.[313] Another part is invested

---

[312] Dixon, Chris (1991), *South East Asia in the World Economy*, Cambridge: Cambridge University Press, pp. 167-236.
[313] Dixon, Chris (1991), *op. cit.*, p. 162.

abroad by the government, to decrease the vulnerability of its resources *vis-à-vis* potential downturns of the Singapore's economy. And a substantial surplus (as much as 24 per cent of total government revenue) is reserved in a Development Fund to stabilise the economy and allow for strategic development expenditures.[314]

The actual dynamism of investment is left to private capital, and particularly to foreign investment, whose flows have significantly increased since 1965. For instance, investment by resident foreigners and foreign corporations has risen from 9 per cent of GDP in 1965 to over 26 per cent during the 1980s. The majority of this investment went into manufacturing, out the period of 1965-90.[315]

The third major contributor to Singapore's economic growth is the expanding external sector, which enables the state to generate foreign currencies. This is particularly important, when one considers the fact that Singapore is relatively a small city-state with no natural resources. Thus, it can be concluded that the main sources of Singapore's economic success were its labour force, capital investment mainly forced savings and FDI, and integration into the new international division of labour.

Determinants of FDI Inflow

As noted, the causes of inward direct investment into Singapore's economy has been both historical and state-led. Historical in the sense that, the factors which enables the city-state to function as an entrepot and associated regional and international nodality, established in the colonial period, have continued to act as an attraction for FDI until the present day. Under the colonial regime the factors that conferred Singapore's comparative advantage for FDI inflow were its natural harbour and strategic location as an entrepot-trading nation. This led to an early form of investment, which specialised in the importing and re-exporting of primary products from Southeast Asia to Europe, the US and other parts of the world. At the same time, it imported and re-exported manufactured goods from the industrialised countries to the Asian neighbours.[316]

However, with the achievement of sovereignty in 1965, its locational advantage as an entrepot trading zone, its hardworking workforce, competitive labour costs, open investment policy, infrastructure, and the state became the main forces behind its comparative advantage for FDI in the 1960s. The state,

---

[314] Castells, Manuel (1988), *op. cit.*, p. 6.
[315] Dixon, Chris (1991), *op. cit.*, p. 162.
[316] Tan, Augustine H. H. (1985), *op. cit.*

in particular, through its various policies, institutional networks and incentives gradually created and shaped Singapore's comparative advantage in labour-intensive industries during the 1970s, and capital-intensive manufacturing in the 1980s and onwards. However, the response from the foreign investors was phenomenal. Since the late 1960s, FDI has dominated investment commitments in manufacturing, especially in export-oriented industries. Between 1970 and 1990, FDI has accounted for over 85 per cent of the total manufacturing investment. Among the different types of manufacturing establishments, wholly foreign firms were by far the largest, accounting for 60 per cent of cumulative investment over the period 1975-88. As in 1988, wholly foreign firms accounted for one-half of all employment, 62 per cent of all value added, and three-quarters of all exports. In other words, wholly foreign establishments are characterised by relatively high levels of labour productivity, capital intensity, and are export oriented while the reverse was true for wholly local establishments.[317]

However, such heavy dependence on FDI calls in question not only the continuing ability of Singapore to attract sizable foreign investments, but also the desirability of continuing with large scale inflows. As pointed out by Lim, such large inflows may in the long run amount to net loss as Singapore may attempt to increase its tax incentives to match the international competition for FDI.[318] However, the government justifies the high presence of foreign TNCs in Singapore's manufacturing sector by pointing to the contribution of these firms to its citizens high standard of living which is the second highest in Asia after Japan; the high economic growth averaging 7-10 per cent between 1960-92, and employment. On the other hand, the government has allowed the large influx of foreign firms into Singapore for its own electorial success. For the power and its popularity of the PAP government is closely tied to that of foreign capital. Thus, the government electoral success depends on foreign capital success in Singapore. Moreover, to ensure the success of the foreign capital, the state has played an effective role by pursuing economic policies, which will be suitable to the needs of foreign TNCs.

By contrast, the neoclassical account of the rapid economic growth in Singapore is that the state has allowed the efficiencies derived from market based resource allocations to be maximised.[319] The Friedmans go further, arguing that the successful Asian economies such as Malaysia, Korea, Taiwan, Hong Kong, Singapore, and Japan, are those which rely heavily on private

---

[317] Naya, Seiji and Ramstetter (1988), *op. cit.*, p. 60.

[318] Lim, Chong Yah (1988), *op. cit.*

[319] Balassa, Bela (1981), *Newly Industrialising Countries in the World Economy*, New York: Pergamon Press.

markets.[320] By contrast, India, Indonesia and Communist China, all rely heavily on central planning, and as such, experienced economic stagnation.[321] By this, Friedman equates state-led economies to economic stagnation and private-led economies to economic growth. The fundamental problem with such dichotomy is that it fails to recognise the fact that the state does not necessarily need to be involved in the production process, but can intervene in other aspects of the market. For instance, Taiwan and Korea are by every market indicator, guided market economies. They are market economies in the sense that initiative rests mainly with the enterprise, profits remain the enterprise's main motive, and enterprise's which do not make profits will in most cases go out of business. Therefore, the state influences the market by shifting the composition of what is profitable, rather than by direct regulation or direct production as postulated by Friedman.[322]

In Singapore, the role of the state has been both more overt and pervading. It has been described by Mirza as a miracle by design where: "the state apparatus is one of the most powerful in the Third World and can indeed be regarded as the epitome of the "hard state" described in the development literature. The government uses the apparatus to exert considerable control over the economy and this is reflected in the scale of state expenditure, the activities of the state-owned enterprises and even in the rate of national savings".[323]

Indeed, the state has been involved in direct production just as much as the private firms. In fact, this has given Singapore's economy the unique element, which consist of the state, TNC and local private firms, which in the last three decades has changed in shape and size. However, the neoclassical economists may argue that the changing patterns of the state, foreign TNCs and local private firms involvement in production is irrelevant, because ownership structure of firms is an immaterial factor in their contribution to the country's output. However, this ignores the fact that economic change and policies affect different players in the economy in different ways.[324] Thus, when the state introduced the high-wage policy in the late 1970s and early 1980s to restructure the Singapore's economy, it failed to take into account the relative importance of the different sizes and shapes of state-owned and

---

[320] Friedman, Milton and Rose (1980), *Free to Choose: A Personal statement*, New York: Harcourt Brace, p. 57.

[321] Ibid.

[322] White, Gordon (1988), *Developmental States in East Asia*, London: Macmillan, p. 6.

[323] Mirza, H. (1986), *op. cit.*, p. 35.

[324] Ho, Kwon Ping (1992), *Comment on Singapore: The Year in Review 1991*, Singapore: Institute Policy Studies.

foreign corporations, and private local firms. The policy was introduced as a blunt instrument disregarding the differential status of firms for instance, the expanding and unexpanding and profitable and unprofitable firms were all treated alike.[325]

However, while the view that the state has played a major role in the development of Korea, Taiwan and Singapore, it has also been argued that the state in Hong Kong has been a major forced behind its development.[326] The difference between Hong Kong and the other East Asian NIEs is that the role of the state in Hong Kong is more deeply based and subtle in its application. However, the persistence of the myth of the Asian NIEs "lean state" development has four main roots. Firstly, the states themselves made considerable efforts to project liberal economic images so that other countries would have as few grounds as possible to improve trade restrictions and attract investment. Secondly, the neoclassical economists merely looked at the apparently liberal external trade regimes to the exclusion of the internal economic and social structures that lay behind them. Thirdly, those writers who accepted that there was state intervention during the 1950s and early 1960s which was largely eliminated have generally confused a limited degree of liberalisation with a liberal trade policy.[327] Fourthly, there is considerable vested interest on the part of international agencies, developed world governments, and associated experts to present the "Asian miracle economies" as the product of free market capitalism.[328]

Determinants of Overseas Direct Investment

As pointed out in chapters 4 and 5, two major phenomena determine outward direct investment by firms based in Singapore: objective and subjective conditions for capital. Objectively, it was argued that labour-intensive firms' in Singapore invested abroad because of Singapore's loss of comparative advantage in labour-intensive production, which has severely reduced firm's profitability since the introduction of a high wage policy in 1979. As confirmed by the OLS regression, many labour-intensive firms in Singapore have relocated to areas where profitability potential is greater than in Singapore. This puts in question the high wage policy, which priced out Singapore in the labour-intensive production.

---

[325] Tan, Augustine H. H. (1985), *op. cit.*, p. 34.
[326] Dixon, Chris and Smith, David (1993), *Economic and Social Development in Pacific Asia*, London: Routledge.
[327] Ibid.
[328] Dixon, Chris and Smith, David (1993), *op. cit.*

Although the high-wage policy introduced in 1979, led to greater use of capital equipment, the pertinent question is whether the policy forced the premature exit of the existing industries without a sufficiently offsetting expansion of the desired high technology industries. Before the introduction of the wage increases, Singapore was experiencing labour shortage. During the high wage period, labour shortage became severe and it led to the serious competition for labour between the foreign and local firms. Thus, most local firms who could not compete with the going factor prices had to relocate overseas.[329]

Another major effect of the high-wage policy was the 1985 recession. The economy for the first time experienced a negative growth that was registered, as the worst in Southeast Asia. Every sector of the economy experienced a downturn. According to the Economic Committee set up in 1986 to investigate the causes and the possible solutions to the recession, two major factors emerged as the causes. Firstly, Singapore's higher business costs, particulary labour costs, eroded its international competitiveness. Between 1979-84, Singapore's competitive position weakened by 50 per cent against Hong Kong; 15 per cent against Taiwan and 35 per cent against Korea.[330] Moreover, during the 1979-84 period, real labour costs rose faster than productivity growth and, together with a strong currency, contributed to an erosion of Singapore's international competitiveness and business profitability. Secondly, it was found that Singapore's excessive dependence on FDI and trade (between 1979-84, trade was more than 3 times its GDP size compared to 1.7 for Hong Kong; 0.9 for Taiwan and 0.7 for Korea) made it easier for Singapore to "sneeze" when world trade "caught a cold".

Even after economic growth was restored in the late 1980s, firms were still relocating abroad because of labour and skill shortages, which eased during the recession, but re-emerged with the economic growth. Many measures have been introduced to resolve the problem on both the supply and demand sides. On the supply side, the government has been encouraging economically inactive families into the labour market for full and part-time employment, it has raised the overall retirement age, and allowed a liberal inflow of foreign workers. On the demand side, firms were encouraged to use labour efficiently through automation, mechanisation and computerisation. Even these measures were not enough to save the relocation of labour-intensive activities abroad.

---

[329] Tan, Augustine H.H. (1985), op. cit , p. 33; Ong, Nai Pew and Lim, Cin (1985), "Slack Demand is Only Half the Story", *Straits Times*, July 31.

[330] Development Bank of Singapore 1987, *Outlook for the Singapore Economy*, Singapore: Economic Research Department, p. 3.

Subjectively, the Student t-test and the multiple regression presented in chapter 5 confirms the theoretical framework that firm's decisions to invest abroad are also governed by the availability of cheap labour, raw materials, growing internal and regional markets, political stability and shared language, culture and religion in the neighbouring countries. Furthermore, most of the regional countries have improved their investment policies by changing their industrial strategies from import-substitution to export-led growth, and by carefully executed structural adjustment programmes. Thus, labour-intensive firms from Singapore enjoyed foreign status incentives that would not have been available if they were still located in Singapore. As pointed out in chapter 5, most of these firms that relocated because of the tax incentives were local firms. This is not surprising, as the bulk of these firms were not entitled to tax benefits in Singapore.

The Outlook into the Next Millennium

A key component of the economic strategy for the year 2000 is the promotion of outward investment to enable Singapore to overcome domestic constraints to economic growth posed by land and labour shortages, and to help secure access to foreign markets, resources and technologies. The year 2000 strategy fits in with Lee Kuan Yew's vision of Singapore as the economic hub of South East Asia through which TNCs:[331] "can serve not only their home market, but also the regional and world market. Furthermore, they can tap the region's bigger and cheaper labour pool. Labour-intensive parts of a product can be done in neighbouring countries and exported to Singapore for more capital-or skill-intensive operations".[332]

According to the Department of Statistic's own figures, Singapore's direct investment between 1976 and 1990 has grown on average 16 per cent a year. The bulk of the investment occurred between 1989-90, when the compound rate has been more than 20 per cent a year. Over half of the direct investment has been in the Asian region, particularly in the growth triangle. Although there is no separate data showing Singapore's direct investment in the growth triangle, it is believed that over 50 per cent of the investment in the ASEAN is in the growth triangle zones. Although, the growth triangle between Singapore-Johor-Batam is not a determinant of FDI from Singapore, it has helped to facilitate the flow of FDI within these countries. The main aim of the growth triangle has been to exploit the mutual advantage, the compli-

---

[331] Cited by Dixon, Chris and Smith (1993), *op. cit.*

[332] Lee, Kuan Yew (1989), speech delivered in Tokyo, cited in the *Far Eastern Economic Review*, 18 August, p. 77.

mentary mix of resources, labour, skills, infrastructure and services available in Singapore, Johor and the Riau islands. From Singapore's viewpoint, the growth triangle is essential for its year 2000 development programme.

Thus, it is logical to predict that Singapore's direct investment in the growth triangle will increase by 50 per cent of the present level by the year 2000. It is believed the growth triangle will account for over 55 per cent of Singapore's investment in the Asian region. The reason for such high hopes is that Singapore's incorporation into the NAFTA will entail direct competition with some of the Latin American countries: in particular, Mexico where labour costs are relatively cheaper in labour-intensive production. Singapore will need the growth triangle to enable it to compete in the world market in labour-intensive production. It is also speculated that Singapore's direct investment in North America and in particular, the US will increase by as much as 5 to 8 times the present level. This is because America is the most important export market for Singapore manufacturers. However, Singapore's investment in the EC is expected to be increasing at a decreasing rate of 3-8 per cent by the year 2000. The reason is because of the current recession in almost all-European countries. However, countries such as UK, Germany, France, Netherlands, and Denmark are expected to be the main recipient of Singapore's FDI. Furthermore, Singapore's direct investment in Eastern Europe is expected to improve slightly by 3 per cent because of the availability of skilled and unskilled labour force, infrastructure, and markets. However, the region's political instability is bound to be a major set back to investment flows. Lastly, Singapore's investment in Asia is expected to grow at an annual rate of 20-30 per cent. This will be due to the fact that the region has the fastest growing economies in the world: and because the US will be focusing their year 2000 international economic priorities in the Asia Pacific rim. Apart from the growth triangle states, Vietnam, Cambodia, Malaysia, China, Hong Kong and Philippines are expected to be the biggest recipients of the new wave of Singapore's direct investment by the year 2000.

The preceding globalisation plan is in accordance with the domestic economic year 2000 strategy. According to the National Day Rally speech presented by Singapore's Prime Minister in 1992, Singapore's Development Plan for the year 2000 is to achieve a developed country status and Switzerland's 1984 per capita income of US$ 31,800.[333] To achieve this target, Singapore needs to maintain its present level of FDI inflow, achieve average growth rate of 7 per cent per year, and productivity increases of 4 per cent a year. Presently, the economy is growing at an average rate of 5 to 6 per cent, per

---

[333] Prime Minister's National Day Rally Speech, 1992.

capita income is about two-thirds (US$ 20,400 in 1991) that of Switzerland (US$ 31,800), and productivity is also about half (US$ 23,900 output per worker) those of the G7 countries of US, Japan, Germany, France, Britain, Italy and Canada (for instance, Japan at US$ 47,000).[334] Currently, the competition for international direct investment is not only from the NIEs but also from the semi-industrialising countries of Malaysia, Indonesia, Thailand, China and Philippines, and the DCs.

However, judging from Singapore's economic records for the last three decades, it is believed that Singapore's economic planners will be able to achieve their targets for the year 2000.

Further Studies

The aim of this book has been to examine the main determinants of inward and outward direct investment in Singapore's economy. This has been achieved by examining Singapore's economic success since 1965, and the objective and subjective factors, which influence a firm's decision to invest abroad. It was also possible to investigate the difference between foreign and local firm's motivations for FDI. As confirmed by the two cross-tabulation tables in chapter 5, there are similarities between foreign and local firm's motivating push factors for FDI. It was found that there is a relatively weak correlation between foreign TNCs and local firm's decisions to invest abroad. The reason for this was because of the fact that local firms based in Singapore particularly prefer economic areas where cultural, language and religion are similar. However, based on the issues raised and the findings in the book, one can identify a number of possible areas for further research. The first of these will be to investigate the possible influence of country and/or regional specific factors as a major pull factor for Singapore's direct investment. For instance, the research can concentrate on Singapore's direct investment in the EC where the present level of FDI is low. The focus on the EC will allow one to examine the effect of the Single Market on Singapore's overseas direct investment. Also, it will address the issue of whether the creation of a Single Market is indeed a protectionist measure against Singapore's exports. Moreover, it will provide the opportunity to examine Singapore's direct investment in the EC as a desperate measure to overcome trade barriers.

On the other hand, the research can focus on one or two countries where Singaporean investment has been highly successful. As noted in chapter 4, Singapore's investment in Malaysia is among the top ten major investors and in Indonesia, Singapore firms are the largest group of investors. These

---

[334] Ibid.

two countries can be examined in more detail to investigate whether Singapore's direct investment is really responding to objective and subjective conditions for capital as identified in the book. The results from this investigation will be very interesting in that it will provide the opportunity to compare the results with the findings of this book. Furthermore, the result will focus on one or two countries rather than a broad account of Singapore's globalisation strategy. The research will also concentrate on investigating the different types of technology used by foreign TNCs and local firm's abroad.

By contrast, the research investigation can focus on why Singapore firms have a relatively low level or no direct investment in certain economic regions such as Sub-Saharan, West and Southern African countries. To what extent could investment opportunities provided by the new South Africa act as an incentive to Singapore investors?

Previously, the economic sanctions imposed by the international community through the United Nations (UN) and the political uncertainty made South Africa unattractive for FDI. This is despite its many resources and viable investment opportunities. However, the removal of sanctions, and the on-going transition from the "white" minority rule to a "multi-racial" form of government has created an environment within which all foreign firms are actively encouraged to invest in South Africa. Furthermore, investors are also guaranteed that their investment in the country will be safe.

Overall, South Africa seems to be one of the most promising and profitable investment sites in Africa. This is due to its advantages of well-developed infrastructure, banking, technology, link with developed countries and availability of cheap labour. Moreover, this is an area, which will provide a possible outcome, which can be used to compare the African and Southeast Asian countries' investment policies.

The book can also be extended to incorporate some of the recent economic developments in the Asian region and the wider world economic issues such as the new American initiative to form the Asia Pacific Rim Common Market by the year 2000. It will also be interesting to know how these new developments complement Singapore's year 2000 strategy. Also, it will be interesting to know if it is realistic for the USA to propose a Pacific Rim Common Market in the face of the existing Common Markets. What effect the new Common Market will have on the existing NAFTA and EC? In the case of the Asian region, the research can examine the fact that while there is competition between Hong Kong, Tokyo and Singapore there is also an increasing degree of complementarity. Singapore for instance, specialises in the Asian currency and Asian bond markets, while Hong Kong has become the East Asian centre for fund management and loan syndication.

The book has also highlighted the fundamental role of the state in shaping and creating Singapore's comparative advantage in attracting FDI. Also, it was mentioned that the state is a major producer in the local economy and an international investor abroad. Future studies may investigate the extent to which the state-owned corporations are involved in overseas production. However, given the resources, time and visa constraints in Singapore it was not possible to investigate what motivates state corporations to invest abroad. This is an area, which can be expanded by subsequent research. The findings can also be used to compare with TNCs and private local firms' motivation for FDI.

However, the strength of the empirical evidence used in support of the book could be questioned on the grounds that the conclusion is based on just two case studies. Therefore, the conclusion of the empirical chapter should be used with caution, as the sample of the firms selected is biased. Furthermore, due to time, financial and visa constraints, it was not possible to investigate those firms that might have relocated entire production activities before the time of the survey, and those firms which did not relocate at all. In addition, although the questionnaire was particularly designed to investigate the motivating push and pull factors for FDI, it neglected certain possible factors such as the use of ownership specific advantages by firms to carry out FDI. Finally, it possible that the official statistics used in the book may not reflect the extent of Singapore's overseas investment, as there is no regulation requiring firms investing abroad to provide documentation of such activities.

Overall, one can conclude that the successful use of FDI by the Singapore government to achieve economic success could be a model for any country, which intends to pursue economic development. Although Singapore's characteristics are unique in their own way, the fundamental aspects of a favourable investment climate and the successful manipulation of foreign investment to contribute to local development are all useful insights which can be exploited by many developing nations. However, it would not be advisable for a country to copy exactly Singapore's model without a serious modification to incorporate that country's culture and local linkages. That is, FDI should be pursued to incorporate local manufacturing contents rather than forming a foreign enclave, which may result in technological, social and economic dualism between the foreign TNCs on the one hand and the private local firms on the other. In fact, FDI should be seen to represent the transmission of capital, managerial and technical skills which takes account of local resources thus providing real linkages with domestic firms and overall development.

Bibliography

Adam, Gy (1974), "Some Reasons for Foreign Investment", *Acta Oeconomica*, 13 (3-4), pp. 323-37.

Agarwal, Jamuna P. and Gubitz, Andrea and Nunnenkamp, Peter (1991), *Foreign Direct Investment in Developing Countries: The Case of Germany*, Tubingen: Mohr (Siebeck).

Aggarwal, Raj (1984), "The Strategic Challenge of Third World Multinationals: A New Stage of the Product Life Cycle of Multinationals?", *Advances in International Comparative Management*, 1 (4), pp. 103-22.

Aggarwal, Raj (1985), "Emerging Third World Multinationals: A Case Study of the Foreign Operations of Singapore Firms", *Journal of Contemporary Southeast Asia*, 7 (3), pp. 193-208.

Agodo, Oriye (1978), "The Determinants of U.S. Private Manufacturing Investments in Africa", *Journal of International Business Studies*, 9 (3), pp. 95-107.

Aharoni, Yair (1966), *The Foreign Investment Decision Process*, Boston: Harvard Business School.

Amsden, A. H. (1985), "The State and Taiwan's Economic Development" in Rueschemeyer, P., Evans, D. and Skocpol, T. (eds.), *Bringing The State In*, London: Cambridge University Press.

Amsden, A. H. (1989), *Asia's Next Giant: South Korea and Late Industrialisation*, Oxford: Oxford University Press.

Appelbaum, R. P. and Henderson, J. (1992), *States and Development in the Asian-Pacific Rim*, Newbury Park: Sage Publications.

Areskoug, Kaj (1976), "Private Foreign Investment and Capital Formation in Developing Countries", *Economic Development and Cultural Change*, 24 (3), pp. 539-47.

Argawal, A. P. (1980), "Determinants of Foreign Direct Investment: A Survey", *Weltwirtschaftliches Archive*, Band 116, pp. 739-773.

159

Arndt, H. W. (1974), "Professor Kojima on the Macroeconomic of Foreign Direct Investment", *Hitotsubashi Journal of Economics*, 15 (2), pp. 26-35.

Arrighi, G. (1978), "Towards a Theory of Capitalist Crisis", *New Left Review*, 111, pp. 3-24.

Arrow, K. J. (1969), *The Organisation of Economic Activity: Issues Pertinent to the Choice of Market Versus Nonmarket Allocation*, United States Congress, Joint Economic Committee, pp. 47-64.

Arrow, K. J. (1974), *The Limits of Organisation*, New York: W. W. Norton & Company.

Avery, William P. and Rapkin, David P. (1989), *Markets, Politics, and Change in the Global Political Economy*, London: Rienner.

Bain, Joe S. (1979), *Barriers to New Competition*, Cambridge, Mass.: Harvard University Press.

Balassa, Bela (1978), "Export Incentives and Export Performance in Developing Countries: A Comparative Analysis", *Weltwirtschaftliches Archiv*, 114(1), pp. 24-61.

Balassa, Bela (1981), *Newly Industrialising Countries in the World Economy*, New York: Pergamon Press.

Baldwin, Robert E. (1979), "Determinants of Trade and Foreign Investment: Further Evidence", *Review of Economics and Statistics*, 61(1), pp. 40-48.

Bandera, Valdimir N. and White, Joseph T. (1968), "U. S. Direct Investments and Domestic Markets in Europe", *Economia Internazionale*, 21 (3), pp. 117-33.

Bandera, Valdimir N. and Lucken, J. A. (1972), "Has U.S. Capital Differentiated between EEC and EFTA?", *Kyklos* 25 (1), pp. 306-14.

Barlow, E. R. and Wender, Ira T. (1955), *Foreign Investment and Taxation*, Englewood Cliffs: Prentice-Hall Inc.

Bauer, John (1990), "Demographic Change and Asian Labour Markets in the 1990s", *Population and Development Review* 16(4), pp. 615-45.

Baumol, William (1967), *Business Behaviour, Value, and Growth*, New York: Harcourt, Brace, & World.

Bennett, Peter D. and Green, Robert T. (1972), "Political Instability as a Determinant of Direct Foreign Investment in Marketing", *Journal of Marketing Research*, 9(2), pp. 182-86.

Bergsten, C. Fred, Horst, Thomas and Theodore, H. Moran (1978), *American Multinational and American Interests*, to Washington, D.C.: Brookings Institution.

Berle, A. and Means, G. (1968), *The Modern Corporation and Private Property*, New York: Transaction Publishers.

Bhagwati, Jagdish N. and Dinopoulos, Elias and Wong, Kar Yiu (1992), "Quid Pro Quo Foreign Investment", *American Economic Review*, 82(2), pp. 186-90.

Birch, Melissa H. (1991), "Change Patterns of Foreign Investment in Latin America", *Quarterly Review of Economics and Business*, 31 (3), pp. 141-58.

Blais, Jeffery P. (1975), *A Theoretical and Empirical Investigation of Canadian and British Direct Foreign Investment in Manufacturing in the United States* (Ph.D Dissertation, University of Pittsburgh).

Bloomfield, Arthur I. (1963), *Short-Term Capital Movements Under the Pre-1914 Gold Standard*, New Jersey: Princeton University Press.

Brech, Michael and Sharp, Margaret (1984), *Inward Investment: Policy Options for the United Kingdom*, London: The Royal Institute of International Affairs and Routledge & Kegan Paul.

Buckley, Peter J. (1983), "Macroeconomic versus International Business Approach to Direct Foreign Investment: A Comment on Professor Kojima's Interpretation", *Hitotsubashi Journal of Economics*, 24(1), pp. 95-100.

Buckley, Peter J. (1989), *The Multinational Enterprise: Theory and Applications*, London: The Macmillan Press.

Buckley, Peter. J. (1990), *International Investment*, Aldershot: Elgar.

Buckley, Peter. J. and Casson, M. C. (1976), *The Future of the Multinational Enterprise*, London: The MacMillan Press.

Buckley, Peter J. and Mirza, Hafiz (1985), "The Wit and Wisdom of Japanese Management: An Iconoclastic Analysis", *Management International Review*, 25, pp. 16-32.

Buffie, Edward F. (1987), "Labour Market Distortions, the Structure of Protection and Direct Foreign Investment", *Journal of Development Economics*, 27(1-2), pp. 149-63.

Casson, Mark (1991), "General Theories of the Multinational Enterprise: Their Relevance to Business History", in Wilkins, Mira (ed.), *The Growth of Multinationals*, London: Elgar Reference Collection, Chapter 3.

Castells, Manuel (1988), *The Developmental City-State in An Open World Economy: The Singapore Experience*, University of California, Berkeley Working Paper, no. 31.

Caves, Richard E. (1971), "International Corporations: The Industrial Economics of Foreign Investment", *Economica*, 38 (1), pp. 1-27.

Caves, Richard E. (1974), Multinational Firms, Competition and Productivity in Host Country Markets, *Economica*, 41, pp. 176-93.

Caves, Richard E. (1982), *Multinational Enterprise and Economics Analysis*, Cambridge: Cambridge University Press.

Chamberlin, Edward H. (1933), *The Theory of Monopolist Competition*, Cambridge: Harvard University Press.

Chan, Steve, Clark, Cal and Davis, David R. (1990), "State Entrepreneurship, Foreign Investment, Export Expansion, and Economic Growth: Granger Causality in Taiwan's Development", *Journal of Conflict Resolution*, 34(1), pp. 102-29.

Chan, Heng Chee (1971), *Singapore: The Politics of Survival 1965-1967*, Singapore: Oxford University Press.

Chaponniere, Jean-Raphael (1992), "The NIEs Go International", paper prepared for the conference on *Europe, U.S. and Japan in the Asia Pacific Region: Current Situation and Perspectives*, held at the INSEAD Euro-Asia Centre, Fontainebleau, France.

Chatterji, Monojit and Lahiri, Sajal (1989), "Private Foreign Investment and Welfare in LDCs", in Singer, Hans W. and Sharma, Soumitra (eds.), *Growth and External Debt Management*, London: St. Martin's Press.

Chen, Peter S. J. (1983), "Singapore's Development Strategies: A Model for Rapid Growth", in Chen, Peter S. J. (ed.), *Singapore Development Policies and Trends*, Singapore: Oxford University Press, pp. 3-26.

Chen, Thomas P. (1989), "The Internationalization of the Taiwanese Economy", in Lee, Cheng F. and Hu, Sheng Cheng (eds.), *Taiwan's Foreign Investment, Exports and Financial Analysis*, London: JAI Press.

Cheng, Siok Hwa (1979), "Economic Change in Singapore, 1945-1977", *Southeast Asian Journal of Social Science*, 7(1-2), pp. 81-113.

Chew, Soon Beng and Chew, Rosalind (1983), "Income Policy: The Singapore Experience", mimeo, National University of Singapore.

Chia, Siow Yue (1971), "Growth and Pattern of Industrialization", in You Poh Seng and Lim Chong Yah (eds), *The Singapore Economy*, Singapore: Eastern Universities Press, pp. 189-223.

Chia, Siow Yue (1972), "Export Performance of the Manufacturing Sector and of Foreign Investment", in Wong Kum Poh and Maureen Tan (eds), *Singapore in the International Economy*, Singapore University Press, pp. 33-47.

Chia, Siow Yue (1981), "Foreign Investment in Manufacturing in Developing Countries: The Case of Singapore", in F. E. I. Hamilton and G. J. R. Linge (eds), *Spatial Analysis, Industry and the Industrial Environment*, vol. 11, International Industrial Systems, New York: John Wiley & Sons, pp. 439-64.

Chia, Siow Yue (1986), "Direct Foreign Investment and the Industrialisation Process in Singapore", in Lim Chong Yah and Peter J. Lloyd (eds.), *Singapore: Resources and Growth*, Oxford: Oxford University Press.

Chng, Meng Kng, Low, Linda and Toh, Mun Heng (1988), *Industrial Restructuring in Singapore: For ASEAN-Japan Investment and Trade Expansion*, Singapore: Chopmen.

Chong, Li Choy (1986), "Singapore's Development: Harnessing the Multinationals", *Contemporary Southeast Asia: A Quarterly Journal of International and Strategic Affairs*, 8 (1), pp. 56-69.

Chou, Tein-Chen (1988), "American and Japanese Direct Foreign Investment in Taiwan: A Comparative Study", *Hitotsubashi Journal of Economics*, 29(2), pp. 165-79.

Chow, Kit Boey and Tyabji, Amina (1980), *External Linkages and Economic Development: The Singapore Experience*, Economic Research Centre, Monograph Series 8.

Chua, Beng Huat (1982), "Singapore in 1981: Problems in New Beginnings", *Southeast Asian Affairs*, pp.315-35.

Clammer, John (1985), *Singapore: Ideology, Society and Culture*, Singapore: Chapmen Publications.

Clegg, Jeremy (1987), *Multinational Enterprise and World Competition: A Comparative study of the USA, Japan, the UK, Sweden and West Germany*, London: St. Martin's Press.

Cline, William R. (1982), "Can the East Asian Model of Development Be Generalized?", *World Development*, 10(2), pp. 81-90.

Coase, R. H. (1937), "The Nature of the Firm", *Economica*, 4 (1), pp. 386-405.

Commons, John R. (1959), *Institutional Economics*, Madison: University of Wisconsin Press.

Crew, Michael A. (1975), *Theory of the Firm*, London: Longman.

Cyert, R. M. and March, J. G. (1963), *A Behavioural Theory of the Firm*, New York: Prentice Hall.

Dell, Sidney (1991), *International Development Policies: Perspectives for Industrial Countries*, Durham: Duke University Press.

Department of Statistics, *Destination, Activity, and Returns of Singapore's Direct Investments Abroad*, Singapore: National Printers, 1992.

Department of Statistics, *Yearbook of Statistics Singapore*, Singapore National Printers, various years.

Department of Statistics 1993, *Singapore's Investment Abroad 1976-1989*, Singapore: National Printers.

Department of Statistics 1988, *Singapore National Accounts 1987*, Singapore: Singapore National Printers.

Department of Statistics 1983, *Economic & Social Statistics Singapore 1960-1982*, Singapore: Singapore National Printers.

Development Bank of Singapore (1987), *Outlook for the Singapore Economy*, Singapore: Economic Research Department.

Development Bank of Singapore (1989), *An Integrated European Market in 1992: Implications for Singapore*, Singapore: DBS Bank.

Deyo, F. C. (1989), *Beneath the Miracle: Labour Subordination in the New Asia Industrialism*, Berkeley: University of California Press.

Diaz-Alejandro, C. F. (1977), "Foreign Direct Investment by Latin Americans", in T. Agmon and C. P. Kindleberger (eds.), *Multinationals from Small Countries*, Cambridge, Mass.: MIT Press.

Dickie, Robert B. and Layman, Thomas A. (1988), *Foreign Investment and*

Government Policy in the Third World: Forging Common Interests in Indonesia and Beyond, London: St. Martin's Press.

Dinopoulos, Elias and Lane, Timothy D. (1992), "Market Liberalization Policies in a Reforming Socialist Economy", *International Monetary Fund Staff Papers*, 39(3), pp. 465-94.

Disney, Richard and Ho, Soo Kiang (1990), "Do Real Wages Matter in an Open Economy? The Case of Singapore: 1966-1987", *Oxford Economic Papers*, 42(3), pp. 635-57.

Dixon, Chris (1991), *South East Asia in the World Economy*, Cambridge: Cambridge University Press.

Dixon, Chris and Smith, David (1993), *Economic and Social Development in Pacific Asia*, London: Routledge.

Dominic, M. P. (1977), "Singapore: Foreign Investment and Tax Treaties", *Bulletin for International Fiscal Documentation*, 31(6), pp. 268-75.

Drake, Tracey A. and Caves, Richard E. (1992), "Changing Determinants of Japanese Foreign Investment in the United States", *Journal of the Japanese and International Economy*, 6(3), pp. 228-46.

Drucker, Peter (1974), "Multinational and Developing Countries: Myths and Realities", *Foreign Affairs*, 53 (1), pp. 121-34.

Drysdale, John (1979), "Singapore's Low-Level Wage Problem", *ASEAN Business Quarterly*, pp. 37-45.

Drysdale, John (1984), *Singapore: Struggle For Success*, Singapore: Times Books International.

Dunning, John H. (1970), *Studies in International Investment*, London: Allen and Unwin.

Dunning, John H. (1971), *Multinational Enterprise*, London: Allen and Unwin.

Dunning, John H. (1973), "The Determinants of International Production", *Oxford Economic Papers*, 25(3), pp. 289-336.

Dunning, John H. (1974), *Economic Analysis and the Multinational Enterprise*, London: Allen and Unwin.

Dunning, John H. (1980), "Towards an Eclectic Theory of International Production: Some Empirical Tests", *Journal of International Business Studies*, 11(1), pp. 9-31.

Dunning, John H. (1981), *International Production and the Multinational Enterprise*, London: Allen & Unwin.

Dunning, John H. (1983), "Changes in the Level and Structure of International Production: The Last One Hundred Years", in Casson, M. (ed.), *The Growth of International Business*, London: Croom Helm, pp. 84-139.

Dunning, John H. (1986), *Japanese Participation in British Industry*, London: Croom Helm.

Dunning, John H. (1986), "The Investment Cycle Revisited", *Weltwirtschaftliches Archiv*, Band 122, pp. 667-77.

Dunning, John H. (1988), *Multinational, Technology and Competitiveness*, London: Allen and Unwin.

Dunning, John H. (1993), *Multinational Enterprise and the Global Economy*, London: Addison-Wesley.

Economic Development Board, *Annual Report*, 1965, pp. 5-6.

Economic Development Board, *Economics Development Board Report*, Singapore: Economic Development Board, various years.

Economic Development Board, *Economic Development Board Yearbook*, Singapore: Economic Development Board, various years.

Economic Development Board, *Report on the Census of Industrial Production*, Singapore: Singapore National Printers, various years.

Ee, Hock Chye (1991), "*Foreign Direct Investment from Singapore Manufacturing Sector*" (MBA dissertation, National University of Singapore).

Embassy of the United States of America, Singapore Office (1992), *The Growth Triangle: Singapore-Johor-Riau*, Report prepared as a guide to U.S. investors, May.

Emmanuel, A. B. C. (1984), "Advantages Offered to Foreign Investment", *Bulletin for International Fiscal Documentation*, 39(3), pp. 113-16.

Evans, David and Alizadeh, Parvin (1984), "Trade, Industrialisation, and the Visible Hand", *The Journal of Development Studies*, 21(1), pp. 22-46.

Friedman, Milton (1981), *The Invisible Hand in Economics and Politics*, Inaugural Singapore Lecture, Singapore: Institute of Southeast Asian Studies.

Friedman, Milton and Rose (1980), *Free to Choose: A Personal Statement*, New York: Harcourt Brace.

Frobel, F., Heinricks, J. and Kreyo, O. (1980), *The New International Division of Labour*, Cambridge: Cambridge University Press.

Gaisford, James D. (1991), "Asymmetric Effects of Endowment Changes on Foreign Investment Source and Host Countries", *Canadian Journal of Economics*, 24(4), pp. 940-57.

Gehrels, Franz (1983), "Foreign Investment and Technology Transfer: Optimal Policies", *Weltwirtschaftliches Archiv*, 119(4), pp. 663-85.

George, T. S. (1975), *Lee Kuan Yew's Singapore*, London: Andre Deutsch.

Giddy, Ian H. and Young, Stephen (1982), "Conventional Theory and Unconventional Multinationals: Do New Forms of Multinational Enterprise Require New Theories?", in Rugman, Alan M. (ed.), *New Theories of the Multinational Enterprise*, London: Croom Helm.

Giovannini, Alberto (1991), "International Capital Mobility and Tax Avoidance", *Banca Nazionale del Lavoro Quarterly Review* (177), pp. 197-223.

Glade, William P. (1987), "Multinationals and the Third World", *Journal of Economic Issues*, 21(4), pp. 1889-1920.

Goldberg, A. (1985), *The Chinese Connection: Getting Plugged into Rim Real Estate, Trade and Capital Markets*, Vancouver: University of British Columbia Press.

Goodman, Louis W. (1987), *Small Nations, Giant Firms*, London: Holmes & Meier.

Gray, H. P. (1982), "Macroeconomic Theories of Foreign Direct Investment: An Assessment", in Alan M. Rugman (ed.), *New Theories of the Multinational Enterprise*, London: Croom Helm, Chapter 8.

Grubaugh, Stephen G. (1987), "Determinants of Direct Foreign Investment", *Review of Economics and Statistics*, 69(1), pp. 149-52.

Haggard, Stephan (1986), "The Newly Industrializing Countries in the International System", *World Politics*, XXXVIII (2), pp. 343-70.

Hamilton, Clive (1983), "Capitalist Industrialisation in East Asia's 'Four Little Tigers'", *Journal of Contemporary Asia*, 13(1), pp. 35-73.

Harvey, John T. (1990), "The Determinants of Direct Foreign Investment", *Journal of Post Keynesian Economics*, 12(2), pp. 260-72.

Hein, Simeon (1992), "Trade Strategy and the Dependency Hypothesis: A Comparison of Policy, Foreign Investment, and Economic Growth in Latin America and East Asia", *Economic Development and Cultural Change*, 40(3), pp. 495-521.

Heineberg, Heinz (1988), "Singapore: From the British Colonial Base to the Up-and-Coming 'Chinese' City-State", *Applied Geography and Development*, 31 (1), pp. 15-36.

Helleiner, G. K. (1973), "Manufactured Exports from Less Developed Countries and Multinational Firms", *The Economic Journal*, 83(329), pp. 21-47.

Helleiner, Gerald Karl (1989), "Transnational Corporations and Direct Foreign Investment", in Hollis Chenery and T. N. Srinivasan (eds.), *Handbook of Development Economics*, Oxford: Elsevier Press.

Helleiner, Gerald Karl (1990), *The New Global Economy and the Developing Countries: Essays in International Economics and Development*, Aldershot: Elgar.

Heyzer, Noeleen (1984), "The Merging of State with Foreign Investment: Building a Technocratic Elite in Singapore", in Ngo, Manh Lan (ed.), *Unreal Growth: Critical Studies in Asian Development*, New Delhi: Hindustan Publishing.

Hicks, John (1974), "The Future of Industrialism", *International Affairs*, 50 (2), pp. 218-29.

Hiemenz, Ulrich and Langhammer, Rolf J. et-al. (1987), *The Comparative Strength of European, Japanese and U.S. Suppliers on ASEAN Markets*,

Tubingen: Mohr (Siebeck).

Hill, Hal (1990), "Foreign Investment and East Asian Economic Development", *Asian Pacific Economic Literature*, 4(2), pp. 21-58.

Hill, Hal and Johns, Brian (1985), "The Role of Direct Foreign Investment in Developing East Asian Countries", *Weltwirtschaftliches Archiv*, 121(2), pp. 55-81.

Hill, Hal and Pang, Eng Fong (1991), "Technology Exports from a Small, Very Open NIC: The Case of Singapore",*Working Paper in Trade and Development*, no.8916, Australia National University.

Ho, Kwon Ping (1992), *Comment on Singapore: The Year in Review 1991*, Singapore: Institute Policy Studies.

Hood, Neil and Young, Stephen (1979), *The Economics of Multinational Enterprise*, London: Longman.

Horstmann, Ignatius J. and Markusen, James R. (1989), "Firm-Specific Assets and the Gains from Direct Foreign Investment", *Economica*, 56(221), pp. 41-48.

Hsiao, Frank S. T. and Mei, Chu W (1989), "Japanese Experience of Industrialization and Economic Performance of Korea and Taiwan: Tests of Similarity", in Lee, Cheng F. and Hu, Sheng Cheng (eds.), *Taiwan's Foreign Investment, Exports and Financial Analysis*, London: JAI Press.

Huang, S. H. (1971), 'Measure to Promote Industrialisation', in You Poh Seng and Lim Chong Yah (eds.), *The Singapore Economy*, Singapore: Eastern Universities Press.

Hufbauer, G. C. (1966), *Synthetic Materials and the Theory of International Trade*, London: Gerald Duckworth.

Hughes, Helen (1969), "From Entrepot Trade to Manufacturing", in Helen Hughes and You Poh Seng (eds), *Foreign Investment and Industrialisation in Singapore*, Canberra: Australian National University Press, pp. 1-45.

Hughes, Helen and Ohlin, Goran (1980), "Adjustment to the Changing International Structure of Production", *Finance and Development*, pp. 21-4.

Hughes, Helen and Waelbroeck, Jean (1981), "Can Developing-Country Exports keep Growing in the 1980s?", *The World Economy*, pp. 127-47.

Huizinga, Harry (1991), "Foreign Investment Incentives and International Cross-Hauling of Capital", *Canadian Journal of Economics*, 24(3), pp. 710-16.

Hultman, Charles W. and McGee, L. Randolph (1988), "Factors Influencing Foreign Investment in the U.S., 1970-1986", *Rivista Internazionale di Scienze Economiche e Commerciali*, 35(10-11), pp. 1061-66.

Hymer, Stephen H. (1971), "The Multinational Enterprise and the Law of Uneven Development", in Bhagwati J. (ed.), *Economics and the World Order*, New York: World Law Fund.

Hymer, Stephen H. (1976), *The International Operations of National Firms: A Study of Direct Foreign Investment*, Mass, Cambridge: M.I.T. Press.

International Bank for Reconstruction and Development, *The Report of the International Bank for Reconstruction and Development on the Economic Development of Malaya*, Baltimore: John Hopkins University Press, 1955.

International Bank for Reconstruction and Development (1955), *The Economic Development of Malaya*, Chapter 6, pp. 84-95, and Technical Report 8, pp. 301-16.

International Bank for Reconstruction and Development/ The World Bank 1992, *World Development Report 1992*, Oxford: Oxford University Press.

International Monetary Fund, *Balance of Payments Statistics*, Computer Tape, Washington, D.C.: International Monetary Fund, various years.

International Monetary Fund, *Direction of Trade Statistics Yearbook*, Washington D.C.: International Monetary Fund, various years.

International Monetary Fund, *International Financial Statistics Yearbook*, Washington, D.C.: International Monetary Fund, various years.

Iverson, Carl (1953), *Aspects of the Theory of International Capital Movements*, London: Oxford University Press.

John, R. (1959), *Institutional Economics*, Madison: University of Wisconsin Press.

Jones, Geoffrey (1988), "Foreign Multinationals and British Industry before 1945", *Economic History Review*, 41 (3), pp. 429-53.

Jones, Ronald, W. and Anne O. Krueger (1990), *The Political Economy of International Trade: Essays in Honour of Robert E. Baldwin*, Cambridge, Mass.: Blackwell.

Jones, Ronald W. and Dei, Fumio (1983), "International Trade and Foreign Investment: A Simple Model", *Economic Inquiry*, 21(4), pp. 449-64.

Joo-Jock, Lim A. (1991), "Geographical Setting", in Ernest C. T. Chew and Edwin Lee (eds.), *A History of Singapore*, Oxford: Oxford University Press.

Josey, Alex (1972), *The Singapore General Elections 1972*, Singapore: Eastern University Press.

Josey, Alex (1974), *Lee Kuan Yew: The Struggle For Singapore*, Sydney: Angus & Robertson.

Kahley, William J. (1990), "Foreign Investment: What Are the Benefits?", *Regional Science Perspectives*, 20(1), pp. 152-93.

Kenwood, A. G. and Lougheed, A. L. (1992), *The Growth of the International Economy 1820-1990*, London: Routledge.

Khalilzadeh, Shirazi Javad and Shah, Anwar (1991), *Tax Policy in Developing Countries*, Washington, D.C.: World Bank.

Kindleberger, Charles P. (1969), *American Business Abroad: Six Lectures on Direct Investment*, New Haven: Yale University Press.

Kindleberger, Charles P. (1969), *Economic Development*, New York: McGraw-Hill.

Kirkpatrick, Colin (1986), 'Singapore at the Cross-roads: The Economic Challenges Ahead, *National Westminster Bank Quarterly Review*, pp. 46-57.

Klanova, Eva and Vtipilova, Lenka (1992), "Do You Need Foreign Capital?", *Czechoslovak Economic Digest*, (3), p. 8.

Klodt, Henning (1991), "Comparative Advantage and Prospective Structural Adjustment in Eastern Europe", *Economic Systems*, 15(2), pp. 265-81.

Koechlin, Timothy (1992), "The Determinants of the Location of USA Direct Foreign Investment", *International Review of Applied Economics*, 6(2), pp. 203-16.

Koekkoek, Ad and Mennes, L. B. M. (1991), *International Trade and Global Development: Essays in Honour of Jagdish Bhagwati*, London: Routledge.

Kogut, B. and Chang, S. J. (1991), "Technological Capabilities and Japanese Direct Investment in the United States", *Review of Economics and Statistics*, LXXIII, pp. 401-13.

Kohlhagen, Steven W. (1977), "Exchange Rate Changes, Profitability, and Direct Foreign Investment", *Southern Economic Journal*, 44(1), pp. 43-52.

Kojima, Kiyoshi (1973), "A Macroeconomic Approach to Foreign Direct Investment", *Hitotsubashi Journal of Economics*, 14 (2), pp. 1-20.

Kojima, Kiyoshi (1973), "Reorganisation of North-South Trade: Japan's Foreign Economic Policy for the 1970s", *Hitotsubashi Journal of Economics*, 13 (1), pp. 1-35.

Kojima, Kiyoshi (1975), "International Trade and Foreign Investment: Substitutes or Complements", *Hitotsubashi Journal of Economic*, 16 (1), pp. 1-12.

Kojima, Kiyoshi (1977), "Japanese type versus American type", *Hitotsubashi Journal of Economic*, 17 (2), pp. 1-14.

Kojima, Kiyoshi (1980), "Japanese Direct Foreign Investment in Asian Developing Countries", *Rivista Internazionale di Scienze Economiche e Commerciali*, 27(7-8), pp. 629-41.

Kojima, Kiyoshi (1982), "Macroeconomic Versus International Business Approach to Direct Foreign Investment", *Hitotsubashi Journal of Economics*, 23 (2), pp. 1-19.

Kojima, Kiyoshi and Ozawa, Terutomo (1984), "Micro-and Macro-Economic Models of Direct Foreign Investment: Towards a Synbook", *Hitotsubashi Journal of Economics*, 25 (2), pp. 1-20.

Kojima, Kiyoshi (1985), "The Allocation of Japanese Direct Foreign Investment and Its Evolution in Asia", *Hitotsubashi Journal of Economics*, 26(2), pp. 99-116.

Kojima, Kiyoshi (1985), "Japanese and American Direct Investment in Asia:

A Comparative Analysis", *Hitotsubashi Journal of Economics*, 26 (2), pp. 1-35.

Kojima, Kiyoshi (1990), *Japanese Direct Investment Abroad,* Tokyo: International Christian University, Social Science Research Institute.

Komaran, R. V. (1986), *Singapore Investment in China,* a dissertation submitted to the National University of Singapore, as a partial fulfilment of the Advanced Study Project, for the Master in Business Administration.

Krause, Lawrence B., Koh, Ai Tee and Lee, Tsao Yuan (1988), *The Singapore Economy Reconsidered,* Singapore: Institute of Southeast Asian Studies.

Kravis, Irving B. (1970), "Trade as a Handmaiden of Growth: Similarities between the Nineteenth and Twentieth Centuries", *Economic Journal,* 80 (320), pp. 850-872.

Kreinin, Mordechai E. and Plummer, Michael G. (1992), "Effects of Economic Integration in Industrial Countries on ASEAN and the Asian NIEs", *World Development,* 20(9), pp. 1345-66.

Kumar, K. and Mcleod, M. G. (1981), *Multinationals from Third World Countries,* Lexington: Heath.

Kumar, Sree and Lee, Tsao Yuan (1991), "A Singapore Perspective", in *Growth Triangle: The Johor-Singapore-Riau Experience,* in Lee Tsao Yuan (ed.), Singapore: Institute of Southeast Asian Studies.

Kumar, Sree and Lee, Tsao Yuan (1991), "Growth Triangles, Belts and Circles", *Trends,* Singapore: Institute of Southeast Asian Studies.

Kwack, Sung Y. (1972), "A Model of US Direct Investment Abroad: A Neoclassical Approach", *Western Economic Journal,* 10 (4), pp. 373-83.

Lall, Rajiv B. (1986), *Multinationals from the Third World: Indian Firms Investing Abroad,* Oxford: Oxford University Press.

Lall, Sanjaya (1980), "Monopolistic Advantages and Foreign Involvement by U.S. Manufacturing Industry", *Oxford Economic Papers,* 32, pp. 102-22.

Lall, Sanjaya (1982), "Export of Capital from Developing Countries: India", in J. Black and John H. Dunning (eds.), *International Capital Movements,* London: Macmillan.

Lall, Sanjaya (1983), *The New Multinationals: The Spread of Third World Enterprises,* Singapore: John Wiley.

Lall, Sanjaya and Siddharthan, N. S. (1982), "The Monopolistic Advantages of Multinationals: Lessons from Foreign Investment in the U.S.", *Economic Journal,* 92(367), pp. 668-83.

Lall, Sanjaya and Streeten, Paul (1980), *Foreign Investment, Transnational and Developing Countries,* London: The Macmillan Press.

Langhammer, Rolf J. (1991), "Competition among Developing Countries for Foreign Investment in the Eighties: Whom Did the OECD Investors Prefer?", *Weltwirtschaftliches Archiv,* 127(2), pp. 390-403.

Langhammer, Rolf J. (1992), "Salient Features of Trade Among Former Soviet Union Republics: Facts, Flaws and Findings", *Aussenwirtschaft*, Band 47, pp. 253-77.

Lau, Geok Theng, et al (1991), *Marketing the Growth Triangle: The Batam Case*, Faculty of Business Administration, National University of Singapore, mimeo.

Lecraw, D. (1985), "Singapore", in Dunning, J. H. (ed.), *Multinational Enterprises, Economic Structure and International Competitiveness*, London: Wiley.

Lee, Chung H. (1980), "Direct Foreign Investment and Its Economic Effects: A Review", *Journal of Economic Development*, 5(2), pp. 139-50.

Lee, Chung H. (1984), "Direct Foreign Investment and Industrial Development in the Pacific Basin", in Benjamin, Roger and Kudrle, Robert T. (eds), *The Industrial Future of the Pacific Basin*, London: Westview Press.

Lee, Chung H. (1984), "On Japanese Macroeconomic Theories of Direct Foreign Investment", *Economic Development and Cultural Change*, 32(4), pp. 713-23.

Lee, Chung H. (1990), "Direct Foreign Investment, Structural Adjustment, and International Division of Labor: A Dynamic Macroeconomic Theory of Direct Foreign Investment", *Hitotsubashi Journal of Economics*, 31(2), pp. 61-72.

Lee, J. and Go, E. M. (1988), "Foreign Capital, Balance of Payments and External Debt in Developing Asia", in shinichi ichimura (ed.), *Challenge of Asian Developing Countries*, Tokyo: Asian Productivity Organization, pp. 227-297.

Lee, Kuan Yew (1989), Speech Delivered in Tokyo, Far Eastern Economic Review, 18 August.

Lee, Lai To (1984), "Singapore's Continuous Search For Quality", *Southeast Asian Affairs*, pp. 279-93.

Lee, Soo Ann (1973), *The Industrialisation of Singapore*, Camberwell: Longman.

Lee, Soo Ann (1977), "Effects of the British Withdrawal", in Adult Education Board, Singapore, *Papers on Economic Planning and Development in Singapore* (Singapore: Adult Education Board, pp. 44-51).

Lee, Soo Ann (1977), *Singapore Goes Transnational*, Singapore: Eastern Universities Press.

Lee, Tsao Yuan (1988), "The Government in Labour Market", in Lawrence B. Krause, Koh Ai Tee and Lee Yuan (eds.), *The Singapore Economy Reconsidered*, Singapore: Institute of Southeast Asian Studies.

Lee, Tsao Yuan (1990), "EC-1992: The Perspective of the Asian NIEs", Paper prepared for a conference on *The EC After 1992: Perspective from the*

Outside, by University of Basel.

Lee, Tsao Yuan (1991), *Growth Triangle: The Johor-Singapore-Riau Experience,* Singapore: Institute of Southeast Asian Studies.

Lee, Tsao Yuan (1992), "Global Regionalism and Regional Economic Zones in the Asia-Pacific: The Promise and Challenge of the 90s", *Business Times,* 15 April 1992.

Lee, Tsao Yuan (1992), "Regional Economic Zones in the Asia-Pacific: A Conceptual Overview", paper presented at the conference on *Regional Cooperation and Growth Triangles in ASEAN,* jointly organised by Centre for Business Research and Development, Faculty of Business Administration and the Centre for Advanced Studies, Faculty of Arts & Social Sciences, National University of Singapore, 23-24 April.

Lee, Tsao Yuan (1992), *Singapore: The Year in Review 1991,* Singapore: The Institute of Policy Studies.

Levinsohn, James A. (1989), "Strategic Trade Policy When Firms Can Invest Abroad: When Are Tariffs and Quotas Equivalent?", *Journal of International Economics,* 27(1-2), pp. 129-46.

Levy, Santiago and Sean Nolan (1992), "Trade and Foreign Investment Policies Under Imperfect Competition: Lessons for Developing Countries", *Journal of Development Economics,* 37 (1-2), pp. 31-62.

Liew, S. L. (1990), "Charting a Global Strategy: Creating Competitive Advantage through the Growth Triangle", *Economic Bulletin Special Report,* November, pp. 14-18.

Lim, Chong Yah (1983), "Singapore's Economic Development: Retrospect and Prospect", in Peter S. J. Chen (ed.), *Singapore Development Policies and Trends,* Singapore: Oxford University Press, pp. 89-104.

Lim, Chong Yah (1984), *Economic Restructuring in Singapore,* Singapore: Federal Publication.

Lim, Chong Yah (1988), *Policy Options for Singapore Economy,* London: McGraw-Hill Company.

Lim, David (1992), "Capturing the Effects of Capital Subsidies", *Journal of Development Studies,* 28(4), pp. 705-16.

Lim, H. K. (1988), *Problems and Prospects of Singapore Multinationals,* a dissertation submitted to National University of Singapore, as a partial fulfilment of the Advanced Study Project for the degree of Master of Business Administration.

Lim, Linda Yuen-Ching (1978), *Multinational Firms and Manufacturing for Export in Less-Developed Countries,* vols. 1 and 11 (PhD book, University of Michigan).

Lim, Linda Yuen-Ching (1983), "Singapore's Success: The Myth of the Free

Market Economy", *Asian Survey*, 23 (6), pp. 753-70.

Lim, Mab Hui (1979), *Ownership and Control of the One Hundred Largest Corporations in Malaysia*, Oxford: Oxford University Press.

Lim, M. H. and Teoh, K. F. (1986), "Singapore Corporations go Transnational", *Journal of Southeast Asian Studies*, 17 (2), pp. 336-365.

Little, I. M. D. (1981), "The Experience and Causes of Rapid Labour-Intensive Development in Korea, Taiwan province, Hong Kong and Singapore; and the Possibilities of Emulation" in Eddy Lee (ed.), *Export-Led Industrialisation and Development*, Geneva: International Labour Organisation, pp. 23-46.

Little, Jane Sneddon (1985), "Multinational Corporations and Foreign Investment: Current Trends and Issues", in Adams, John (ed.), *The Contemporary International Economy: A Reader*, London: St. Martin's Press.

Livingstone, J. M. (1989), *The Internationalization of Business*, New York: St. Martin's Press.

Lundgren, N. (1977), "Comment",in *The International Allocation of Economic Activity*, Ohlin, B., Hesselborn, P.O. and Wijikman, P.M. (eds.), London: MacMillan.

MacCharles, Donald C. (1987), *Trade among Multinationals: Intra-industry trade and national competitiveness*, London: Croom Helm.

Markusen, James R. (1984), "Multinationals, Multi-Plant Economies, and the Gains from Trade", *Journal of International Economics*, 16, pp. 205-226.

Marris, Robin (1964), *The Economic Theory of "Managerial" Capitalism*, London: MacMillan Press.

Martin, Stephen (1991), "Direct Foreign Investment in the United States", *Journal of Economic Behaviour and Organization*, 16(3), pp. 283-93.

McClintock, Brent (1988), "Recent Theories of Direct Foreign Investment: An Institutionalist Perspective", *Journal of Economic Issues*, 22(2), pp. 477-84.

McClintock, Brent (1989), "Direct Foreign Investment: Reply", *Journal of Economic Issues*, 23(3), pp. 885-89.

McManus, J. C. (1972), *The Theory of the Multinational Firm and the Nation State*, Toronto: Collier, MacMillan.

McMillan, Carl H. (1987), *Multinationals from the second world: Growth of Foreign Investment by Soviet and East European Enterprises*, London: St. Martin's Press.

Milkman, Ruth (1992), "The Impact of Foreign Investment on U.S. Industrial Relations: The Case of California's Japanese-Owned Plants", *Economic and Industrial Democracy*, 13(2), pp. 151-82.

Milne, R. S. (1966), "Singapore's Exit From Malaysia: The Consequences of Ambiguity", *Asian Survey*, VI (3), pp. 175-84.

Ministry of Communications and Information, *Singapore*, Singapore:

Ministry of Communications and Information, various years.

Ministry of Finance, *State of Singapore Development Plan 1961, 1961-1964,* Singapore: Ministry of Finance.

Ministry of Finance (1964), *Development Plan 1961-1964,* Singapore: Government Printer.

Ministry of Information and the Arts (1991), *Singapore 1991,* Singapore: Ministry of Information and the Arts.

Ministry of Trade and Industry (1986), *The Singapore Economy: New Directions,* Singapore: National Printers.

Ministry of Trade and Industry, *Economic Survey of Singapore,* Singapore: National Printers, various years.

Mirus, Rolf (1980), "A Note on the Choice between Licensing and Direct Foreign Investment", *Journal of International Business Studies,* 11(1), pp. 86-91.

Mirza, Hafiz (1986), *Multinationals and the Growth of the Singapore Economy,* London: Croom Helm.

Mirza, Hafiz (1989), "The Strategy of Pacific Asian Multinationals", in Peter J. Buckley (ed.), *The Multinational Enterprise: Theory and Applications,* London: MacMillan.

Miyagiwa, Kaz (1990), *International Capital Mobility and National Welfare,* London: Garland.

Moran, Theodore H. (1986), *Investing in Development: New Roles for Private Capital?,* Oxford: Transaction Books.

Morck, Randall and Yeung, Bernard (1991), "Why Investors Value Multinationality", *Journal of Business,* 64(2), pp. 165-87.

Morris, Jonathan (1991), *Japan and the Global Economy: Issues and Trends in the 1990s,* London: Routledge.

Mubariq, Ahmad (1992), Economic Cooperation in the Southern Growth Triangle: An Indonesian Perspective", paper presented at a Conference on *Regional Cooperation and Growth Triangles in ASEAN,* jointly organised by Centre for Business Research & Development, Faculty of Business Administration and Centre for Advanced Studies, Faculty of Arts & Social Sciences, National University of Singapore, 23-24 April.

National Research Council (1990), *The Internationalization of U.S. Manufacturing: Causes and Consequences,* Washington, D.C.: National Academy Press.

National Wage Council (1978), *Information Booklet,* Singapore: National Printers.

Naya, Seiji and Eric D. Ramstetter (1988), "Policy Interactions and Direct Foreign Investment in East and Southeast Asia", *Journal of World Trade,* 22

(2), pp. 57-71.

Ng, Chee Yuen and Wong, Poh Kam (1991), "The Growth Triangle: A Market Driven Response", *Asia Club Papers 2*, Tokyo: Asia Club, pp. 123-52.

Nyaw, Mee-Kau (1979), *Industrial Growth and Export Expansion in Singapore*, Hong Kong: Kingsway International.

Ong, Nai Pew and Lim, Cin (1985), "Slack Demand is Only Half the Story", *Straits Times*, July 31.

Ozawa, Terutomo (1972), "Labour Resource Oriented Migration of Japanese Industries to Taiwan, Singapore and South Korea", *Economics Staff Working paper*, World Bank, no. 134.

Ozawa, Terutomo (1975), "The Emergence of Japan's Multinationalism: Patterns and Competition, *Asian Survey*, 15, pp. 1036-53.

Ozawa, Terutomo (1979), "International Investment and Industrial Structure: New Theoretical Implications from the Japanese Experience", *Oxford Economic Papers*, 31 (1), pp. 72-92.

Ozawa, Terutomo (1982), "A Newer Type of Foreign Investment in Third World Resource Development", *Rivista Internazionale di Scienze Economiche e Commerciali*, 29(12), pp. 1133-51.

Ozawa, Terutomo (1991), "The Dynamics of Pacific Rim Industrialisation: How Mexico can join the Flock of Flying Geese" in Roett, R. (ed.), *Mexico's External Relations in the 1990's*, London: Lynne Reinner.

Ozawa, Terutomo (1991), *Japanese Multinationals and 1992*, in Brugenmeier, B. and L.M. Mucchielli (eds), Multinationals and Europe 1992, London: Routledge.

Pang, Eng Fong (1978), "Changing Patterns of Industrial Relations in Singapore", in   Peter S. J. Chen and Hans-Dieter Evers (eds), *Studies in ASEAN Sociology*, Singapore:Chopmen, pp. 422-36.

Pang, Eng Fong (1980), "Factors Which Hinder or Help Productivity Improvement in the Asian Region: A Review and the Prospects", *APO Basic Research Project*, National Report.

Pang, Eng Fong (1981), "Economic Development and the Labour Market in a Newly Industrializing Country: The Experience of Singapore", *The Developing Economies*, XIX (1), pp. 3-15.

Pang, Eng Fong (1981), "Foreign Indirect Investment in Singapore: A Preliminary Report", mimeo, *Economic Research Centre*, National University of Singapore.

Pang, Eng Fong and Komaran, R. V. (1985), "Singapore Multinationals", *Columbia Journal of World Business*, 20 (2), pp. 35-42.

Pang, Eng Fong and Lim, Linda (1981), "Rapid Growth and Relative Price Stability in a Small Open Economy: The Experience of Singapore", Paper prepared for the *Conference on Experiences and Lessons of Small Open*

Economies, organised by the Faculty of Economic and Administrative Sciences of the Catholic University of Chile, Santiago, 11-13 November.

Pang, Eng Fong and Lim, Linda (1982), "Political Economy of a City-State", *Singapore Business Yearbook 1982*, Singapore: Times Periodicals, pp. 7-33.

Pang, Eng Fong and Tan, Chwee Huat (1983), "Trade Unions and Industrial Relations", in Peter S. J. Chen (ed.), *Singapore Development Politics and Trends*, Singapore: Oxford University Press, pp. 227-39.

Papanastassiou, M. and Pearce, R. D. (1990), "Host Country Characteristics and the Sourcing Behaviour of UK Manufacturing Industry", University of Reading, Discussion papers in *International Investment and Business Studies*, Series B, no. 140.

Park, Eul Y. (1984), "Patterns of Foreign Direct Investment, Foreign Ownership, and Industrial Performance: The Case of the Korean Manufacturing Industry", in Benjamin, Roger and Kudrle, Robert T. (eds), *The Industrial Future of the Pacific Basin*, London: Westview Press.

Partadiredja, Ace and Yeoh, Caroline (1991), *Migrant Workers in a Corner of the Growth Triangle*, Faculty of Business Administration, National University of Singapore, mimeo.

Patterson, Seymour (1989), *The Microeconomics of Trade*, Kirksville, Mo.: Thomas Jefferson University Press.

Pazos, Felipe (1988), "Foreign Investment Revisited", in Jorge, Antonio and Salazar-Carrillo, Jorge (eds.), *Foreign Investment, Debt and Economic Growth in Latin America*, London: St. Martin's Press.

Pearce, R. D. (1989), *The Internationalisation of Sales by Leading Enterprises: Some Firm, Industry and Country Determinants*, University of Reading, Discussion papers in *International Investment and Business Studies*, Series B, no. 135.

Penrose, Edith T. (1959), *The Theory of the Growth of the Firm*, Oxford: Basil Blackwell.

Perry, Martin (1991), "The Singapore Growth Triangle: State, Capital and Labour at a New Frontier in the World Economy", *Singapore Journal of Tropical Geography*, 12 (2), pp. 138-151.

Popkin, J. (1965), *Interfirm Differences in Direct Investment Behaviour of US Manufacturers* (Ph.D Dissertation, submitted to University of Pennsylvania).

Porter, Michael E. (1980), *Competitive Strategy: Techniques for Analyzing Industries and Competitors*, New York: Free Press.

Porter, Michael E.(1983), *Transnational Corporations in World Development: Third Survey*, New York: United Nations.

Porter, Michael E.(1989), *Transnational Corporations in World Development: A Reexamination*, New York: United Nations.

Prime Minister's National Day Rally Speech, Singapore: Ministry of Information, 1992.

Probert, Jocelyn (1991), *Asian Direct Investment in Europe*, a research carried out for Euro-Asia Centre, INSEAD.

Ragazzi, Giorgio (1973), "Theories of the Determinants of Direct Foreign Investment", *International Monetary Fund Staff Papers*, 20(2), pp. 471-98.

Rajaratnam, S. (1972), *Singapore: Global City*, Address to Singapore Press Club, February, Ministry of Culture.

Ramstetter, Eric D. (1991), *Direct Foreign Investment in Asia's Developing Economies and Structural Change in the Asia-Pacific Region*, Boulder and Oxford: Westview Press.

Ranis, Gustav (1985), "Can the East Asian Model of Development be Generalised? A Comment", *World Development*, 13(4), pp. 543-5.

Regnier, Philippe (1987), *Singapore: City-State in Southeast Asia*, London: Hurst & Company.

Reuber, G. L. et al (1973), *Private Foreign Investment in Development*, Oxford: Clarendon Press.

Richardson, J. D. (1971), "On 'Going Abroad': The Firm's Initial Foreign Investment Decision", *Quarterly Review of Economics and Business*, 11(4), pp. 7-22.

Riedal, James (1984), "Trade as the Engine of Growth in Developing Countries, Revisited", *Economic Journal*, 94 (373), pp. 56-73.

Riedel, James (1991)", "Intra-Asian Trade and Foreign Direct Investment", *Asian Development Review*, 9 (1), pp. 1-30.

Rivera-Batiz, Francisco L. and Rivera-Batiz, Luis A. (1992), *International Economic Journal*, 6(1), pp. 45-57.

Robert, Vicat Turrell and Jean Jacques Van-Helten (1987), "The Investment Group: The Missing Link in British Overseas Expansion Before 1914?", *Economic History Review*, 40 (2), pp. 267-274.

Rodan, Garry (1985), "Industrialisation and the Singapore State in the context of the New International Division of Labour", in R. Higgott and R. Robison (eds), *Southeast Asia: Essays in the Political Economy of Structural Change*, London; Routledge & Kegan Paul, pp. 172-94.

Rodan, Garry (1987), "The Rise and Fall of Singapore's Second Industrial Revolution", in Richard Robison, Kevin Hewison and Richard Higgott (eds), *Southeast Asia In the 1980s: The Politics of Economics Crisis*, Sydney: Allen & Unwin, pp. 149-76.

Rodan, Garry (1989), *The Political Economy of Singapore's Industrialisation: National State and International Capital*, London: MacMillan.

Roemer, John E. (1976), "Japanese Direct Foreign Investment in Manufactures: Some Comparisons with the US Pattern", *Quarterly*

Review of Economics and Business, 16(2), pp. 91-111.

Root, Franklin R. (1990), *International Trade and Investment*, Cincinnati: South-Western.

Root, Franklin R. and Ahmed, A. A. (1979), "Empirical Determinants of Manufacturing Direct Foreign Investment in Developing Countries", *Development and Cultural Change*, 27 (4), pp. 751-67.

Safarian, A. E. and Bertin, Gilles Y. (1987), *Multinationals, Governments and International Technology Transfer*, London: St. Martin's Press.

Sassen, Saskia (1988), *The Mobility of Labour and Capital: A Study in International Investment and Labour Flow*, Cambridge: Cambridge University Press.

Scaperlanda, Anthony E. and Mauer, Lawrence J. (1969), "The Determinants of US Direct Investment in the EEC", *The American Economic Review*, 59 (2), pp. 558-68.

Schaefer, Jeffrey M. and Strongin, David G. (1989), "Why all the Fuss about Foreign Investment", *Challenge*, 32(3), pp. 31-35.

Schive, Chi and Majumdar, Badiul A. (1990), "Direct Foreign Investment and Linkage Effects: The Experience of Taiwan", *Canadian Journal of Development Studies*, 11(2), pp. 325-42.

Schmitz, Andrew and Bieri, Jurg (1972), "EEC Tariffs and US Direct Investment", *European Economic Review*, 3 (1), pp. 259-70.

Scott, Norman (1992), "Implications of the Transition for Foreign Trade and Investment", *Oxford Review of Economic Policy*, 8(1), pp. 45-57.

Shapiro, Daniel M. (1980), "Domestic Determinants of U.S. Direct Foreign Investment Outflows", *Economia Internazionale*, 33(1), pp. 58-70.

Shee, Poon Kim (1979), "Singapore 1978: Preparation For The 1980s", *Asian Survey*, XIX (2), pp. 124-30.

Singapore Business, *Global Opportunities*, September 1989.

Smith, M., McLoughlin, Lange, J. P. and Chapman, R. (1985), Asia's New, Industrial World, London: Methleen.

Stevens, Guy V. G. (1969), *US Direct Manufacturing Investment to Latin America: Some Economic and Political Determinants* (mimeographed, June).

Stevens, Guy V. G. (1969), "Fixed Investment Expenditure of Foreign Manufacturing Affiliates of US Firms: Theoretical Models and Empirical Evidence", *Yale Economic Essays*, 9 (1), pp. 137-200.

Stevens, Guy V. G. (1972), "Capital Mobility and the International Firm", in *The International Mobility and Movement of Capital* (ed.), by F. Machlup, et al., New York: Columbia University.

Stevens, Guy V. G. (1974), "Determinants of Investment", in *Economic Analysis and the Multinational Enterprise* (ed.), by John Dunning, London: Allen & Unwin.

Stevens, Guy V. G. and Lipsey, Robert E. (1992), "Interactions between Domestic and Foreign Investment", *Journal of International Money and Finance*, 11(1), pp. 40-62.

Stulz, Rene M. (1983), "On the Determinants of Net Foreign Investment", *Journal of Finance*, 38(2), pp. 459-68.

Svedberg, Peter (1978), "The Portfolio-Direct Composition of Private Foreign Investment in 1914 Revisited", *The Economic Journal*, 88, pp. 763-777.

Swedenborg B. (1979), *The Multinational Operations of Swedish Firms: An Analysis of Determinants and Effects*, Stockholm: Industrial Utrednings-institut.

Tan, Augustine H. H. (1985), "Singapore's Economy: Growth and Structural Change", paper prepared for a Conference on *Singapore and the United States into the 1990s*, November 6-8.

Tan, Augustine H. H. and Hock, Ow Chin (1982), 'Singapore', in Bela Belassa and Associates, *Development Strategies in Semi-Industrial Countries*, World Bank: The John Hopkins University Press.

Tan, Loong-Hoe (1992), "Single European Market in 1992: Implications and Responses from Singapore", paper presented at *Colloquium on ASEAN and Europe 1992*, Kuala Lumpur.

Tokunaga, Shojiro (1992), *Japan's Foreign Investment and Asian Economic Interdependence: Production, Trade, and Financial Systems*, Tokyo: University of Tokyo Press.

Torrisi, C. R. (1985), "The Determinants of Direct Foreign Investment in a Small LDC", *Journal of Economic Development*, 10(1), pp. 29-45.

Trevor, Malcolm (1987), *The internationalization of Japanese business: European and Japanese perspectives*, Boulder, Colo.: Westview Press.

Turnbull, C. M. (1977), *A History of Singapore, 1819-1975*, London: Oxford University Press.

Turner, Louis (1973), *Multinational Companies and the Third World*, New York: Hill & Wang.

United Nations (1963), *A Proposed Industrialisation Programme for the State of Singapore*, New York: UN Industrial Survey Mission.

United Nations (1992), *World Investment Report 1992*, New York: United Nations.

United Nations Industrial Development Organization (1985), *Regional industrial co-operation: Experiences and Perspective of ASEAN and the Andean pact*, Vienna: UNIDO Publication.

Uno, Kimio (1987), *Japanese Industrial Performance*, Oxford: Elsevier Science.

Van-Thiel, Servaas (1984), "Tax Incentives for Foreign Investment", Bulletin for International Fiscal Documentation, 38(11), pp. 497-500.

Vatikiotis, M. (1991), "Search For a Hinterland: Singapore Appeals to

Neighbours' Enlightened Self-interest", *Far Eastern Economic Review*, 3rd January.

Vernon, Raymond (1966), "International Investment and International Trade in the Product Cycle", *Quarterly Journal of Economics*, 80, pp. 190-207.

Vernon, Raymond (1971), "The Multinational Enterprise: Power vs. Sovereignty, *Foreign Affairs*, 49, pp. 736-51.

Vernon, Raymond (1971), *Sovereignty at Bay: The Multinational Spread of U.S. Enterprises*, London: Longman.

Vernon, Raymond (1974), "Competition Policy Toward Multinational Corporations", *The American Economic Review*, 64 (2), pp. 276-82.

Vernon, Raymond (1979), "The Product Cycle Hypothesis in a New International Environment", *Oxford Bulletin of Economics and Statistics*, 41 (4), pp. 255-67.

Von-Furstenberg, George M. (1980), "Domestic Determinants of Net U.S. Foreign Investment", *International Monetary Fund Staff Papers*, 27(4), pp. 637-78.

Wade, R. (1990), *Governing the Market: Economic Theory and the Role of Government in East Asian Industrialisation*, Princeton: Princeton University Press.

Wain, Barry (1979), "The ASEAN Report", *The Asian Wall Street Journal*, 1, pp. 1-5.

Walia, Tirlochan S. (1976), *An Empirical Evaluation of Selected Theories of Foreign Direct Investment by U.S. Based Multinational Corporations* (Ph.D Dissertation, New York University, Graduate School of Business Administration).

Wang, Jian Ye and Blomstrom, Magnus (1992), "Foreign Investment and Technology Transfer: A Simple Model", *European Economic Review*, 36(1), pp. 137-55.

Weintraub, Robert (1967), "Studio empirico sulle relazionidi lungo andare tra movimenti di capitali e rendimenti differenziali", *Rivista Internazionale di Scienze Economiche e Commerciali*, 14 (2), pp. 401-15.

Wells, Louis T., Jr. (1978), "Foreign Investment from the Third World: The Experience of Chinese Firms from Hong Kong", *Columbia Journal of World Business*, pp. 39-49.

Wells, Louis T., Jr. and Wint, Alvin G. (1990), *Marketing a Country: Promotion as a Tool for Attracting Foreign Investment*, Washington, D.C.: Multilateral Investment Guarantee Agency.

Wheeler, David and Mody, Ashoka (1992), "International Investment Location Decisions: The Case of U.S. Firms", *Journal of International Economics*, 33(1-2), pp. 57-76.

White, Gordon (1988), *Developmental States in East Asia*, London: Macmillan.

Wie, Thee Kian (1991), "The Surge of Asian NIC Investment into Indonesia", *Bulletin of Indonesian Economic Studies*, 27(3), pp. 55-88.

Wildsmith, J. R. (1973), *Managerial Theories of the Firm*, New York: Dunellen, p. 409.

Wilkins, Mira (1988), "The Free-Standing Company, 1870-1914: An Important Type of British Foreign Direct Investment", *Economic History*, 41 (2), pp. 259-82.

Wilkins, Mira (1989), *The history of foreign investment in the United States to 1914*, Cambridge, Mass. and London: Harvard University Press.

Williamson, Oliver E. (1967), *Economics of Discretionary Behaviour: Managerial Objectives in a Theory of the Firm*, Chicago: Markham.

Williamson, Oliver E. (1970), *Corporate Control and Business Behaviour*, Englewood Cliffs, N.J.: Prentice-Hall.

Williamson, Oliver E. (1971), "The Vertical Integration of Production: Market Failure Considerations", *American Economic Review*, 61 (2), pp. 112-27.

Williamson, Oliver E. (1975), *Markets and Hierarchies: Analysis and Anti-Trust Implications: A Study in the Economics of Internal Organisation*, New York: Free Press.

Williamson, Oliver E. (1979), "Transaction-cost Economics: The Governance of Contractual Relations", *Journal of Law and Economics*, 22 (2), pp. 233-61.

Williamson, Oliver E. (1981), "The Modern Corporation: Origins, Evolution, Attributes", *Journal of Economic Literature*, 19 (4), pp. 1537-68.

Wong, K. P. (1980), *The Cultural Impact of Multinational Corporations in Singapore*, Paris: United Nations Educational, Scientific and Cultural Organization.

Wong, Weng Kong, et al (1991), "Transnational Investments in Johor Opportunities and Strategies for Singapore Entrepreneurs", paper presented at the World Conference on *Entrepreneurship and Innovative Change*, organised by NTU-Peat Marwick Entrepreneurship Development Centre, Nanyang Technological University, Singapore, July 3-5.

World Bank (1989), *World Development Report 1989*, Oxford: Oxford University Press.

World Bank (1992), *World Development Report 1992*, Oxford: Oxford University Press.

World Bank (1993), The East Asian Miracle, Washington.

Wu, De Min (1989), "An Empirical Analysis of Japanese Direct Investment in Taiwan: A Neoclassical Approach", in Lee, Cheng F. and Hu, Sheng Cheng (eds.), *Taiwan's Foreign Investment, Exports and Financial Analysis*, London: JAI Press.

181

Yeoh, Caroline, et al (1990), "Batam: A New Dimension in ASEAN Economic Co-operation", Paper presented at the conference on *Industrial and Trade Policies for the 1990s: Prospects and Implications for Developed and Developing Countries*, 19-21 September, Maastricht, the Netherlands.

Yeoh, Caroline, et al (1992), *Strategic Business Opportunities in the Growth Triangle*, Singapore: Longman.

Yoshihara, Kunio (1976), *Foreign Investment and Domestic Response: A Study of Singapore's Industrialisation*, Singapore: Eastern Universities Press.

You, Poh Seng and Lim, Chong Yah (1984), *Singapore: Twenty-five years of Development*, Singapore: Nan Xing Zhou Lianhe Zaobao.

Young, Alwyn (1992), *A Tale of Two Cities: Factor Accumulation and Technical Change in Hong Kong and Singapore*, Unpublished Material for the National Bureau of Economic Research.

Young, Kan H. and Steigerwald, Charles E. (1990), "Is Foreign Investment in the U.S. Transferring U.S. Technology Abroad?", *Business Economics*, 25(4), pp. 28-30.

Zhuravlev, S. N. (1992), "Foreign Investments in the Economy: Methods for Regulating Their Volume and Structure", *Matekon*, 28 (2), pp. 45-63.

Appendices

Appendix A1 Singapore: General Elections, 1955 - 91

	No. of Seats[1]	No. of Parties Contesting	Party Returned	No. of Seats Won	% Votes Won
Legislation Assembly					
1955 April 2	25[2]	5&11 Independents	Labour Front	10	26.7
1959 May 30	51	10&39 Independents	PAP	43	53.4
1963 Sept 21	51	8&16 Independents	PAP	37	46.5
Parliament					
1968 April 13	7 + (51)	2&5 Independents	PAP	58	84.4
1972 Sept. 2	57 + (8)	6&2 Independents	PAP	65	69.0
1976 Dec. 23	53 + (16)	7&2 Independents	PAP	69	72.4
1980 Dec. 23	38 + (37)	8	PAP	75	75.6
1984 Dec. 22	49 + (30)	9	PAP	77	62.9
1988 Sept. 3	70 + (11)[3]	7	PAP	80	61.8
1991 Aug. 31	40 + (41)		PAP	77	61.0

Notes:
1 Uncontested seats in brackets.
2 The 1955 Legislation Assembly consisted of one Speaker, three *ex-officio* members, 25 elected members, and four nominated members.
3 Includes 13 group representation.

Sources: Ministry of Culture (1992), *Singapore 1989: Country Profile 1991/92* and *Country Profile 1992*, London: The Economist Intelligent Unit.

Appendix A2 Singapore: Principal Statistics of Manufacturing, 1960 - 90

Year	Establishments	Workers	Materials	Output	Value Added	Direct Exports	Employees' Remuneration	Capital Expenditure
1960	548	27,416	302,846	465,568	142,143	164,310	66,975	9,806
1961	562	27,562	321,143	518,373	174,364	179,068	71,633	10,539
1962	605	28,642	432,626	660,300	201,680	217,501	76,863	33,274
1963	858	36,586	558,560	843,753	252,566	223,807	97,552	17,720
1964	930	41,488	605,744	927,928	282,462	266,422	111,125	52,688
1965	1,000	47,334	693,345	1,086,363	348,361	349,163	131,692	59,226
1966	1,123	52,807	870,605	1,325,782	415,043	404,865	150,754	75,533
1967	1,200	58,347	1,160,857	1,687,234	478,629	508,204	170,310	84,805
1968[1]	1,586	74,833	1,498,244	2,175,668	611,758	598,466	210,699	89,573
1969[2]	1,714	100,758	2,271,584	3,123,899	856,631	1,265,286	319,803	212,578
1970	1,747	120,509	2,668,394	3,891,012	1,093,722	1,523,033	397,618	421,342
1971	1,813	140,522	3,150,082	4,699,246	1,366,520	1,954,683	503,209	460,571
1972	1,931	170,352	3,742,698	5,722,224	1,782,278	2,641,681	648,676	647,961
1973	2,079	198,574	5,064,990	7,938,073	2,540,597	4,269,774	861,407	787,954
1974	2,179	206,067	9,236,569	13,346,913	3,528,220	7,811,939	1,075,892	620,543
1975	2,385	191,528	8,586,011	12,610,144	3,411,129	7,200,693	1,180,524	622,635

Appendix A2 Singapore: Principal Statistics of Manufacturing, 1960 - 90 (Cont'd.)

Year	Establishments	Workers	Materials	Output	Value Added	Direct Exports	Employees' Remuneration	Capital Expenditure
1976	2,505	207,234	10,629,406	15,317,439	3,961,813	9,575,927	1,309,841	618,670
1977	2,638	219,112	12,224,625	17,558,249	4,475,458	10,969,405	1,471,749	751,639
1978	2,946	243,724	13,561,952	19,666,684	5,162,922	12,632,733	1,724,243	821,838
1979[3]	3,122	269,334	17,513,440	25,133,686	6,412,934	16,202,989	2,085,918	1,424,463
1980	3,355	285,250	21,415,150	31,657,895	8,521,888	19,172,916	2,526.8	1,861,859
1981	3,439	281,675	24,891,517	36,787,096	9,720,545	22,375,250	2,938.0	1,966,771
1982	3,586	275,450	24,854,426	36,467,443	9,355,941	21,858,690	3,270.6	2,222,730
1983	3,616	271,106	25,116,313	37,221,519	9,822,090	22,640,771	3,623.6	2,113,351
1984	3,648	274,391	27,474,362	41,077,861	11,106,272	25,057,754	4,045.0	2,986,080
1985	3,504	253,510	25,509,13	38,495,0	10,702,	24,276,	4,053.7	1,977,20
1986	3,449	246,682	23,233,90	37,258,7	11,899,	24,387,	3,769.1	1,746,35
1987	3,514	276,309	29,049,97	46,084,0	14,470,	30,379,	4,176.0	2,725,52
1988	3,624	324,713	35,288,80	56,470,0	17,918,	37,806,	5,056.5	3,546,95
1989	3,678	338,043	41,693.9	63,924.1	19,746.2	5,974.6	4,518.1	42,545.9
1990	3,716	352,067	46,960.9	71,578.5	21,694.3	6,861.9	4,190.3	47,099.9

Notes:

1   Data for the petroleum industry in the 1969 census was extended to include blending activity, which accounted for about 28 percent of the increase in output.

2   Prior to 1970, data included repair and servicing of motor vehicles and other household goods and carpentry and joinery work which accounted for about 0.6 percent of output and 0.1 percent of value added in 1969.

3   Prior to 1980, data on output and sales of petroleum refining industry included the value of products processed for third party overseas.

Source: Singapore, Department of Statistics, *Census of Industrial Production*, 1970-92.

Appendix A3 Singapore: Selected Ratios of Principal Manufacturing Statistics, 1961 - 90

Year	Value Added Per Worker	Output Per Worker	Value Added to Output	Remuneration to Value Added	Remuneration to Output	Direct Exports to Total Sales	Direct Exports to Output
	S$		Percent				
1961	6,100	42,906	14.2	41.9	6.0	58.1	58.6
1962	6,924	50,522	13.7	37.9	5.2	67.3	66.9
1963	6,900	38,258	18.0	37.7	6.8	52.5	52.5
1964	6,845	34,492	19.8	38.3	7.6	52.6	51.9
1965	7,207	33,295	21.6	37.9	8.2	51.6	51.4
1966	7,732	35,228	21.9	36.4	8.0	43.3	42.8
1967	9,192	35,422	22.5	35.6	7.9	41.1	40.7
1968	8,146	35,409	23.0	34.3	7.9	36.3	36.3
1969	8,600	40,522	21.2	36.6	7.8	45.7	46.2
1970	9,029	36,619	24.7	36.4	9.0	44.6	00.2
1971	9,705	36,137	26.9	36.7	9.9	44.1	44.7
1972	10,388	34,962	29.7	36.6	10.9	47.9	47.5
1973	12,856	42,945	29.9	33.8	10.1	54.9	54.9
1974	17,127	67,795	25.3	30.5	7.7	60.7	59.8
1975	17,763	67,679	26.2	34.7	9.1	58.6	57.7
1976	19,168	76,724	25.0	33.0	8.2	61.9	62.8
1977	20,417	82,277	24.8	32.9	8.2	62.8	62.4

Appendix A3 Singapore: Selected Ratios of Principal Manufacturing Statistics, 1961 - 90 (Cont'd.)

	Value Added Per Worker	Output Per Worker	Value Added to Output	Remuneration to Value Added	Remuneration to Output	Direct Exports to Total Sales	Direct Exports to Output
Year	S$		Percent				
1978	21,179	83,144	25.5	33.4	8.5	64.2	63.9
1979[3]	23,992	96,835	24.8	32.3	8.0	64.1	64.2
1980	30,027	113,844	26.4	29.5	7.8	61.9	60.6
1981	34,681	132,488	26.2	30.1	7.9	61.1	60.7
1982	33,966	132,392	25.6	35.0	9.0	60.0	59.9
1983	36,230	137,295	26.4	36.9	9.7	60.5	60.8
1984	40,476	149,706	27.0	36.1	9.8	61.2	61.0
1985	42,436	152,345	27.9	37.7	10.5	63.0	62.8
1986	48,352	151,385	31.9	31.6	10.1	64.7	65.3
1987	52,362	166,801	31.4	28.9	9.0	65.9	65.9
1988	54,370	171,838	31.6	28.2	9.8	67.1	65.9
1989	58,413	189,100	30.9	30.3	9.3	66.9	5.6
1990	61,620	203,309	30.3	31.6	9.6	65.5	65.8

Sources: Department of Statistics, *Census of Industrial Production* and *Yearbook of Statistics*, 1970-92.

Appendix A4 Singapore: Export Performance, 1960 - 90

Value in S$ million	1960	1965	1970	1975	1980	1985	1986	1987	1988	1989	1990	1995	1996
Total export	3,427	3,004	4,756	12,758	41,452	50,179	48,986	60.266	79,051	87.117	95.256	167.515	176.272
Re-export	3,209	2,239	2,924	5,218	15,647	17,603	16,923	21,195	29,496	31,865	32,452	69,042	72,683
Domestic Exports	0,218	0,762	1,832	7,540	25,805	32,576	32,062	39,071	49,555	55,252	62,754	98,473	103,589
Oil (SITC3)	-	-	0,792	3,233	11,612	15,840	11,98020	11,753	11,341	13,224	17,137	13,721	16.551
Non-oil	-	-	1,040	4,307	14,193	16,735	00,082	27,317	32,214	42,028	45,618	84,751	87,038
Exports (SITC 5-8)	0,735	0,935	1,321	5,337	18,522	26,260	24,477	30,501	37,999	42,546	47,520	-	-
Total Imports	4,078	3,807	3,807	19,270	51,345	57,818	55,545	68,415	88,227	96,864	109,806	176,314	185,183

Source: Ministry of Trade and Industry, *Economic Survey of Singapore*, 1975-92.

Appendix A5 Singapore: Income from Direct Investment Abroad by Country, 1981 - 89

	1981	% Share	1982	% Share	1983	% Share	1984	% Share	1985	% Share
Total	104.9	100.0	121.0	100.0	161.8	100.0	161.3	100.0	14.6	100.0
ASIAN COUNTRIES	99.4	94.8	119.9	99.1	110.0	68.0	135.0	83.7	(52.8)	(361.6)
ASEAN	76.6	73.0	78.5	64.9	103.6	64.0	96.0	59.5	(36.6)	(250.7)
Brunei	3.7	3.5	3.5	2.9	0.5	0.3	0.8	0.5	1.3	8.9
Indonesia	2.8	2.7	1.2	1.0	2.2	1.4	(3.6)	(2.2)	(4.6)	(31.5)
Malaysia	69.4	66.2	77.9	64.4	104.2	64.4	100.1	62.1	(34.8)	(238.4)
Philippines	0.0	0.0	(3.5)	(2.9)	(3.6)	(2.2)	(3.3)	(2.0)	1.4	9.6
Thailand	0.7	0.7	(0.6)	(0.5)	0.3	0.2	2.0	1.2	0.1	0.7
Hong Kong	21.5	20.5	34.9	28.8	0.6	0.4	34.0	21.1	(13.8)	(94.5)
Japan	0.0	0.0	(0.3)	(0.2)	0.0	0.0	0.0	0.0	(2.6)	(17.8)
China	0.0	0.0	0.0	0.0	0.0	0.0	0.0	0.0	(5.4)	(37.0)
South Korea	(0.2)	(0.2)	(0.2)	(0.2)	0.0	0.0	0.0	0.0	0.4	2.7
Taiwan	0.7	0.7	2.1	1.7	0.1	0.1	0.8	0.5	(2.2)	(15.1)
Others	0.8	0.8	4.9	4.0	5.7	3.5	4.2	2.6	7.4	50.7
EUROPEAN COUNTRIES	(18.3)	(17.4)	(10.5)	(8.7)	45.1	27.9	(2.2)	(1.4)	24.2	165.8
Netherlands	0.6	0.6	3.8	3.1	0.1	0.1	(0.1)	(0.1)	(0.3)	(2.1)
United Kingdom	(18.9)	(18.0)	(14.3)	(11.8)	44.1	27.3	(5.2)	(3.2)	13.7	93.8
Germany	0.0	0.0	0.0	0.0	0.0	0.0	0.0	0.0	(0.2)	(1.4)
Others	0.0	0.0	0.0	0.0	0.9	0.6	3.1	1.9	11.0	75.3
Australia	3.6	3.4	(11.5)	(9.5)	(20.5)	(12.7)	(8.2)	(5.1)	1.8	12.3
Canada	0.0	0.0	(0.1)	(0.1)	(2.6)	(1.6)	(2.5)	(1.5)	(1.2)	(8.2)
United States	(2.0)	(1.9)	(2.1)	(1.7)	(3.3)	(2.0)	(7.2)	(4.5)	(4.3)	(29.5)
Other Countries	22.2	21.2	25.3	20.9	33.1	20.5	46.4	28.8	46.9	321.2

Appendix A5 Singapore: Income from Direct Investment Abroad by Country, 1981 - 89 (Contd.)

	1986	% Share	1987	% Share	1988	% Share	1989	% Share
Total	204.3	100.0	276.2	100.0	391.1	100.0	505.8	100.0
ASIAN COUNTRIES	111.0	54.3	145.4	52.6	256.2	65.5	396.7	78.4
ASEAN	0.9	0.4	60.5	21.9	151.4	38.7	120.6	23.8
Brunei	0.4	0.2	(8.6)	(3.1)	0.4	0.1	(0.4)	(0.1)
Indonesia	(0.8)	(0.4)	(1.0)	(0.4)	2.2	0.6	(3.0)	(0.6)
Malaysia	(3.4)	(1.7)	60.4	21.9	137.1	35.1	110.5	21.8
Philippines	1.1	0.5	1.9	0.7	3.8	1.0	6.9	1.4
Thailand	3.6	1.8	7.8	2.8	7.9	2.0	6.6	1.3
Hong Kong	124.8	61.1	63.4	23.0	102.8	26.3	136.9	27.1
Japan	(3.0)	(1.5)	0.8	0.3	1.0	0.3	0.9	0.2
China	(9.3)	(4.6)	11.7	4.2	1.2	0.3	4.8	0.9
South Korea	(0.2)	(0.1)	0.1	0.0	(1.6)	(0.4)	(1.2)	(0.2)
Taiwan	(1.3)	(0.6)	7.9	2.9	10.6	2.7	128.6	25.4
Others	(0.9)	(0.4)	1.0	0.4	(9.2)	(2.4)	6.1	1.2
EUROPEAN COUNTRIES	39.4	19.3	58.4	21.1	56.5	14.4	24.9	4.9
Netherlands	(4.9)	(2.4)	(7.3)	(2.6)	(6.7)	(1.7)	9.5	1.9
United Kingdom	18.1	8.9	14.5	5.2	6.9	1.8	10.5	2.1
Germany	0.9	0.4	3.7	1.3	1.2	0.3	3.1	0.6
Others	25.3	12.4	47.5	17.2	55.1	14.1	1.8	0.4
Australia	4.4	2.2	22.4	8.1	33.3	8.5	18.9	3.7
Canada	(2.1)	(1.0)	0.1	0.0	(0.3)	(0.1)	(1.7)	(0.3)
United States	0.2	0.1	2.4	0.9	(21.8)	(5.6)	(22.0)	(4.3)
Other Countries	51.4	25.2	47.5	17.2	67.2	17.2	89.0	17.6

Source: Department of Statistics (1993), *Singapore's Investment Abroad, 1976-90*, Singapore: National Printers.

Appendix A6 Singapore: Number of Companies Established Abroad by Country, 1981 - 90

	1981	% Share	1982	% Share	1983	% Share	1984	% Share	1985	% Share
Total	1,042	100.0	1,090	100.0	1,239	100.0	1,322	100.0	1,621	100.0
ASIAN COUNTRIES	893	85.7	921	84.5	1,056	85.2	1,114	84.3	1,360	83.9
ASEAN	745	71.5	754	69.2	831	67.1	854	64.6	1,009	62.2
Brunei	27	2.6	28	2.6	42	3.4	45	3.4	60	3.7
Indonesia	21	2.0	22	2.0	22	1.8	24	1.8	36	2.2
Malaysia	659	63.2	664	60.9	725	58.5	732	55.5	832	51.3
Philippines	10	1.0	11	1.0	12	1.0	14	1.1	19	1.2
Thailand	28	2.7	29	2.7	30	2.4	39	3.0	62	3.8
Hong Kong	118	11.3	131	12.0	176	14.2	208	15.7	276	17.0
Japan	6	0.6	6	0.6	7	0.6	7	0.5	11	0.7
China	0.0	0.0	0.0	0.0	0.0	0.0	0.0	0.0	16	1.0
South Korea	0.0	0.0	0.0	0.0	0.0	0.0	0.0	0.0	0.0	0.0
Taiwan	12	1.2	17	1.6	19	1.5	23	1.7	29	1.8
Others	12	1.2	13	1.2	23	1.9	22	1.7	19	1.2
EUROPEAN COUNTRIES	30	2.9	35	3.2	34	2.7	46	3.5	55	3.4
Netherlands	7	0.7	8	0.7	6	0.5	5	0.4	7	0.4
United Kingdom	20	1.9	23	2.1	23	1.9	35	2.6	35	2.2
Germany	0.0	0.0	0.0	0.0	0.0	0.0	0.0	0.0	0.0	0.0
Others	3	0.3	4	0.4	5	0.4	6	0.5	13	0.8
Australia	53	5.1	59	5.4	59	4.8	61	4.6	70	4.3
Canada	0.0	0.0	0.0	0.0	7	0.6	7	0.5	7	0.4
United States	15	1.4	22	2.0	29	2.3	37	2.8	46	2.8
Other Countries	51	4.9	53	4.9	54	4.4	57	4.3	83	5.1

Appendix A6 Singapore: Number of Companies Established Abroad by Country, 1981 - 90 (Cont'd.)

	1986	% Share	1987	% Share	1988	% Share	1989	% Share	1990	% Share
Total	1,663	100.0	1,740	100.0	1,787	100.0	1,845	100.0	2,290	100.0
ASIAN COUNTRIES	1,391	83.6	1,441	82.8	1,465	82.0	1,482	80.3	1,884	82.3
ASEAN	1,011	60.8	1,041	59.8	1,046	58.5	1,057	57.3	1,297	56.6
Brunei	60	3.6	58	3.3	59	3.3	60	3.3	50	2.1
Indonesia	34	2.0	32	1.8	33	1.8	32	1.7	50	2.1
Malaysia	831	50.0	860	49.4	863	48.3	878	47.6	1,007	44.0
Philippines	18	1.1	17	1.0	15	0.8	16	0.9	46	2.0
Thailand	68	4.1	74	4.3	76	4.3	71	3.8	144	6.3
Hong Kong	291	17.5	299	17.2	306	17.1	302	16.4	365	15.9
Japan	13	0.8	15	0.9	15	0.8	17	0.9	58	2.5
China	22	1.3	31	1.8	30	1.7	30	1.6	12	0.5
South Korea	0.0	0.0	0.0	0.0	6	0.3	7	0.4	80	3.5
Taiwan	33	2.0	34	2.0	40	2.2	47	2.5	30	1.3
Others	21	1.3	21	1.2	22	1.2	22	1.2	42	1.8
EUROPEAN COUNTRIES	58	3.5	65	3.7	66	3.7	67	3.6	113	4.9
Netherlands	7	0.4	9	0.5	7	0.4	7	0.4	20	0.9
United Kingdom	37	2.2	39	2.2	44	2.5	47	2.5	63	2.8
Germany	0.0	0.0	5	0.3	5	0.3	5	0.3	12	0.5
Others	14	0.8	12	0.7	10	0.6	8	0.4	18	0.7
Australia	73	4.4	81	4.7	72	4.0	70	3.8	88	3.8
Canada	7	0.4	8	0.5	9	0.5	11	0.6	11	0.5
United States	46	2.8	51	2.9	62	3.5	70	3.8	86	3.8
Other Countries	88	5.3	94	5.4	113	6.3	145	7.9	108	4.7

Source: Department of Statistics (1993), *Singapore's Investment Abroad. 1976-90*, Singapore: National Printers.

Appendix A7 Singapore: Direct Foreign Investment Abroad by Country, 1981 - 90

	1981	% Share	1982	% Share	1983	% Share	1984	% Share	1985	% Share
Total	1,677.7	100.0	2,086.9	100.0	2.233.1	100.0	2,399.3	100.0	2,257.2	100.0
ASIAN COUNTRIES	1,289.7	76.9	1,586.7	76.0	1,662.4	74.4	1,805.2	75.2	1,721.4	76.3
ASEAN	1,078.5	64.3	1,233.7	59.1	1,241.7	55.6	1,341.4	55.9	1,133.3	50.2
Brunei	3.7	0.2	6.0	0.3	9.0	0.4	49.1	2.0	52.9	2.3
Indonesia	39.5	2.4	39.7	1.9	44.4	2.0	56.3	2.3	65.0	2.9
Malaysia	1,006.9	60.0	1,162.3	55.7	1,162.6	52.1	1,209.1	50.4	971.8	43.1
Philippines	18.4	1.1	16.1	0.8	17.6	0.8	17.6	0.7	22.4	1.0
Thailand	10.0	0.6	9.6	0.5	8.1	0.4	9.3	0.4	21.2	0.9
Hong Kong	181.8	10.8	316.7	15.2	357.4	16.0	391.3	16.3	460.7	20.4
Japan	0.3	0.0	0.4	0.0	0.6	0.0	0.7	0.0	5.0	0.2
China	0.0	0.0	0.0	0.0	0.0	0.0	0.0	0.0	57.6	2.6
South Korea	0.0	0.0	0.0	0.0	0.0	0.0	0.0	0.0	0.0	0.0
Taiwan	12.9	0.8	14.8	·0.7	24.9	1.1	27.1	1.1	32.9	1.5
Others	16.2	1.0	21.1	1.0	37.8	1.7	44.7	1.9	31.9	1.4
EUROPEAN COUNTRIES	50.7	3.0	58.0	2.8	57.7	2.6	71.5	3.0	89.3	4.0
Netherlands	0.8	0.0	0.8	0.0	12.2	0.5	10.6	0.4	12.0	0.5
United Kingdom	49.7	3.0	57.2	2.7	43.1	1.9	43.9	1.8	45.9	2.0
Germany	0.0	0.0	0.0	0.0	0.0	0.0	0.0	0.0	0.0	0.0
Others	0.2	0.0	0.0	0.0	2.4	0.1	17.0	0.7	31.4	1.4
Australia	62.6	3.7	90.6	4.3	121.4	5.4	132.0	5.5	176.9	7.8
Canada	0.0	0.0	0.0	0.0	11.5	0.5	11.5	0.5	17.6	0.8
United States	31.8	1.9	44.3	2.1	47.5	2.1	54.4	2.3	66.1	2.9
Other Countries	242.9	14.5	307.3	14.7	332.6	14.9	324.7	13.5	185.9	8.2

Appendix A7 Singapore: Direct Foreign Investment Abroad by Country, 1981 - 90 (Cont'd.)

	1986	% Share	1987	% Share	1988	% Share	1989	% Share	1990	% Share
Total	2,597.7	100.0	2,961.5	100.0	2,993.9	100.0	2,943.7	100.0	7,492.2	100.0
ASIAN COUNTRIES	1,836.5	70.7	1,908.5	64.4	1,963.6	65.6	1,968.4	66.9	3,625.7	48.4
ASEAN	1,155.8	44.5	1,180.5	39.9	1,216.0	40.6	1,138.4	38.7	2,094.1	28.0
Brunei	50.0	1.9	54.2	1.8	57.4	1.9	56.6	1.9	69.3	0.9
Indonesia	67.7	2.6	58.6	2.0	59.8	2.0	58.3	2.0	99.1	1.3
Malaysia	985.6	37.9	1,008.4	34.1	1,030.8	34.4	971.6	33.0	1,663.4	22.2
Philippines	22.5	0.9	14.3	0.5	22.5	0.8	22.8	0.8	58.2	0.8
Thailand	30.0	1.2	45.0	1.5	45.5	1.5	34.1	1.2	204.0	2.7
Hong Kong	497.9	19.2	539.9	18.2	545.2	18.2	581.4	19.8	908.5	12.1
Japan	6.0	0.2	16.1	0.5	16.7	0.6	33.9	1.2	222.8	3.0
China	93.8	3.6	101.4	3.4	79.1	2.6	47.4	1.6	61.6	0.8
South Korea	0.0	0.0		0.0	14.8	0.5	15.9	0.5	139.9	1.9
Taiwan	37.8	1.5	26.0	0.9	54.3	1.8	86.0	2.9	66.2	0.9
Others	45.2	1.7	44.6	1.5	37.5	1.3	65.4	2.2	132.7	1.8
EUROPEAN COUNTRIES	167.2	6.4	358.2	12.1	303.4	10.1	203.4	6.9	908.7	12.1
Netherlands	13.8	0.5	165.4	5.6	111.4	3.7	(94.3)	(3.2)	620.4	8.3
United Kingdom	81.8	3.1	48.3	1.6	49.3	1.6	50.4	1.7	187.1	2.5
Germany	0.0	0.0	8.6	0.3	8.6	0.3	23.4	0.8	10.0	0.1
Others	71.6	2.8	135.9	4.6	134.1	4.5	223.9	7.6	90.9	1.2
Australia	175.6	6.8	217.8	7.4	166.1	5.5	138.3	4.7	514.6	6.9
Canada	17.6	0.7	17.6	0.6	29.0	1.0	73.4	2.5	22.6	0.3
United States	65.4	2.5	69.3	2.3	107.7	3.6	160.0	5.4	331.0	4.4
Other Countries	335.4	12.9	390.1	13.2	424.1	14.2	400.2	13.6	2,089.5	27.9

Source: Department of Statistics (1993), *Singapore's Investment Abroad, 1976-90*, Singapore: National Printers.

Appendix A8 Singapore: Distribution of Direct Investment Abroad by Country and Activity, 1990

Country	Total	Manufacturing	Construction	Commerce	Transport	Financial	Real Estate	Business Services	Others
Total	100.0	100.0	100.0	100.0	100.0	100.0	100.0	100.0	100.0
ASIAN COUNTRIES	48.4	90.6	92.3	88.5	64.8	21.2	66.1	40.4	89.5
ASEAN	28.0	56.1	38.7	55.0	21.7	12.1	27.0	13.4	83.2
Brunei	0.9	0.8	4.8	1.2	0.1	1.1	0.0	0.0	0.0
Indonesia	1.3	3.2	0.1	0.3	9.8	0.3	1.4	2.1	3.5
Malaysia	22.2	42.1	28.3	48.2	9.3	9.8	23.8	8.0	58.2
Philippines	0.8	2.1	0.4	0.4	0.1	0.1	0.0	0.2	9.7
Thailand	2.7	7.9	5.2	4.9	2.3	0.7	1.9	3.0	0.4
Hong Kong	12.1	15.7	44.5	10.4	10.3	8.0	38.6	8.8	7.2
Japan	3.0	2.4	6.9	18.8	0.4	0.7	0.0	6.6	0.2
China	0.8	2.7	0.0	1.9	0.0	0.0	0.0	3.1	0.0
South Korea	1.9	5.0	0.8	1.7	9.9	0.0	0.4	5.2	5.7
Taiwan	0.9	0.1	0.2	0.3	21.5	0.4	0.0	3.2	0.0
Others	1.8	8.6	1.1	0.4	1.0	0.0	0.1	0.0	0.0
EUROPEAN COUNTRIES	12.1	2.7	0.0	1.7	2.6	20.2	0.4	2.5	7.3
Netherlands	8.3	0.6	0.0	0.0	0.2	14.8	0.0	0.0	0.0
Switzerland	0.4	0.9	0.0	0.1	0.0	0.4	0.0	0.4	0.0
Germany	0.1	0.0	0.0	01	0.5	0.2	0.0	0.4	0.1
United Kingdom	2.5	0.0	0.0	1.4	1.9	3.8	0.4	0.2	7.2
Others	0.8	1.1	0.0	0.1	0.0	0.9	0.0	1.5	0.0
Canada	0.3	0.6	0.3	0.0	2.6	0.1	0.0	1.3	0.0
Australia	6.9	1.5	0.0	3.8	1.8	8.0	25.1	0.1	0.8
United States	4.4	4.4	0.0	1.2	11.4	2.0	5.4	55.6	0.5
New Zealand	10.7	0.1	0.0	4.3	1.8	18.6	0.0	0.0	0.0
Others	17.2	0.2	7.4	0.6	15.0	29.8	3.0	0.0	0.0

Source: Department of Statistics (1993), *Singapore's Investment Abroad, 1976-90*, Singapore: National Printers.

Appendix A9 Singapore: Diversification in Terms of Types of Companies Set up Abroad, 1990

Activity of Investor in Singapore	No. of Companies Set Up Abroad in a Different Activity	Same Activity	Total
Agriculture	2	6	8
Mining	0	2	2
Manufacturing	140	265	405
Construction	22	54	76
Commerce	150	411	561
Transport	36	120	156
Financial	505	310	815
Real Estate	47	43	90
Business Services	87	71	158

Source: Department of Statistics (1993), *Singapore's Investment Abroad. 1976-90*, Singapore: National Printers.

Appendix A10 Singapore: Rates of Return by Activity Abroad, 1990

Activity	Rate of Return (%)
Total	6.1
Agriculture	1.1
Mining	9.6
Manufacturing	9.5
Construction	-15.9
Commerce	5.1
Transport	11.2
Financial	5.7
Real Estate	2.58
Business Services	6.8
Others	5.2

Source: Department of Statistics (1993), *Singapore's Investment Abroad. 1976-90*, Singapore: National Printers.

Appendix A11 Rates of Return of Major Host Countries

Host Country	Rate of Return (%)	Activity with Highest Rate of Return
Malaysia	9.7	Transport
Hong Kong	21.3	Financial (Investment Holding)
New Zealand	14.5	Financial (Investment Holding)
Netherlands	(2.1)	COMMERCE
Australia	(38.5)	Business Services
USA	29.3	Financial (Investment Holding)
Taiwan	(8.3)	Manufacturing
Thailand	(1.4)	Commerce

Source: Department of Statistics (1993), *Singapore's Investment Abroad, 1976–90*, Singapore: National Printers.

Appendix A12 Total Direct Investment Abroad of Local-Controlled Companies by Country and Activity Abroad, 1995 (All Sectors)

Activity Abroad / Country	Manufacturing	Construction	Commerce	Transport	Financial	Real Estate	Business Services	Others	Total
Total	4,664,503	358,092	2,316,055	885,570	12,633,205	2,248,095	709,418	442,493	24,257,431
Asia	4,213,456	347,743	1,954,370	482,717	6,313,627	1,663,190	366,849	366,843	15,708,795
Asean	2,514,086	236,891	974,802	212,264	3,280,217	778,878	202,665	302,553	8,502,356
Brunei	4,027	32,994	5,388	69	2,389	-	1,974	31,258	78,098
Indonesia	316,884	70,673	90,861	84,042	132,812	300,423	23,308	64,304	1,083,308
Malaysia	1,773,728	38,091	745,442	85,697	2,853,053	433,389	33,375	182,180	6,144,954
Philippines	26,428	87,194	4,525	5,717	114,891	339	126,156	19,961	385,211
Thailand	219,094	5,794	124,240	34,682	52,476	21,645	17,637	1,525	477,090
Vietnam	173,925	2,146	4,346	2,058	124,599	23,083	214	3,325	333,695
Hong Kong	462,767	67,408	231,271	189,264	2,615,229	352,949	58,086	1,087	3,978,060
Taiwan	118,324	23,984	149,338	1,261	19,021	11,558	15,573	340	339,339
China	1,000,627	17,501	433,069	62,806	194,663	490,176	42,952	53,347	2,295,142
Japan	1,761	(245)	31,541	3,204	3,613	-	21,547	-	61,421
Others	115,891	2,205	134,349	13,918	200,885	29,628	26,026	9,516	532,417
Europe	123,532	-	91,640	151,036	1,761,075	344,445	308,661	51,605	2,521,993
Netherlands	4,686	-	7,156	-	799,065	-	-	-	810,907
United Kingdom	57,245	-	35,592	9,684	805,748	17,718	275,581	48,065	1,249,633
Others	61,600	-	48,892	141,352	156,262	16,272	33,081	3,540	461,454
Australia	180,605	762	60,580	2,555	365,369	278,615	20,951	22,165	931,603
United States	110,409	-	176,448	10,655	1,913,070	148,754	(10,406)	1,837	2,350,767
New Zealand	4,551	-	7,943	5,151	138,282	8,681	17,829	-	182,436
Others nec	31,950	9,587	25,073	233,458	2,141,782	114,410	5,533	43	2,561,837

Source: Department of Statistics (1993), *Singapore's Investment Abroad. 1976-90*, Singapore: National Printers.

Appendix A13 Direct Equity Investment Abroad by Country and Activity Abroad, 1995 (All Sectors)

Activity Abroad / Country	Manufacturing	Construction	Commerce	Transport	Financial	Real Estate	Business Services	Others	Total
Total	9,424,433	320,356	3,288.872	860,762	18,996,589	2,534,605	1,084,180	355,660	36,865,458
Asia	8,869,342	313,181	2,957.043	313,158	6,330,003	1,906,392	534,727	287,393	21,511,239
Asean	6,628,901	166,710	1,527,803	179,149	2,879,564	644,330	255,167	185,356	12,466,980
Brunei	3,951	20,547	8,134	(169)	2,521	-	1,522	217	36,722
Indonesia	2,727,204	87,213	72,667	71,323	203,211	235,406	27,327	24,053	3,448,405
Malaysia	3,163,543	27,781	189,595	68,015	2,378,215	294,948	54,618	128,032	7,304,746
Philippines	127,086	51,891	21,468	1,744	145,557	18,354	130,596	22,698	521,393
Thailand	491,215	(22,868)	231,310	34,533	31,726	65,630	24,525	3,834	859,906
Vietnam	113,903	2,146	4,629	3,703	118,335	29,993	16,579	6,521	295,808
Hong Kong	528,475	107,076	587,583	46,454	2,778,249	889,900	138,423	13,202	5,089,360
Taiwan	163,044	18,334	279,884	12,799	29,238	11,360	14,947	340	529,945
China	1,332,504	20,043	389,491	58,018	184,357	11,360	46.848	79,104	2,444,959
Japan	51,597	(245)	68,125	1,692	211,290	334,594	49,523	-	381,982
Others	164,820	1,264	104,157	15,048	247,305	-	29,819	9,391	598,013
Europe	159,737	-	51,401	87,133	3,267,093	26,208	251,914	7,319	3,843,622
Netherlands	4,352	-	914	-	450,516	19,024	-	-	455,782
United Kingdom	47,455	-	23,621	10,320	2,103,117	(828)	245,612	3,779	2,434,732
Others	107,930	-	26,866	76,813	73,461	18,196	6,303	3,540	953,108
Australia	208,205	9,716	111,131	3,115	330,604	385,956	31,806	34,934	1,115,467
United States	89,199	-	139,090	15,285	1,541,928	41,460	208,730	709	2,036,402
New Zealand	12,194	-	21,039	5,650	1,765,911	118,594	17,177	24,327	1,964,891
Others nec	85,756	(2,541)	9,168	436,421	5,761,050	63,179	39,826	978	6,393,837

Source: Department of Statistics (1993), *Singapore's Investment Abroad. 1976-90*, Singapore: National Printers.

Appendix A14 Total Direct Investment Abroad by Country and Activity Abroad, 1995 (All Sectors)

Activity Abroad Country	Manufacturing	Construction	Commerce	Transport	Financial	Real Estate	Business Services	Others	Total
Total	11,396,572	504,732	4,528,270	1,353,48	23,171,832	3,379,577	1,317,474	588,232	46,240,179
Asia	10,636,847	477,629	3,921,046	9	7,913,646	2,433,545	678,547	471,566	27,101,208
Asean	8,024,753	295,024	2,076,251	568,382	3,771,575	944,098	339,851	360,834	16,088,208
Brunei	4,027	32,994	15,438	275,822	3,110	-	4,944	31,258	92,037
Indonesia	3,002,873	93,983	147,164	267	243,088	345,645	36,484	65,574	4,030,947
Malaysia	4,044,990	46,911	1,512,653	96,135	3,182,371	475,731	116,958	205,441	9,715,944
Philippines	162,434	86,223	29,345	130,890	153,667	18,618	138,414	30,258	625,143
Thailand	629,488	32,767	366,960	6,185	64,741	73,641	26,472	20,099	1,252,811
Vietnam	180,942	2,146	4,691	38,642	124,577	30,464	16,579	8,203	371,326
Hong Kong	700,961	135,626	731,630	3,703	3,398,792	928,434	168,393	13,387	6,268,334
Taiwan	170,155	23,984	306,590	191,113	30,162	115,578	17,303	340	573,217
China	1,512,318	21,036	495,151	13,126	222,774	519,827	49,169	83,038	2,968,212
Japan	51,753	(245)	135,142	64,899	211,334	-	62,872	-	465,792
Others	176,906	2,205	176,282	4,936	279,009	29,628	40,959	13,967	737,445
Europe	207,980	-	108,169	18,488	4,636,280	39,765	312,229	52,438	5,550,795
Netherlands	4,352	-	7,625	193,933	1,008,868	-	-	-	1,020,845
United Kingdom	60,574	-	48,625	12,691	2,832,381	18,015	275,364	48,898	3,296,548
Others	143,054	-	51,919	181,242	795,032	21,750	36,866	3,540	1,233,402
Australia	220,972	11,409	195,125	4,943	448,144	488,303	43,444	35,925	1,448,265
United States	121,507	-	207,375	19,962	1,913,594	149,882	221,059	1,837	2,635,217
New Zealand	12,147	-	39,903	5,163	1,890,767	126,988	18,035	25,413	2,118,415
Others nec	197,119	15,694	56,652	561,106	6,369,401	141,094	44,160	1,053	8,386,279

Source: Department of Statistics (1993), *Singapore's Investment Abroad, 1976-90*, Singapore: National Printers.

Appendix A15 Direct Equity Investment Abroad by Country and Activity of Investor in Singapore, 1995 (All Sectors)

Activity Abroad / Country	Manufacturing	Construction	Commerce	Transport	Financial	Real Estate	Business Services	Others	Total
Total	12,841,541	848,456	3,177,943	1,237,943	14,477,091	2,258,123	1,974,658	50,251	36,865,458
Asia	6,198,826	807,440	2,885,203	480,225	9,454,463	500,959	1,146,025	38,097	21,511,239
Asean	4,789,601	73,627	1,401,528	300,545	5,021,375	255,823	595,373	29,107	12,466,980
Brunei	4,996	19,983	4,868	-169	5,897	-	1,148	-	36,722
Indonesia	2,225,167	23,559	73,678	83,732	894,539	51,863	95,798	70	3,448,405
Malaysia	2,132,306	21,008	1,029,258	197,905	3,429,777	204,298	261,414	28,779	7,304,746
Philippines	151,636	-22	51,855	871	175,566	-	141,230	258	521,393
Thailand	202,981	4,706	233,984	17,415	332,557	-338	78,600	-	859,906
Vietnam	72,514	4,393	17,886	792	183,040	-	17,183	-	295,808
Hong Kong	758,219	697,025	1,057,084	101,631	2,169,163	93,822	211,562	853	5,089,360
Taiwan	41,365	11,930	41,982	12,401	243,263	-	178,665	340	529,945
China	504,045	25,090	328,830	57,712	1,346,956	126,716	53,421	2,189	2,444,959
Japan	18,457	-	15,049	1,692	292,476	-	54,307	-	381,982
Others	87,139	-232	40,729	6,243	381,230	24,599	52,697	5,609	598,013
Europe	2,470,638	3,347	34,033	20,413	539,615	58,627	716,979	-	3,843,622
Netherlands	-5,889	-	1,658	-	26,178	-	433,835	-	455,782
United Kingdom	1,946,814	-	1,281	-6,697	260,908	-1,404	233,830	-	2,434,732
Others	529,713	3,347	31,064	27,111	252,529	60,031	49,315	-	953,108
Australia	75,522	5,556	91,521	7,047	849,010	53,125	22,229	11,457	1,115,467
United States	469,573	41	12,284	20,530	957,896	500,320	75,049	709	2,036,402
New Zealand	-8,638	286	124,726	1,369	1,844,617	-199	2,730	-	1,964,891
Others nec	3,635,619	31,786	29,658	708,538	831,491	1,145,291	11,646	-12	6,393,837

Source: Department of Statistics (1993), *Singapore's Investment Abroad, 1976-90*, Singapore: National Printers.

Appendix A16 Number of Affiliates Set up Abroad by Country and Activity of Investor in Singapore, 1995 (All Sectors)

Activity Abroad / Country	Manufacturing	Construction	Commerce	Transport	Financial	Real Estate	Business Services	Others	Total
Total	1,158	118	1,160	335	1,784	199	357	48	5,159
Asia	965	101	1,039	236	1,348	150	294	39	4,172
Asean	645	72	689	138	712	81	156	32	2,525
Brunei	10	5	17	3	19	-	5	-	59
Indonesia	78	17	54	12	75	11	12	2	261
Malaysia	445	39	500	78	475	61	75	28	1,701
Philippines	35	1	27	13	36	-	22	1	135
Thailand	59	7	84	28	89	9	35	1	312
Vietnam	18	3	7	4	18	-	7	-	57
Hong Kong	104	8	128	44	272	47	54	3	660
Taiwan	24	6	31	3	28	-	18	1	111
China	145	14	132	33	237	14	33	-	
Japan									608
Others	12	-	14	4	27	-	5	-	62
Europe	35	1	45	14	72	8	28	3	206
Netherlands	5	-	3	-	16	-	2	-	26
United Kingdom	29	-	8	8	78	7	14	-	144
Others	27	1	29	10	17	5	6	-	95
Australia	37	5	37	9	107	17	12	8	232
United States	49	1	15	11	68	6	15	1	166
New Zealand	6	1	10	5	27	3	2	-	54
Others nec	40	9	19	56	123	11	12	-	270

Source: Department of Statistics (1993), *Singapore's Investment Abroad. 1976-90*, Singapore: National Printers.

Appendix A17 Direct Equity Investment Abroad by Country and Activity of Investor in Singapore, 1995 (All Sectors)

Activity Abroad Country	Manufacturing	Construction	Commerce	Transport	Financial	Real Estate	Business Services	Others	Total
Total	15,040,519	929,158	4,257,790	2,130,994	18,559,191	2,627,286	2,623,849	71,391	46,240,179
Asia	7,597,025	872,939	3,740,050	770,530	11,807,809	753,537	1,512,488	47,009	27,101,208
Asean	5,945,510	131,006	1,930,175	398,671	6,489,288	404,019	751,689	37,849	16,088,208
Brunei	5,321	31,397	11,867	267	39,053	-	4,133	-	92,037
Indonesia	2,446,840	38,995	116,754	110,041	1,162,616	56,870	98,762	70	40,309,472
Malaysia	2,805,596	30808	1402999	266776	4,472,453	330,001	369789	37521	9715944
Philippines	236,480	-1066	59,637	5576	180,731	143528	258	625143	
Thailand	328,203	25,858	319,046	15,220	429,100	17148	118,235	-	1,252,811
Vietnam	123,069	5,014	19,873	792	205,336	-	17,242	-	371,326
Hong Kong	899,300	697,667	1,210,422	286,359	2,676,746	106,815	387,016	1008	6,268,334
Taiwan	49,302	14,739	46,435	12,469	2,711,322	-	178,881	340	573,217
China	572,779	28,818	465,930	60,213	1,549,839	251,044	73,400	2,189	2,968,212
Japan	29,814	-	22,227	4,936	352,523	-	56,291	-	465,792
Others	100,590	709	64,860	7,881	465,091	27,480	65,211	5,624	737,445
Europe	2,862,846	3,347	95,910	496,591	1,046,580	94,104	951,417	-	5,550,795
Netherlands	268,580	-	2,072	-	334,624	-	415,569	-	1,020,845
United Kingdom	1,970,540	-	45,116	454,752	427,813	30,465	367,862	-	3,296,548
Others	623,726	3,347	48,722	41,840	284,143	63,639	167,987	-	1,233,402
Australia	101,537	5,556	138,381	12,668	1,051,496	82,671	33,449	22,507	1,448,265
United States	699,678	41	28,237	29,986	1,242,145	528,559	104,734	1,837	2,635,217
New Zealand	-145	1,086	124,703	10,410	1,974,972	4,601	2,788	-	2,118,415
Others nec	3,779,577	46,189	130,510	810,808	1,436,190	1,163,994	18,973	38	7,386,279

Source: Department of Statistics (1993), *Singapore's Investment Abroad. 1976-90*, Singapore: National Printers.

204

Appendix A18 Number of Affiliates Set up Abroad by Country and Activity Abroad, 1995 (All Sectors)

Activity Abroad / Country	Manufacturing	Construction	Commerce	Transport	Financial	Real Estate	Business Services	Others	Total
Total	1,413	152	1,344	324	982	399	406	139	5,159
Asia	1,291	144	1,148	236	672	258	311	112	4,172
Asean	809	103	723	144	341	158	167	80	2,525
Brunei	7	8	23	3	13	-	4	1	59
Indonesia	137	19	28	12	21	20	16	8	261
Malaysia	514	54	536	79	247	123	92	56	1,701
Philippines	35	7	24	12	26	2	22	7	135
Thailand	94	10	109	33	28	7	27	4	312
Vietnam	22	5	3	5	6	6	6	4	57
Hong Kong	69	15	175	35	258	42	61	5	660
Taiwan	27	11	49	4	9	2	8	1	111
China	333	10	104	28	25	48	40	20	608
Japan	6	1	30	4	12	-	8	1	62
Others	47	4	6,721	27	8	27	5	206	
Europe	45	-	57	21	76	32	23	11	265
Netherlands	2	-	6	-	18	-	-	-	26
United Kingdom	17	-	22	6	49	28	16	6	144
Others	26	-	29	15	9	4	7	5	95
Australia	28	2	64	6	55	48	17	12	232
United States	25	-	42	8	41	16	33	1	166
New Zealand	4	-	10	3	14	16	6	1	54
Others nec	20	6	23	50	124	29	16	2	270

Source: Department of Statistics (1993), *Singapore's Investment Abroad, 1976-90*, Singapore: National Printers.

Index